SKETCHING INTERIORS: COLOURED PENCILS
A STEP-BY-STEP GUIDE

SKETCHING INTERIORS: COLOURED PENCILS - A STEP-BY-STEP GUIDE
Copyright © 2007 Noriyoshi Hasegawa
Copyright © 2007 Graphic-sha Publishing Co., Ltd.

First Asian edition published in 2010 by
Page One Publishing Pte. Ltd.
20 Kaki Bukit View, Kaki Bukit Techpark II,
Singapore 415956
Tel: (65) 6742-2088
Fax: (65) 6744-2088
enquiries@pageonegroup.com
www.pageonegroup.com

First designed and published in 2007 by
Graphic-sha Publishing Co., Ltd.

First English edition was produced in 2010 by
Graphic-sha Publishing Co., Ltd.
1-14-17 Kudankita, Chiyoda-ku, Tokyo 102-0073, Japan
Tel: [81] 3-3263-4318
Fax: [81] 3-3263-5297

Author	: Noriyoshi Hasegawa
Production assistance	: Yoko Seki
Original design and layout	: Yoichi Ito (Onuki Design Office)
English edition layout	: Shinichi Ishioka
English translation	: Lingua fránca, Inc (contact@lingua-franca.co.jp)
Japanese edition editor	: Satoru Ota (Graphic-sha Publishing Co., Ltd.)
Foreign project management	: Kumiko Sakamoto (Graphic-sha Publishing Co., Ltd.)

ISBN 978-981-245-919-0

All rights reserved. No part of this book may be reproduced in any form or by any electronic or mechanical means including information storage and retrieval systems without permission in writing from the publisher, except by a reviewer, who may quote brief passages in a review.

Every effort has been made to ensure that content and credits accurately comply with information supplied. We apologize for any inaccuracies that may have occurred and will resolve inaccurate or missing information in a subsequent reprinting of the book.

First printing: October 2010

Printed and bound in China

SKETCHING INTERIORS: COLOURED PENCILS
A STEP-BY-STEP GUIDE

Introduction

I intended this book to be helpful to interior coordinators and others who work with architectural designs when using coloured pencils at meetings with clients. How to produce fast and concise sketches (in perspective) becomes a vital point when interior coordinators give presentations to their clients. I explain how to do this in another publication that is currently available, entitled *Sketching Interiors: A Step-By-Step Guide*.

Rather than explain sketching techniques, this book covers how to apply colour to sketches in a readily comprehensible manner.

There are two key points to applying colour: 1) how not to over colour a sketch and 2) how to create modulation.

Not over-colouring refers to locating areas where colour will be most effective and then leaving other areas without colour.

One of the problems using coloured pencils poses during client presentations is that colouring takes time.

I suggest reading this book to determine how to prioritize the two techniques.

"Modulation" refers to using the inherent agility that coloured pencils afford and either applying as much vigorous pressure as possible for areas requiring saturated colour or as little pressure as possible for areas requiring little saturation. Since "modulation" is difficult to explain in an aesthetic manner, instead this book explains how to modulate the pressure applied to the pencil in an easy-to-understand fashion using five-grade gradation charts for various hues included at key points.

Chapter I, "Coloured Pencil Sketch Representations à la Carte" contains samples of a host of items, ranging from chairs, tables and other furniture to kitchen, bath, and other plumbing fixtures. The reader must practice sketching each individual element before moving on to practice sketching the space itself.

Chapter II, "Mastering Coloured Pencil Techniques" covers topics ranging from how to hold a coloured pencil to layering colours, leaving designated areas uncoloured, blurring or blending, and other basics in applying colour. Spend extra time on this chapter to learn these techniques thoroughly.

Chapter III, "The Coloured Pencil Perspective Sketching Process" uses clear-cut steps to explain how to draw spaces from the foyer or entrance to the garden. In particular, I provide "tips" for specific points on drawing in perspective, indicated using red arrows to make them easy for the reader to understand.

Chapter IV, "Floor Plans in Coloured Pencil" discusses the colouration of flat, orthogonal floor plans. This chapter explains how to create an orthogonal floor plan that projects warmth and has atmosphere by exploiting the advantages inherent to coloured pencils.

Coloured pencils' biggest advantage is convenience. If you are able to add superior representation skills to convenience, then you will find your perspective sketches have become a powerful weapon for you when doing client presentations.

Contents

Introduction 4

Chapter I

Coloured Pencil Sketch Representations à la Carte 13

Chairs 14

Tables 16

Sofas 18

Storage Units 20

Beds 22

Curtains 24

| Light Fixtures 26

| Kitchens 28

| Bathrooms Vanities 30

| Baths 32

| Toilets 34

Chapter II

Mastering Coloured Pencil Techniques 35

| Colouring with Coloured Pencils: Part I 36

| Colouring with Coloured Pencils: Part II 38

Colouring with Coloured Pencils: Part III 40

Colouring with Coloured Pencils: Part IV 42

Chapter III

The Coloured Pencil Perspective Sketching Process 43

Foyer with a Bench 44

Foyer with Red Chairs 48

Foyer with a Recessed Wall 52

Foyer with a Staircase 54

Foyer with Glass Block 56

Home Theater with *Tatami* Mats	60
Living Room with a Red Spiral Staircase	66
Home Theater/Living Room with a Garden View	70
Living Room with Open Walls	72
Home Theater/Living Room with a Yellow Sofa	76
Living Room/Kitchen Space with an Atrium	78
Room with a Purple Sofa	82
Living /Dining Space with a Red Sofa	84
Blue L-shaped Kitchen Cabinets	88

Kitchen with a Red Island 92

Ample 288 Square Foot Living / 94
Dining /Kitchen/Home Theater Space

Spacious 288 Square Foot Dining Room/Kitchen 98

Kitchen/Dining Room Featuring a Long Table 102

Subdued Kitchen with a Table and Earthen Floor 106

Kitchen with a Large, ... 108
Tranquil Tree Visible from Outside

Embraced by Nature: A Bedroom with a Garden View 112

Eye-catching Bedroom/Bathroom 116

Fantasy Theater Bedroom 118

Room with an *Irori*: 120
Trendy Japanese *Tatami* Mat Room

Giving an Asian Flair 124
to a Living Room/Office Space

The Ultimate Bath Space: Bedroom 126
with an Outdoor Bath

Washroom/Toilet/Bath: 130
Pipelines Unified in One Space

Gardening Space

Living Room and Patio with an Umbrella 134

Dramatizing Details 138

Soothing Plant Life 140

Chapter IV

Floor Plans in Coloured Pencil 141

House with a Garden Patio 142

Condominium Surrounded by Flowers 146

Rectangular House with a Pond 150

House Surrounded by Trees 154

House with a Piano 156

Afterword 160

Chapter I

Coloured Pencil Sketch Representations à la Carte

This chapter covers furniture, fixtures, and other common interior components we encounter on a daily basis. Use photos in catalogues to practice drawing these items. Key points to learn are not to apply too much colour and to modulate the pencils strokes.

Chairs

The key to drawing chairs is to avoid producing a faithful rendition and instead to simplify as much as possible. In truth, you will rarely sketch a chair alone. Typically, you will draw chairs in sets with tables, desks, counters, and other such furniture, so abbreviate extraneous lines and colours.

Basic chair: Draw the seat on the thin side.

Basic chair (Front view): Blur the chair's back.

Do not worry about strokes extending beyond the chair's contour lines.

This shows volume given to the chair's back.

Here, the chair's seat remains uncoloured.

I gave volume to this chair's seat.

This chair's legs remain uncoloured.

Here, I omitted one chair leg.

Sometimes, the lower portions of the chair's legs do not need colour.

Here, I intentionally accentuated the blue on one side.

I used a warm grey to soften this chair.

For this chair, I omitted colouring the seat, itself, and instead applied colour to the seat cushion's sides to create the illusion of volume.

The back and seat of this chair are coloured, while the legs and other areas remain uncoloured.

Different shades of yellow distinguish the various surfaces of this chair.

Tables

I mentioned in the previous pages discussing chairs that chairs and tables typically appear together as a set. First practice drawing the table alone before coupling it with chairs. This will make proportioning easier, which will in turn make the chairs easier to draw. Simplify the chairs and omit the seats and legs when appropriate.

Here, I omitted the chairs' seats and legs.

Above, the tabletop remains uncoloured.

Here, the tabletop's left half has been left white.

I abstracted the chairs' lower halves in this sketch.

Abbreviate as much as possible when you sketch.

Omit extraneous lines.

Above, only the chairs have colour.

Avoid giving table cloths' thickness.

Vary the colour saturation.

Avoid applying too much colour.

Sofas

Many find sofas difficult to draw. However, because we associate sitting and lying down with sofas, including a sofa in a living room gives the space warmth. The key is to make the sofa appear soft. Using light lines for the sofa's exterior contours or omitting those lines altogether will make the sofa seem soft.

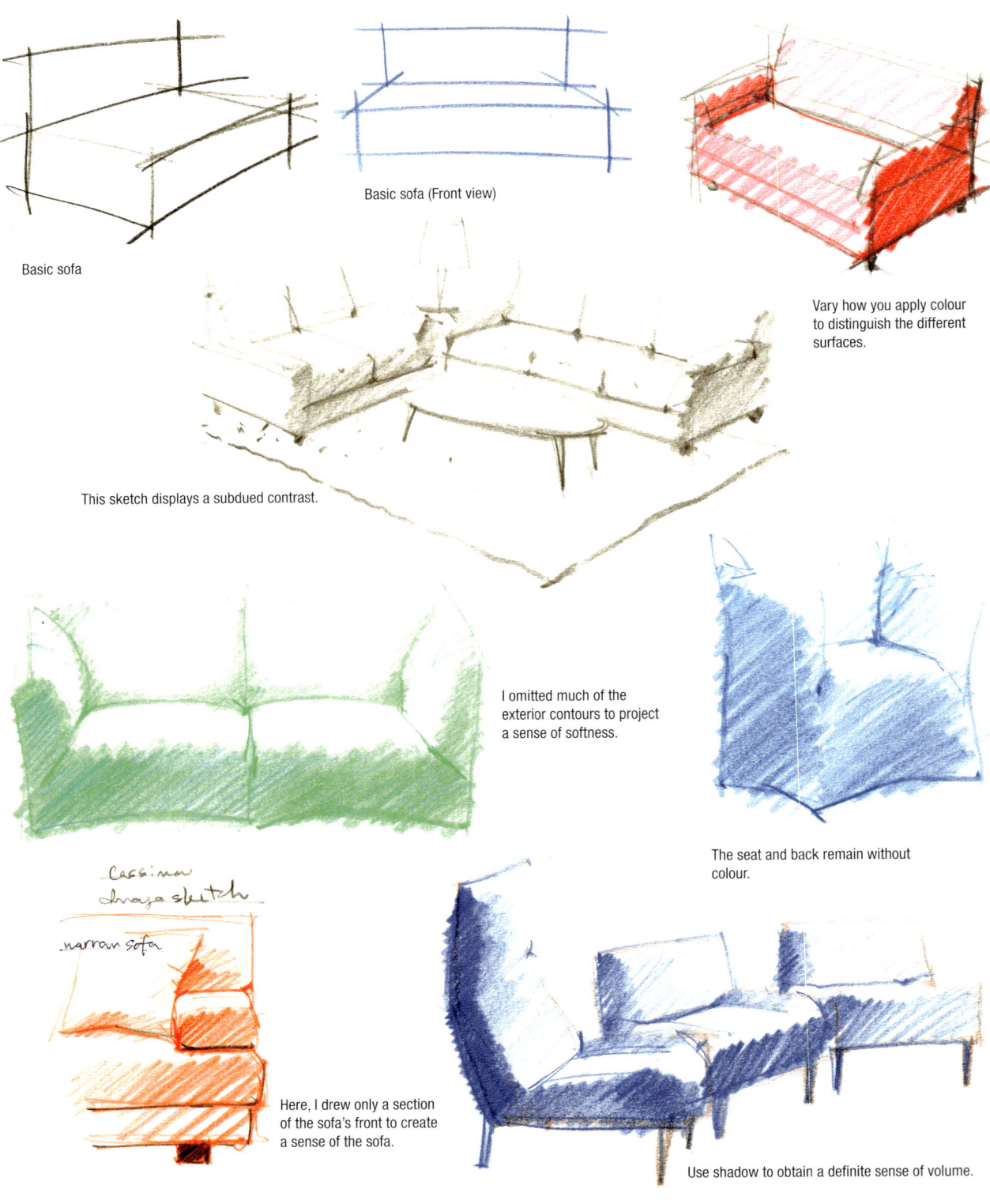

Basic sofa

Basic sofa (Front view)

Vary how you apply colour to distinguish the different surfaces.

This sketch displays a subdued contrast.

I omitted much of the exterior contours to project a sense of softness.

The seat and back remain without colour.

Here, I drew only a section of the sofa's front to create a sense of the sofa.

Use shadow to obtain a definite sense of volume.

Storage Units

The key to drawing storage units is to abstract the doors and shelves to a significant degree. Large storage furniture units call for colouring minimal strategic areas of the piece. Make a point to eliminate extraneous details, while checking the space's overall balance.

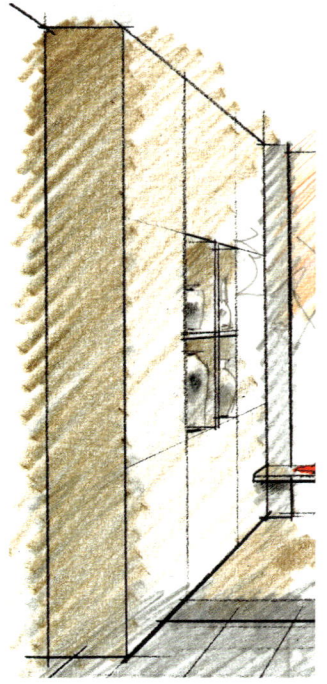

Foyer cabinets: From this angle, the cabinet doors do not require much colouring.

Living room wall unit: Suggest in a simple manner objects displayed on the shelves.

Entertainment cabinet: Shading play a key role in making the shelf holding the TV appear three-dimensional.

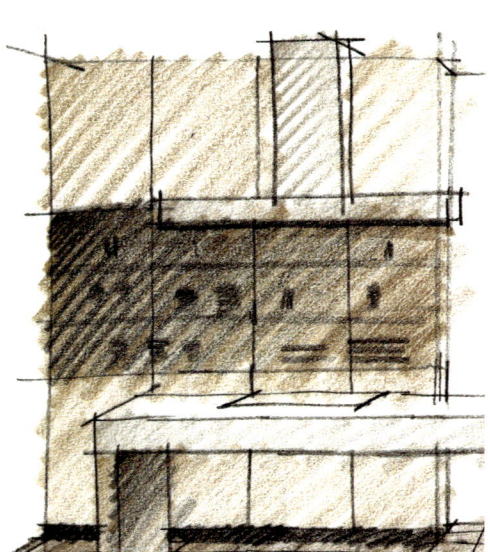

Kitchen cabinets: Suggest kitchen cabinets in an understated manner.

This shows the living room wall unit with displayed objects drawn in relative detail.

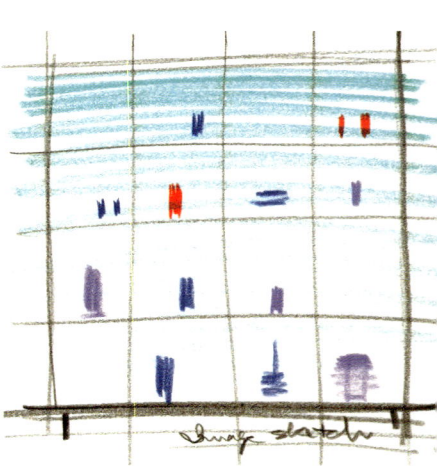

This example shows light blue blurred and gradated to portray glass. I used a variety of bright colours for the objects displayed.

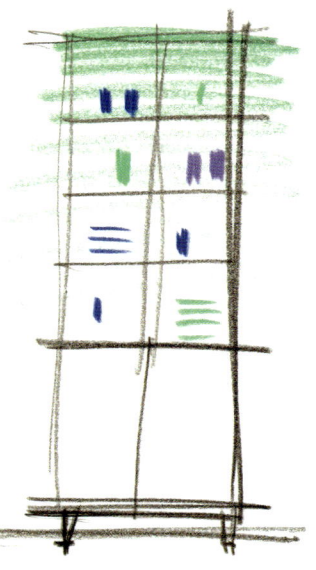

Below, I layered red and yellow to portray the entertainment unit's doors.

Here, I used light green to portray the glass doors.

Wooden armoire: The front is coloured using brown gradated from the upper left.

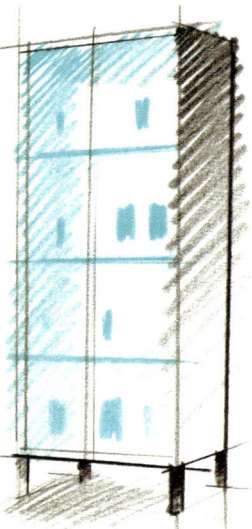
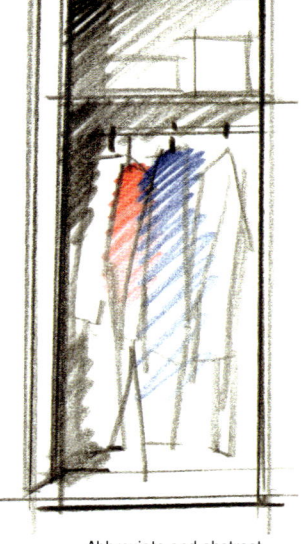

I coloured the cabinet above to give a general idea of how it is constructed.

I used light blue for the glass doors as well as the objects stored inside in this example.

Abbreviate and abstract clothing as much as possible.

In the above, I used correction fluid to portray the down lights and lighting effects.

This shows shelves without doors and with objects displayed.

I used a single shade of blue to colour this living room wall unit.

Your style of portraying books plays a key role in drawing bookshelves.

Beds

Clearly delineating or colouring a bed's contours could make it appear too hard and uncomfortable. The key point here is to make the bed soft.

Suggest bedding creases in an understated fashion.

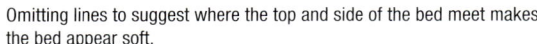

Omitting lines to suggest where the top and side of the bed meet makes the bed appear soft.

I used sepia for this monochrome bed.

This shows an almost perfectly frontal view. The upper left is brighter while the lower right is darker.

Make a point of minimizing contour lines in light areas of a bed.

Used shading to suggest a cutout rectangle on the headboard's right side of this bed.

The lighting effect appearing between the twin beds plays a key role in this composition.

I used warm grey and simple, light strokes to suggest draped bedding.

Colouring only one side of each bed creates a sense of volume.

The above shows a black bed drawn in black coloured pencil. The key to this sketch was that I varied the intensity (colour saturation) at which I applied the pencil.

Light and dark shadows on the bed's side evoke the sense of softness.

I used light shadows to create this grey bed.

Curtains

Overly accentuating curtains can make a space feel oppressive. It is fine to accentuate curtains if you intend them to be the sketch's focus. However, if that is not the case, then it is important that the curtains appear light and airy.

This subdued representation shows the draped folds of a curtain rendered in blue strokes.

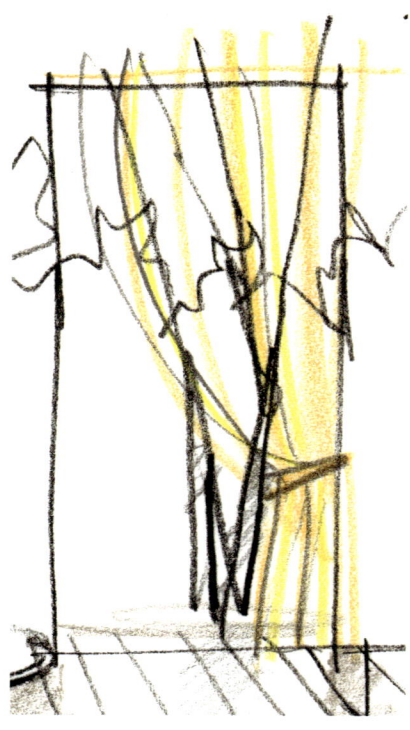

Here, the draped folds are rendered in yellow.

In this sketch, the lines of the draped folds extend beyond the ceiling line.

Rather than using a straightedge, freehand draw draped curtain folds.

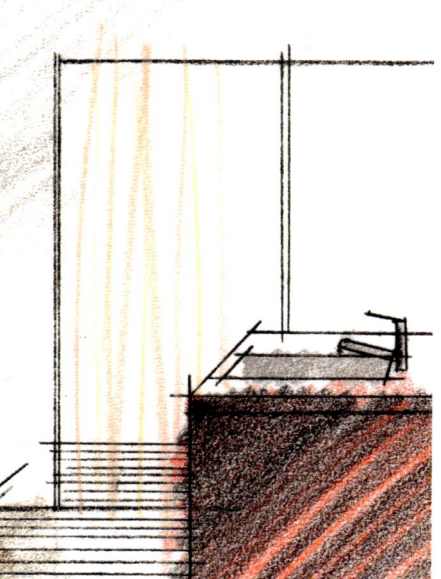

Give the curtains a light and unaffected feel.

Avoid adding too much detail.

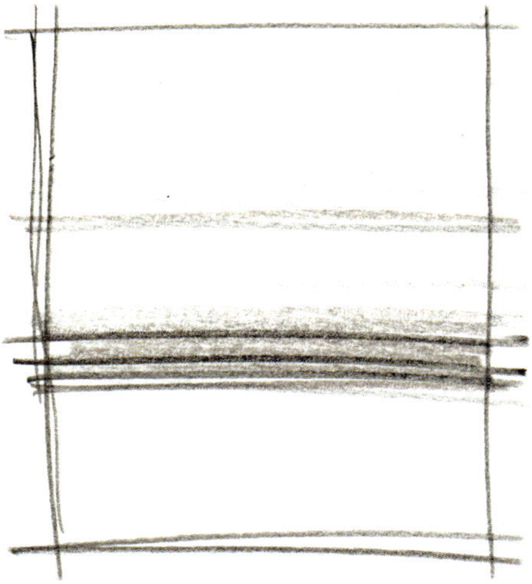

Use as simple representations as possible when drawing blinds.

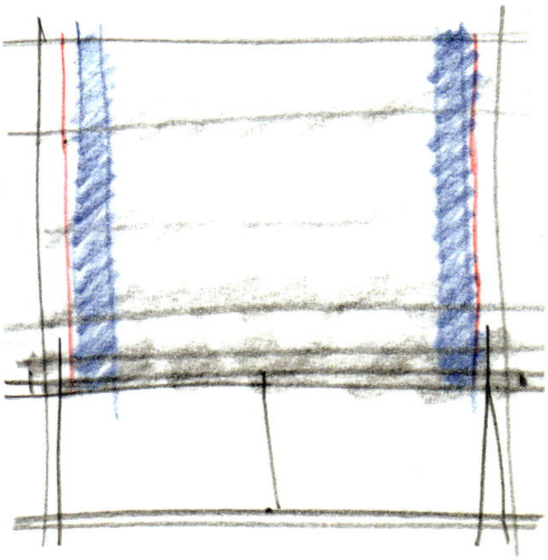

Here, I combined purple with yellow.

Roman blinds: Keep shading on the muted side.

I used blue to create the above curtains. Take care to avoid drawing too many draped folds.

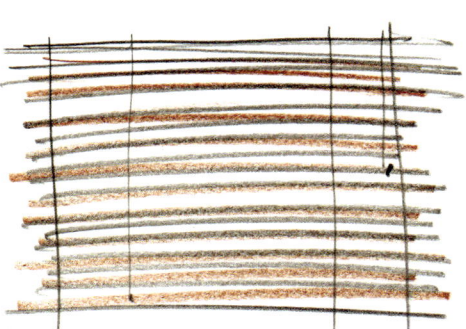

The above shows wood blinds.

Use soft strokes to draw draped folds.

Light Fixtures

People tend to be selective about lighting, so take care not to include too much detail. The key is to portray the distinctive characteristics of the lighting using simple lines.

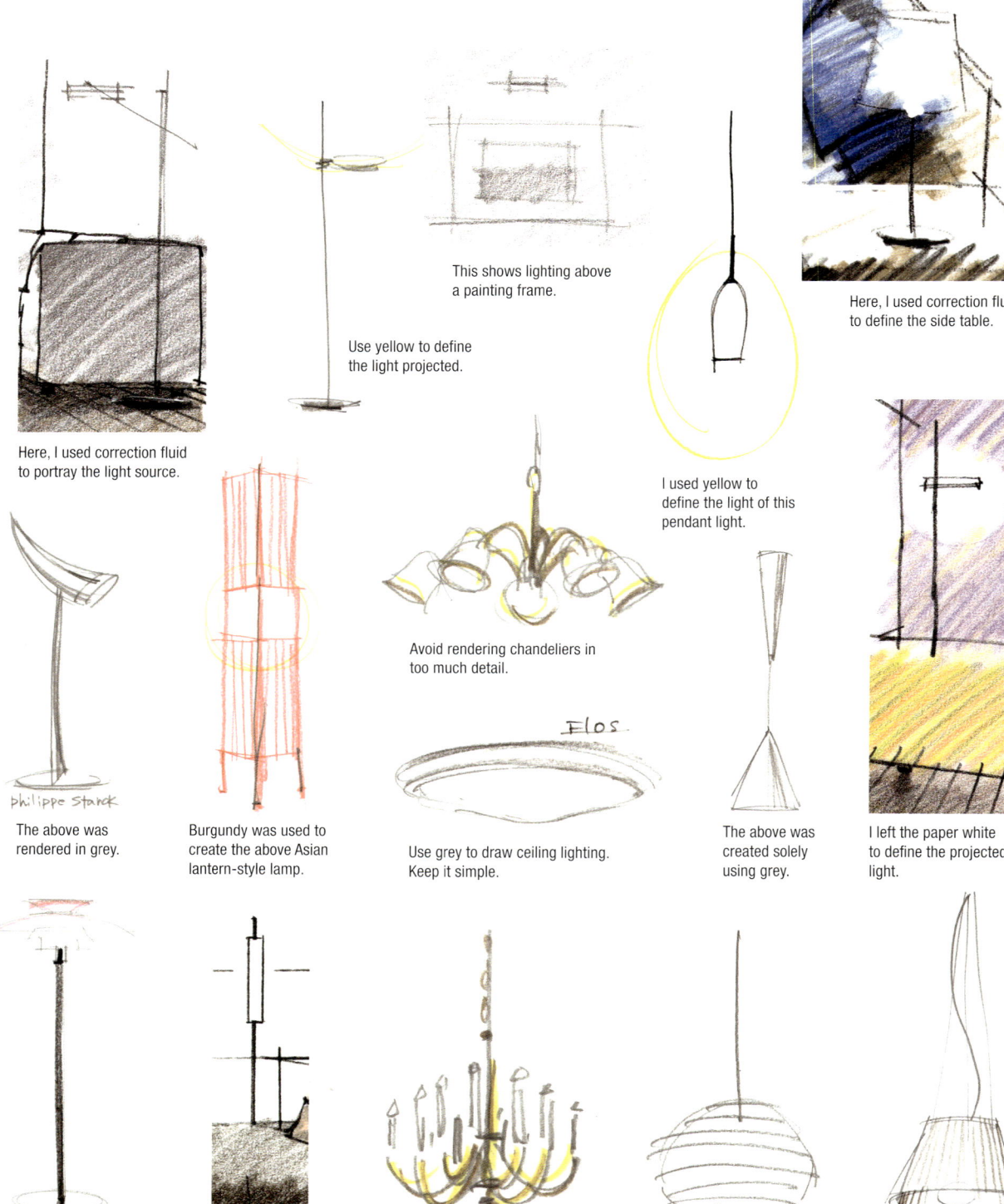

This shows lighting above a painting frame.

Use yellow to define the light projected.

Here, I used correction fluid to define the side table.

Here, I used correction fluid to portray the light source.

I used yellow to define the light of this pendant light.

Avoid rendering chandeliers in too much detail.

The above was rendered in grey.

Burgundy was used to create the above Asian lantern-style lamp.

Use grey to draw ceiling lighting. Keep it simple.

The above was created solely using grey.

I left the paper white to define the projected light.

Lightly apply colour.

This shows a floor lamp.

Omit details when portraying lighting.

I drew the above using a regular pencil.

When drawing pleats, avoid using overly bold strokes.

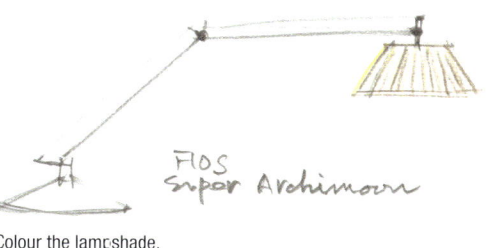

Colour the lampshade.

I sketched the above using only a black coloured pencil.

Bamboo lighting

To portray brightness, leave a portion of the floor lamp's neck white.

Colour the ceiling fan's blades.

A coloured chandelier

Colour was applied to suggest an antique-style chandelier.

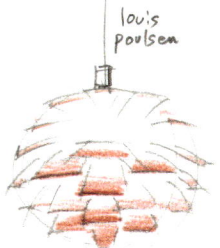

Gradated colour applied to the miniature glass panels produced the above lighting effect.

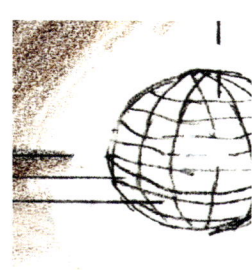

Leaving the paper surrounding the lamp white creates the illusion of light.

This Asian lantern-style lamp has colour applied to the lamp, itself, while yellow was used to portray the light projected.

Here, the light source is rendered using correction fluid.

Here, I used correction fluid to define the light source but left the paper white to portray the surrounding projected light.

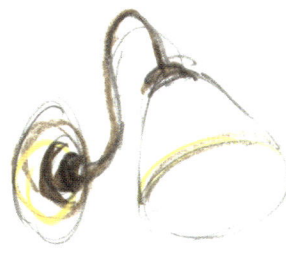

Coloured pencil was used solely to create the contours of this wall sconce rather than on its surfaces.

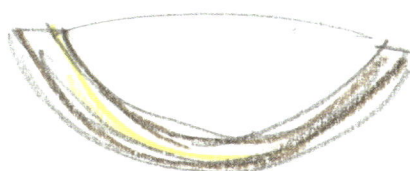

Simplify ceiling lights.

Use light applications of yellow and brown to portray bamboo in lighting.

Kitchens

Kitchens tend to reflect strongly the sensibilities and preferences of the homeowner. Until recently, kitchens components were treated as appliances in sketches. However, nowadays, kitchen components have come to be regarded as furniture and an interior design component. The key sketching point lies in how to portray cabinet doors. Always strive to sketch kitchens in as simple terms as possible, just like you would with other furniture.

Modulating the saturation of the blue play a key role in this sketch.

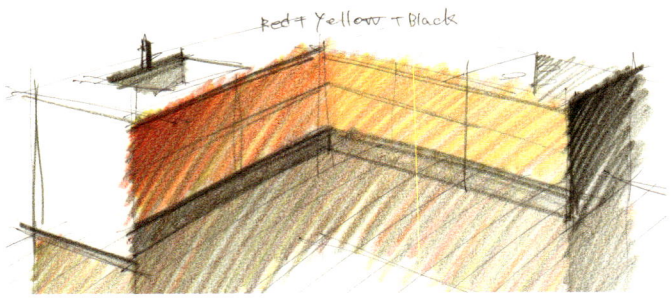

I combined red and yellow to create these cabinet doors.

Modulating the saturation of red created these cabinet doors.

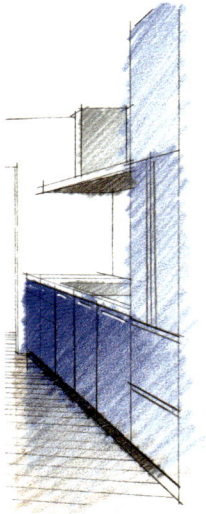

In this example, the blue closer to the picture plane is lighter.

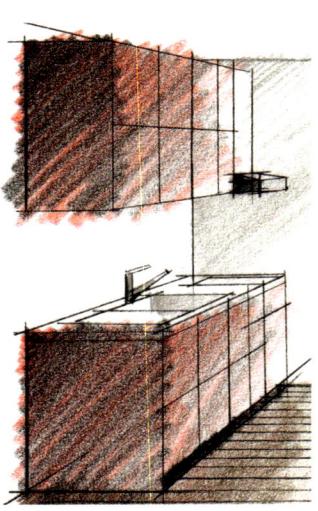

Mix red and black to create wine.

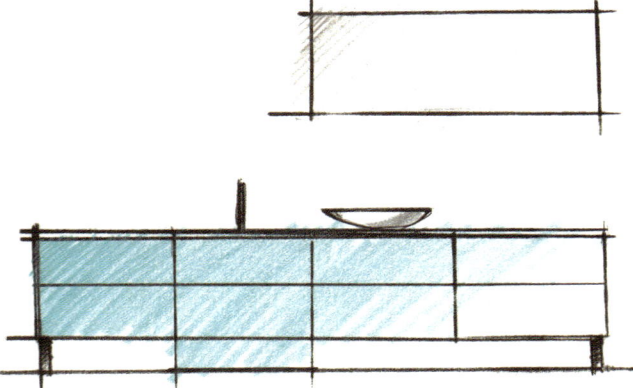

Avoid adding too much detail when sketching modern kitchens.

I left the countertop uncoloured to achieve a bright finish.

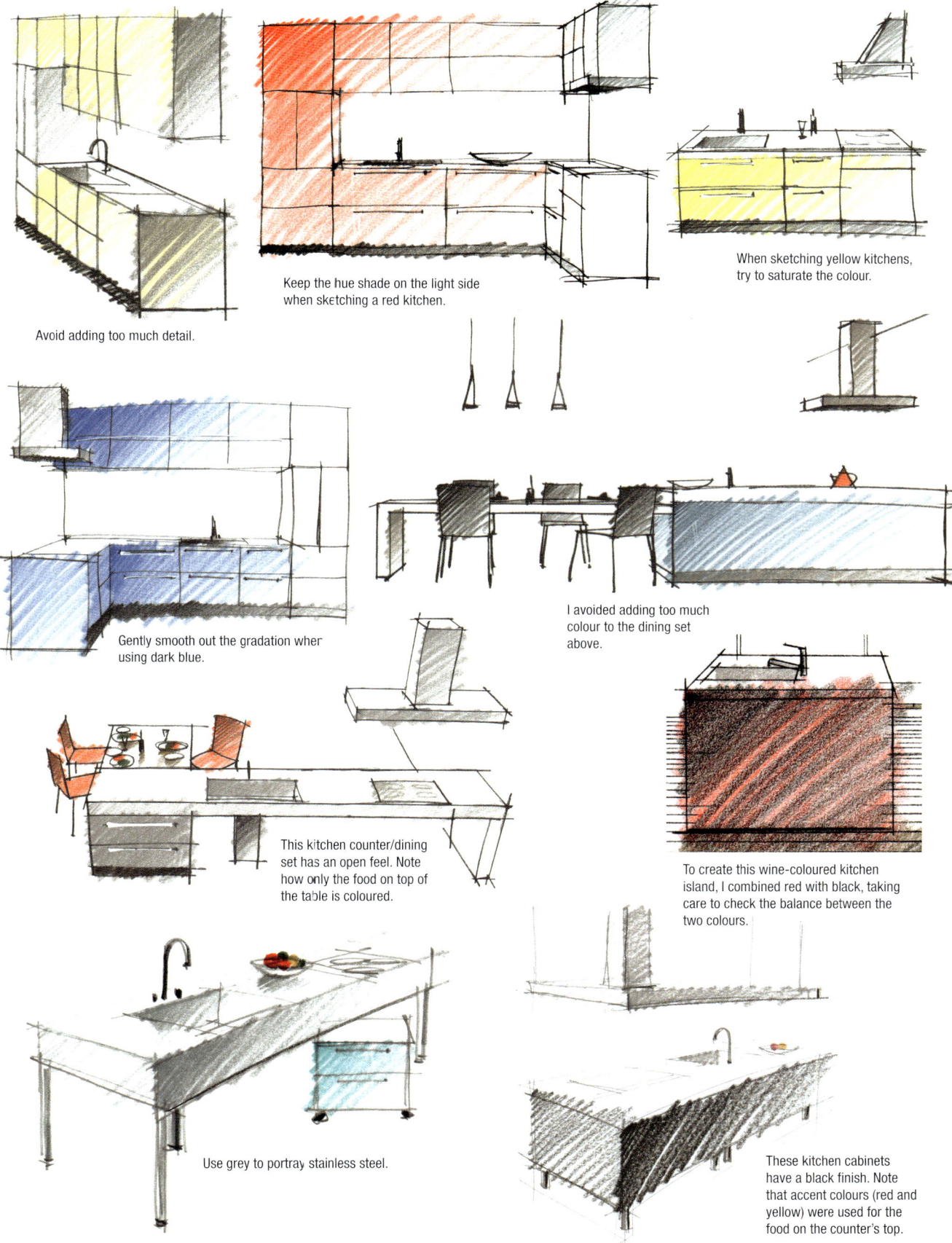

Bathrooms Vanities

Bathroom vanities are another interior component that comes in an array of designs. However, I limited the extent and purposes of those I presented in this book. I suggest that the reader first become proficient in drawing a basic vanity and then use that as a springboard for attempting a variety of other designs.

While vanities comprise a multiple components, including a mirror, a counter or table, a sink, a faucet, and cabinet doors, you will rarely need to draw all of them. You will instead sketch the vanity according to the theme required at that given time, such as focus on the cabinet doors or accentuate the mirror.

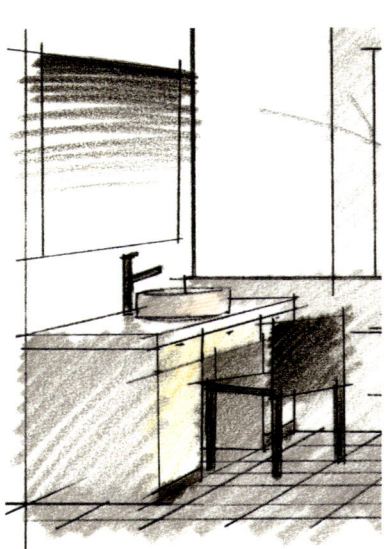
Here, the cabinet doors are rendered in light yellow.

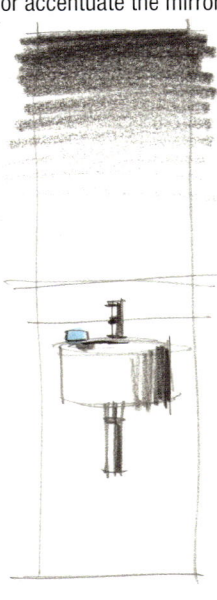
The soap is the only point of colour on this simple sink.

The flowers and stool seat are coloured red.

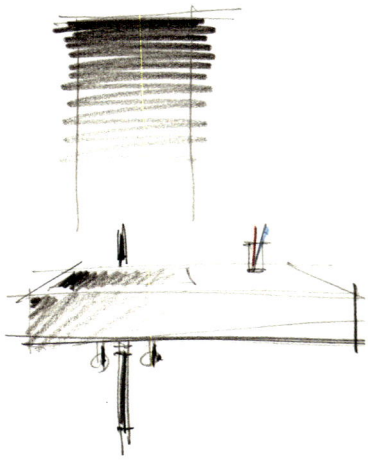

Here, I varied the saturation of the blue to give the cabinet volume.

Here, the overall vanity is monochrome, while the toothbrushes are rendered in different colours.

Use aquamarine to render the sides of glass shelves.

Here, the drawers and soap are coloured.

I lightly coloured the vanity above to achieve a bright and fresh finish.

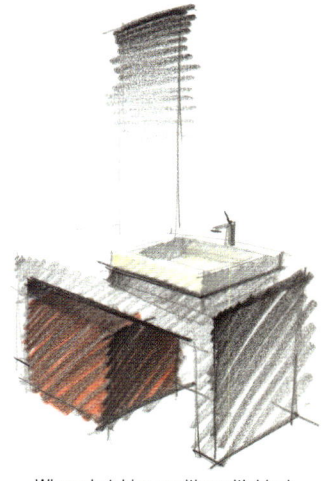

When sketching vanities with black finishes, make the vanity top bright.

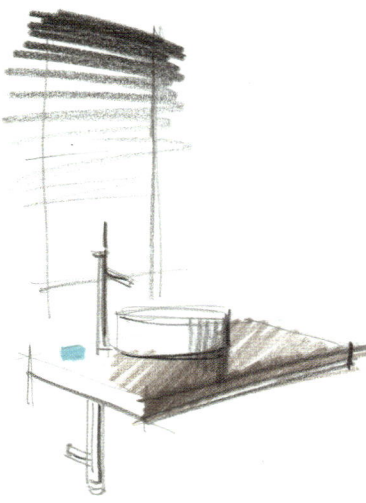

Here, soap appears as a visual accent.

The flowers appear as a visual accent.

In this sketch, I made the shadow underneath the vanity light on the dark side.

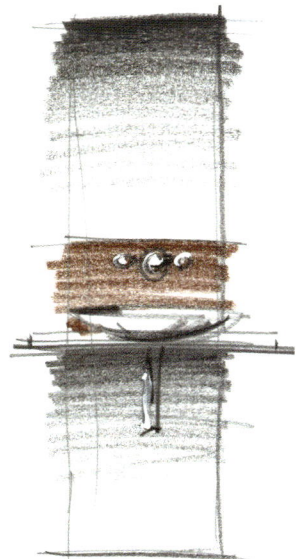

Apply the coloured pencil using vertical strokes when drawing a narrow vanity.

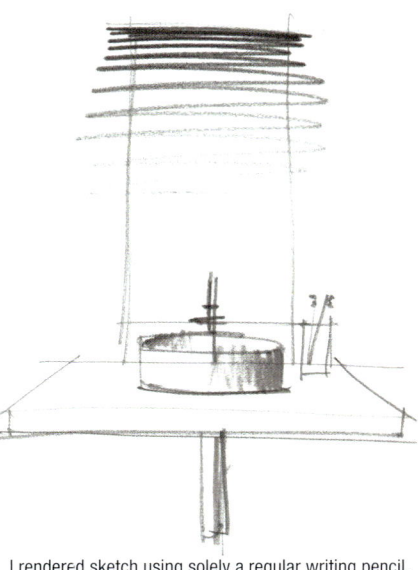

I rendered sketch using solely a regular writing pencil.

Use gradated yellow to colour indirect ceiling lighting.

Baths

Bathrooms have become much more open, when compared to previous bathroom plans. Bathtubs also now come in a host of designs. However, when drawing bathtubs, abbreviate lines and pare down details as much as possible. Instead, colour the water to make it a visual accent.

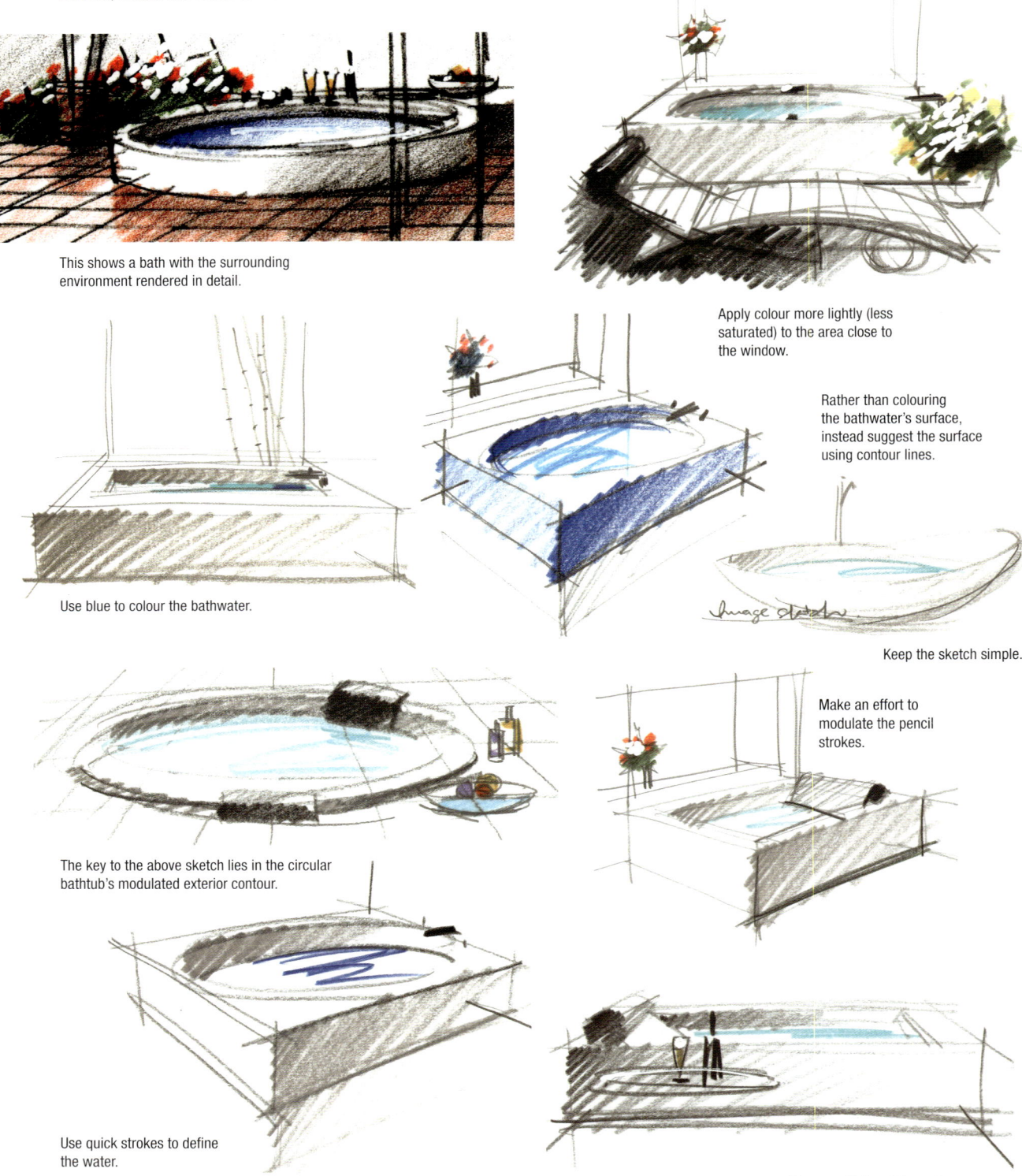

This shows a bath with the surrounding environment rendered in detail.

Apply colour more lightly (less saturated) to the area close to the window.

Rather than colouring the bathwater's surface, instead suggest the surface using contour lines.

Use blue to colour the bathwater.

Keep the sketch simple.

Make an effort to modulate the pencil strokes.

The key to the above sketch lies in the circular bathtub's modulated exterior contour.

Use quick strokes to define the water.

Use smooth transitions when gradating shadows.

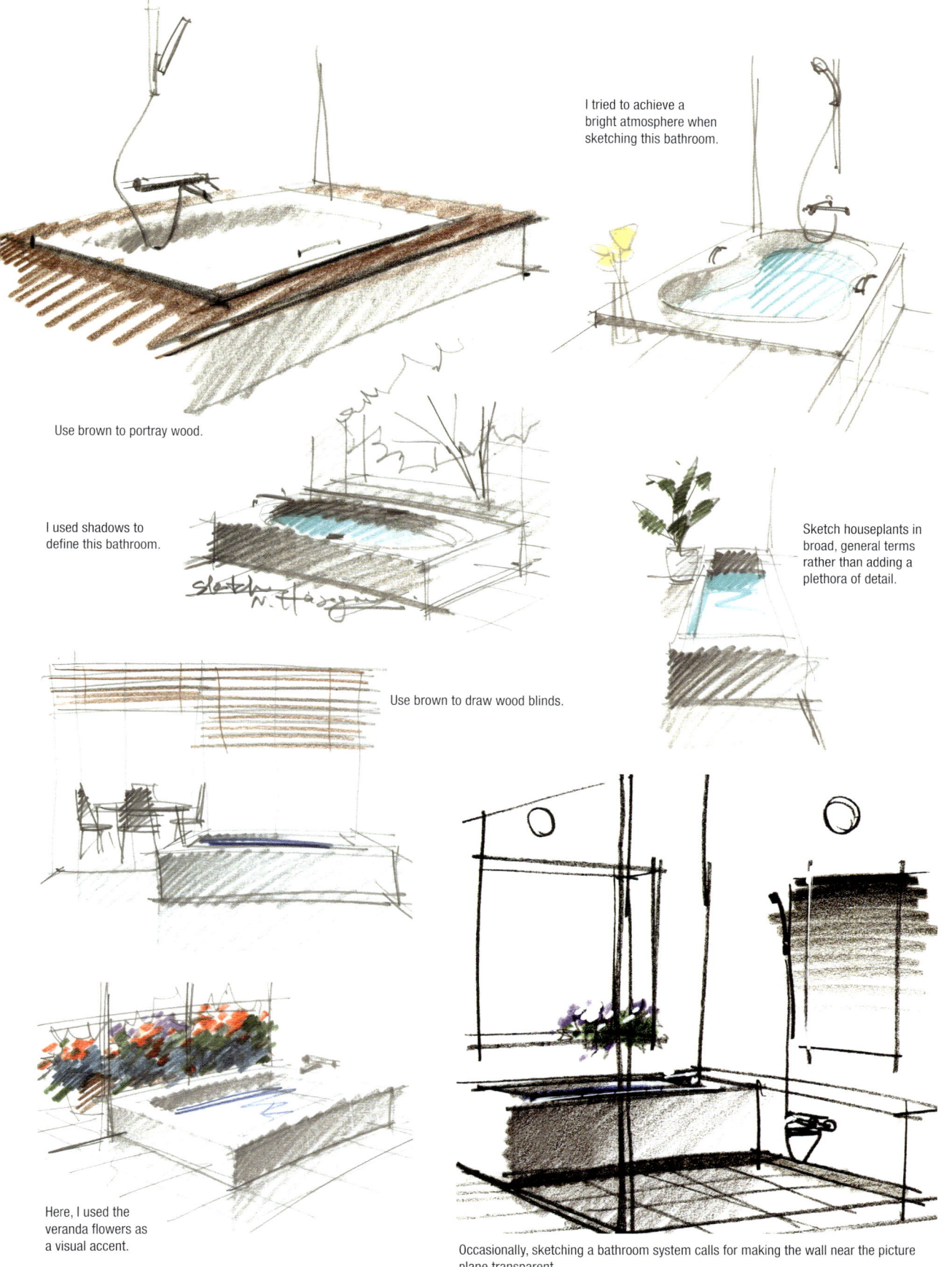

Toilets

Toilets are regarded as having become a particularly developed space in recent years. They are now occasionally even referred to as "the ultimate private space." These days we also see unenclosed toilets with open, airy designs, skillfully integrated within the same space as sinks. Draw toilets using solely contour lines or adding shadow to achieve a suggestion of volume.

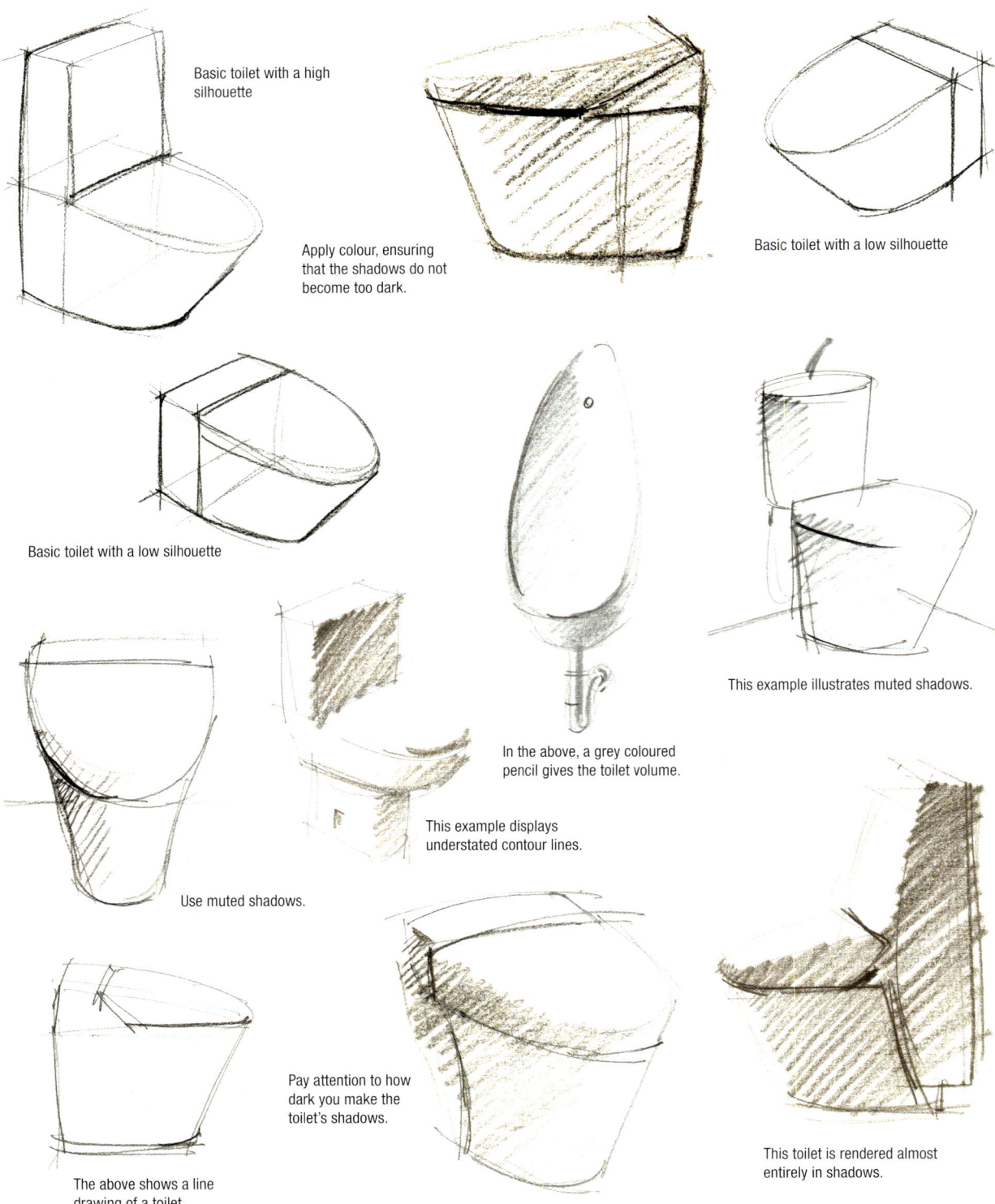

Chapter II

Mastering Coloured Pencil Techniques

While the most appealing aspect of coloured pencils is that they are a convenient way to colour a sketch, the unfortunate fact is that coloured pencil sketches leave a relatively weak impression. Furthermore, coloured pencils do lend themselves well to drawing lines but not so well to coloured large surfaces.

This chapter discusses how to take advantage of the coloured pencils' inherent strengths as well as colouring techniques ranging from basic methods in applying colour. It also teaches how to master colouring with coloured pencils to create sketches with impact.

Colouring with Coloured Pencils: Part I

Colouring with coloured pencils consists more of drawing with connected lines rather than filling a surface area with colour. Use strokes drawn at a 45° angle when colouring.

Holding the Pencil

❶ When colouring with coloured pencils, practice using strokes that move at a 45° angle from the lower left to the upper right. (Left-handed people would probably feel more comfortable moving from the lower right to the upper left.)

❷ Holding a Coloured Pencil: Technique A
Hold a coloured pencil as you would regularly hold a pencil when writing. This is primarily the angle you would use when drawing lines. Some people hold the back of the pencil when sketching, but I cannot recommend this technique for colouring if you intend to modulate the colour's saturation (intensity).

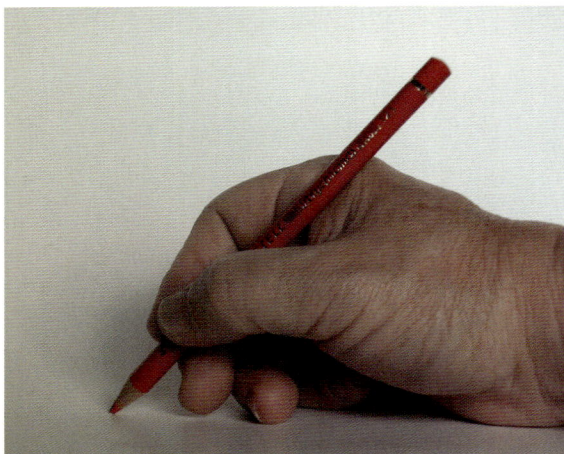

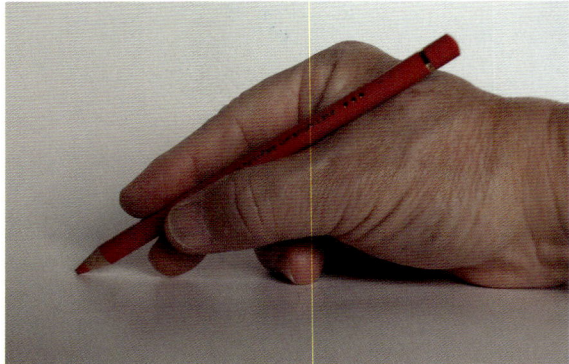

❸ Holding a Coloured Pencil: Technique B
This is the angle you would use to hold a coloured pencil when drawing wide lines or colouring. This is the way I typically hold a coloured pencil and the angle I normally use. To hold the pencil, extend your forefinger, laying it along the coloured pencil, and hold the pencil at a low angle. To draw lines, use the technique described under Technique A. To colour, use the technique described under Technique B.

Leaving Portions White

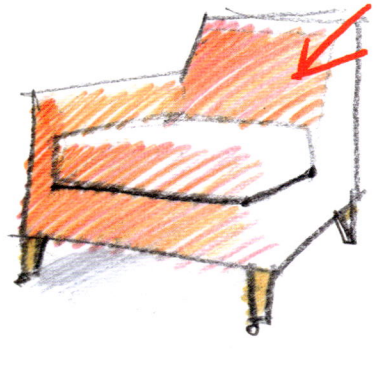

❹ A key point in applying colour with coloured pencils is strategically leaving white areas. Coloured pencils make it difficult to go back and colour light areas, so predetermine which areas you intend to make light, and do not apply colour, as shown in the orange upholstered chair. In this example, the light source is located to the upper right (as the red arrow indicates), so I left the seat uncoloured.

❺ In addition to the seat, light touches the back, the arms, and the right side, so I left these areas uncoloured.

Make a point of observing objects on a regular basis.

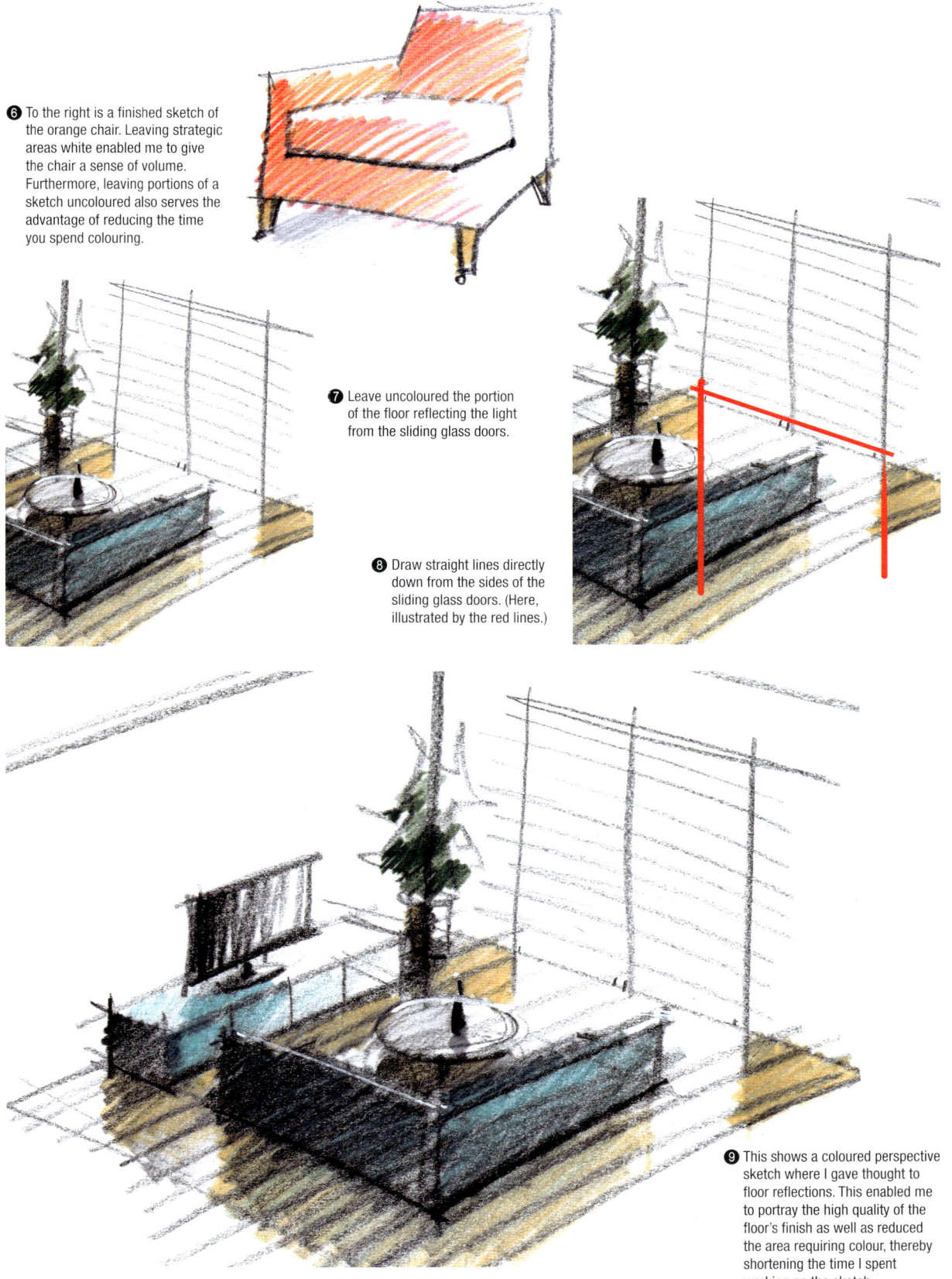

❻ To the right is a finished sketch of the orange chair. Leaving strategic areas white enabled me to give the chair a sense of volume. Furthermore, leaving portions of a sketch uncoloured also serves the advantage of reducing the time you spend colouring.

❼ Leave uncoloured the portion of the floor reflecting the light from the sliding glass doors.

❽ Draw straight lines directly down from the sides of the sliding glass doors. (Here, illustrated by the red lines.)

❾ This shows a coloured perspective sketch where I gave thought to floor reflections. This enabled me to portray the high quality of the floor's finish as well as reduced the area requiring colour, thereby shortening the time I spent working on the sketch.

Colouring with Coloured Pencils: Part II

Modulating the pressure applied to the pencil enables you to lighten or darken the colour.

Modulating Colour

Practice applying different pressures until you are able to produce 5 gradated shades of a single hue. This illustrates five gradated shades for each of the 12 hues of coloured pencils I use. Feel free to use these as reference when you practice. The most saturated shade is just a hair shy of breaking the pencil's point, while the lightest is so light that it is almost difficult to distinguish with the naked eye. The key is to become proficient in modulating the pressure you apply to the pencil. Mastering control over how much pressure to apply will enable you to produce a wide range of representations using colour. When using water colours, the amount of water added allows you to modulate the colour's saturation (intensity). However, in the case of coloured pencils, simply modifying the pressure applied to the pencil enables you to adjust the shade. This is another advantage that coloured pencils afford.

❶ Modifying a colour's saturation enables you to give an object volume, shade an object, and suggest depth.

 **Violet**

 **Red**

 **Mustard**

 **Yellow**

 **Light Green**

 **Dark Green**

 **Black**

 **Brown**

 **Light Peach**

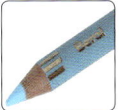 **Light Blue**

 **Blue**

 **Gray**

❷ Layering multiple shades of various hues enhances your ability to portray spaces. Once you are able to modify pencil pressure and produce five shades of a given hue, then go ahead and combine different hues when colouring a sketch. Try combining two colours, three colours, or even four colours. Layering multiple hues enables to produce subtle variations. However, the truth is that many colours will be just impossible. While there are palette limitations, all you need to do is maintain awareness of these limitations when you colour a sketch.

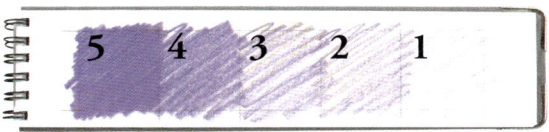

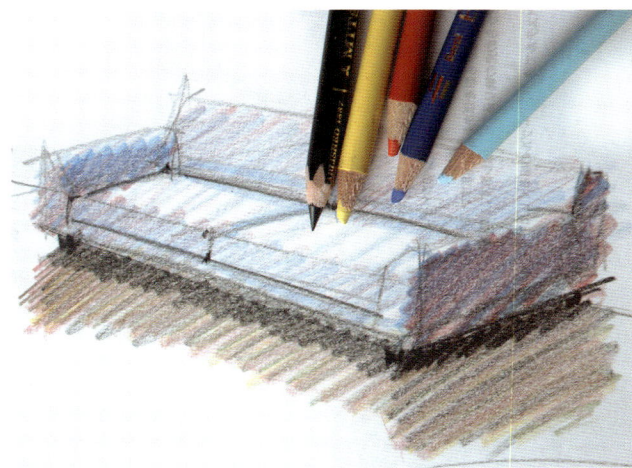

❸ While combining different hues using water colours can produce muddied colours, lightly applying multiple coloured pencil hues gives you clean colours.

Colouring with Coloured Pencils: Part III

Becoming able to modify pressure applied to the pencil as discussed in the previous pages (pp. 38-39) and layering shades of different hues enables you to suggest distance and create sketches with depth. Using colours to suggest depth requires a certain amount of experience. Practice beforehand to determine which colour combinations will be effective for a given interior.

Layering Colours

I combined red and yellow to create the red sofa seen here.

Pencil pressure "grade 5" requires pressure that is just slightly shy of breaking the pencil point. The key is to become proficient in applying this degree of pressure.

Becoming able to modulate the pressure you apply to the pencil will widen your colour repertoire. Combine the five gradated shades of the twelve colours presented when colouring your sketches.

I layered different shades of a single grey hue to create this bedroom. Initially, I used a light shade of the grey and then went back with a second layer, giving thought to the overall visual balance.

The floor, drawn in perspective, was coloured using a combination of brown, grey, and yellow.

This illustrates a variety of colours that can be created by layering different hues.

Colouring with Coloured Pencils: Part IV

The key to gradating (blurring or blending) colours lies in pencil pressure.

How to Gradate (Blur Effect)

Hold the pencil at an angle between 45° and 60° to control the pencil point's width and then gradate or blend the colours. Gradating allows you to produce a range of palettes from vivid colours to transparent colours.

Experiment with gradating a variety of colours.

Use relatively light colours such as yellow, light green, light blue, light peach, mustard, grey, and purple as the base colours.

Red, black, blue, and dark brown make good top layers. Applying the darkest colours last should make it easier to control the results.

Chapter III

The Coloured Pencil Perspective Sketching Process

While coloured pencils are a familiar medium, for some reason they have the reputation of yielding light and weak results.

To use coloured pencils effectively in a perspective sketch, rather than attempting to cover the entire composition with colour, instead, minimize the amount of area actually coloured. In addition, make areas of saturated colour even more saturated and make areas of light colour even lighter to achieve visual variety.

Foyer with a Bench

In this plan, I turned shoe cubbies into a curio shelf, creating a miniature art gallery. Bright sunlight enters from the garden, which is visible from the foyer's opposite side, producing a refreshing a comfortable space. I also included a single plank of wood that I originally intended to display a large urn or other art object but ultimately used as a bench, creating a place for people to rest.

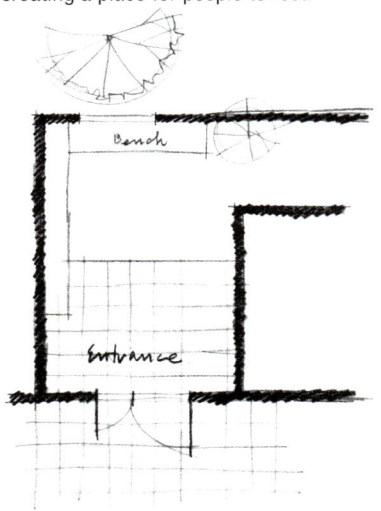

❶ I started by drawing a floor plan.

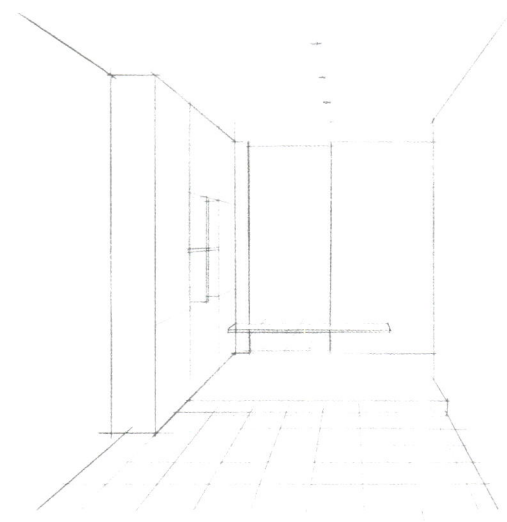

❷ Next, I produced a one-point perspective under drawing.

❸ Then, I added a flower vase alongside the bench to brighten the composition.

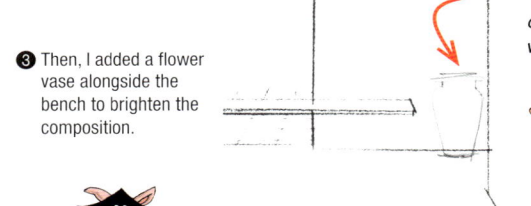

Take careful note of overall proportioning when adding elements.

Use somewhat light strokes for tree and other foliage contours.

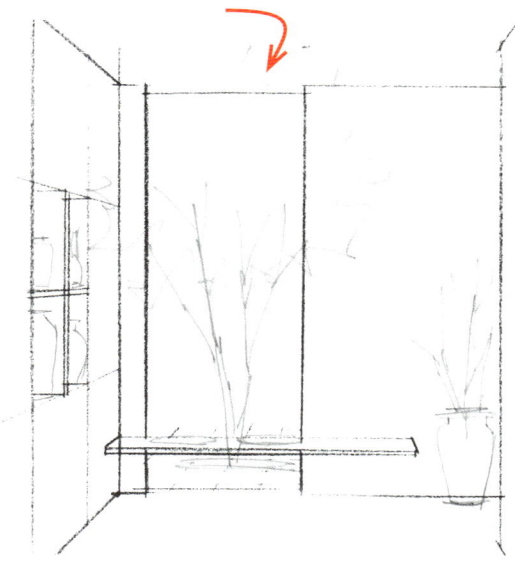

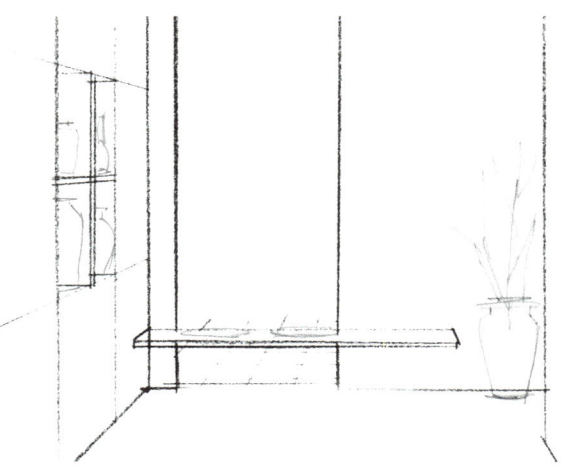

❹ Next, I added details such as art objects (urns and other ceramics) to the curio shelf, the bench cushions, and flowers to the flower vase next to the bench.

❺ I then added the tree in the garden.

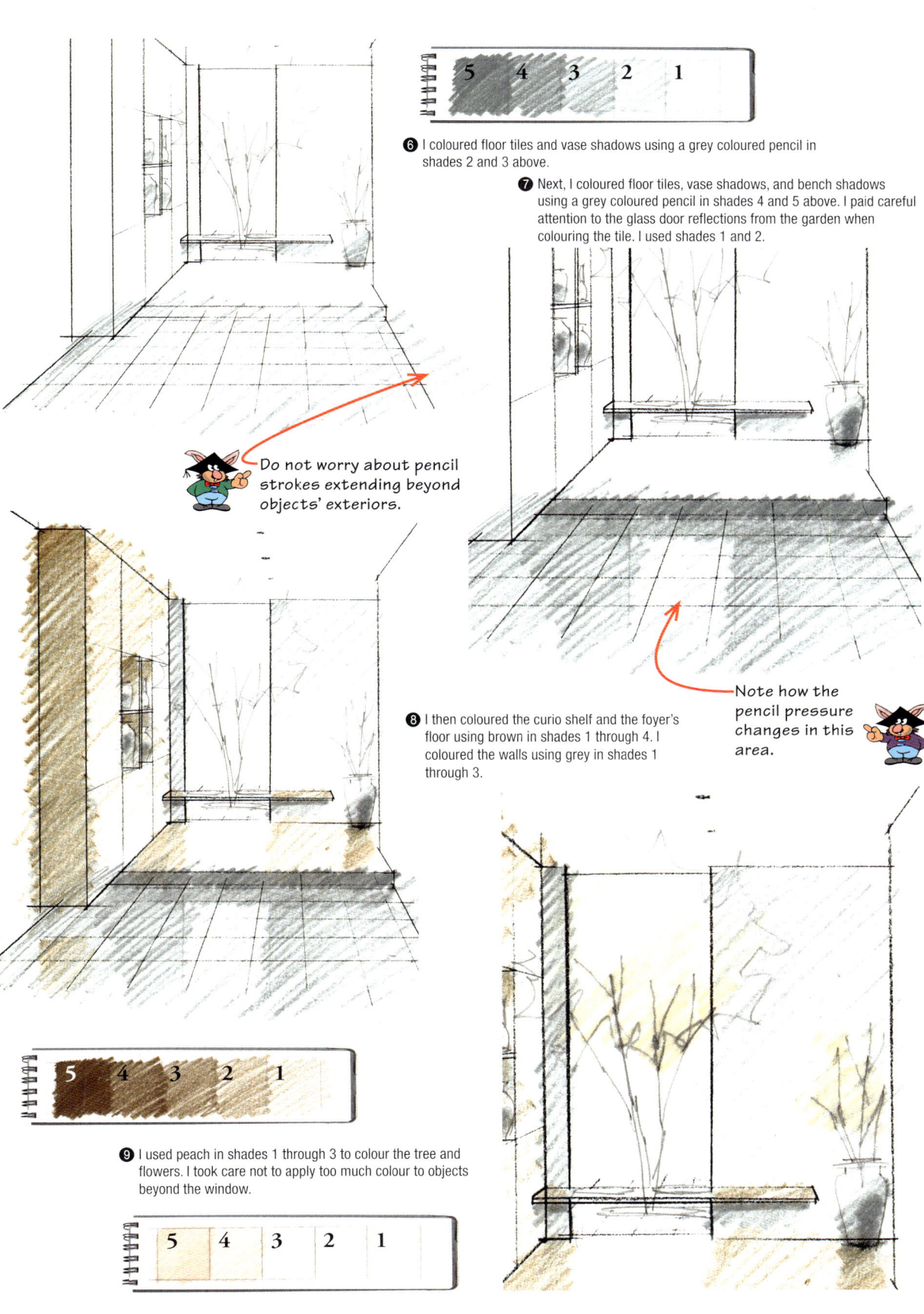

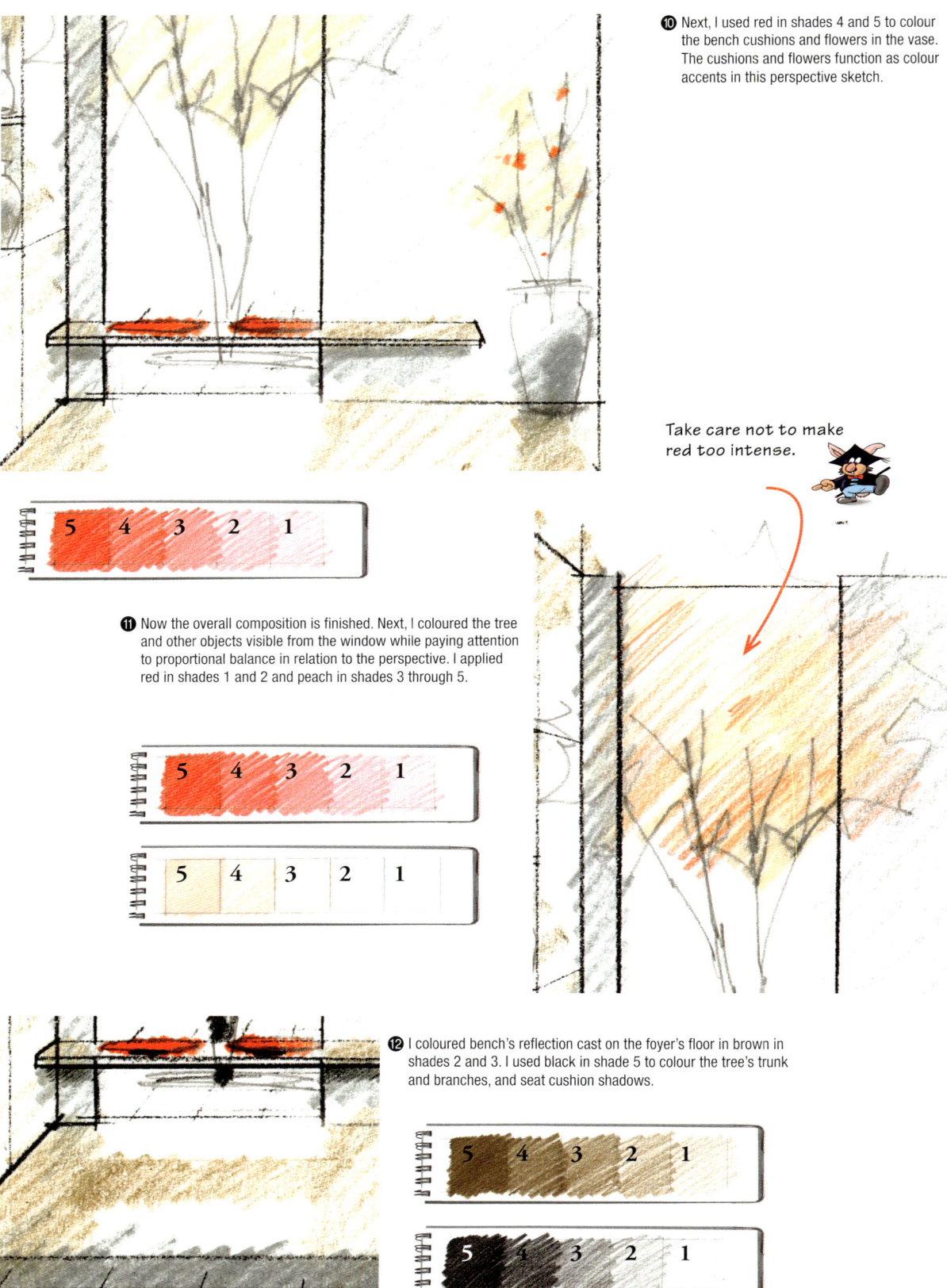

❿ Next, I used red in shades 4 and 5 to colour the bench cushions and flowers in the vase. The cushions and flowers function as colour accents in this perspective sketch.

Take care not to make red too intense.

⓫ Now the overall composition is finished. Next, I coloured the tree and other objects visible from the window while paying attention to proportional balance in relation to the perspective. I applied red in shades 1 and 2 and peach in shades 3 through 5.

⓬ I coloured bench's reflection cast on the foyer's floor in brown in shades 2 and 3. I used black in shade 5 to colour the tree's trunk and branches, and seat cushion shadows.

13 Finally, I made minor adjustments to each colour, while checking the overall finished look to complete the sketch. The tree visible from the foyer's entrance constitutes the focal point. To make the garden appear bright, coloured the floor and walls in a relatively saturated grey in shades 3 and 4.

Foyer with Red Chairs

I added red chairs and a round table to the layout in order to expand upon the foyer's original function (that of entrance/exit and reception room for guests) and redefine this space with an earthen floor into a "living space."
I depicted the overall space in monochrome, giving colour only to the chairs to make them symbolic.

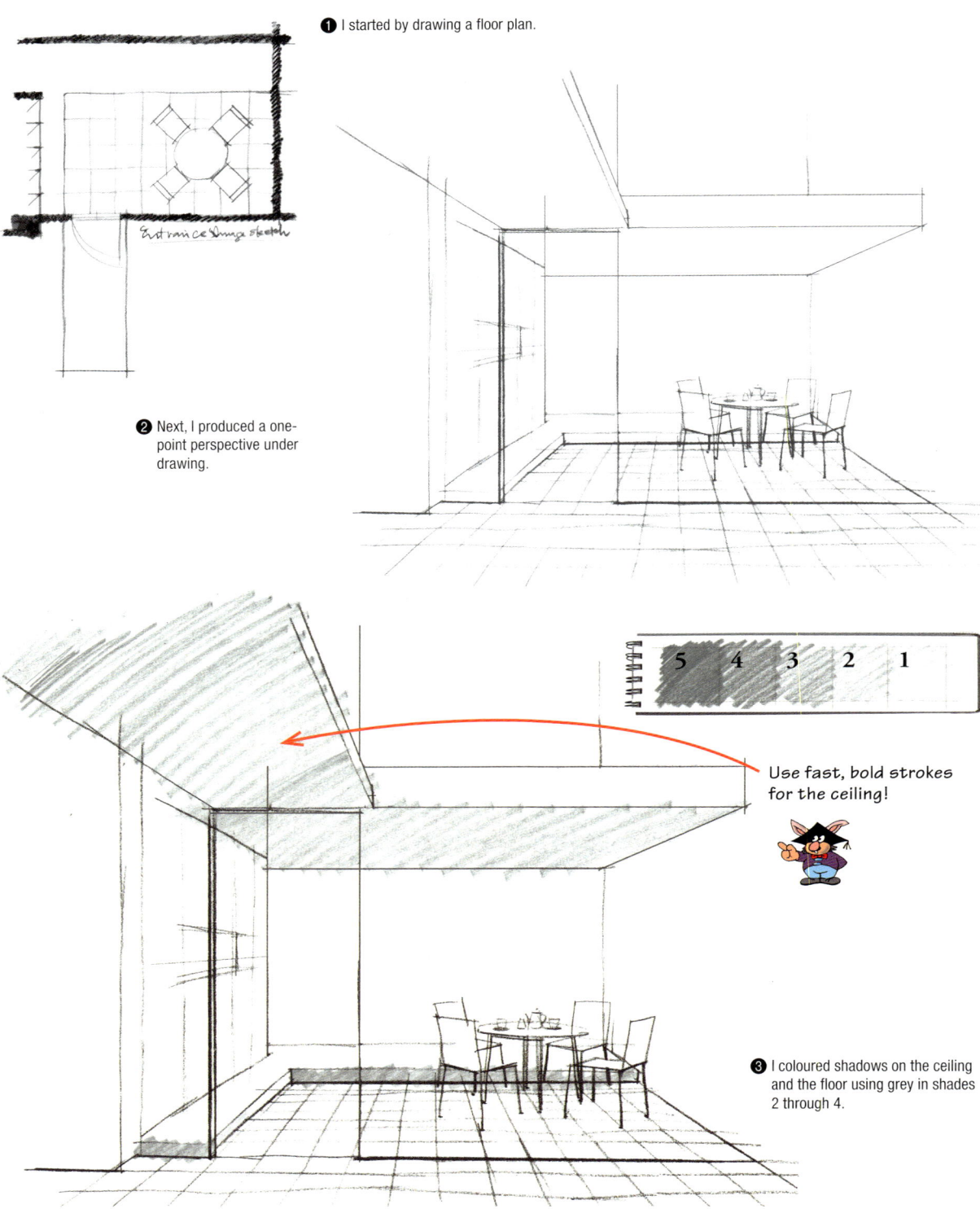

❶ I started by drawing a floor plan.

❷ Next, I produced a one-point perspective under drawing.

Use fast, bold strokes for the ceiling!

❸ I coloured shadows on the ceiling and the floor using grey in shades 2 through 4.

The red may extend beyond the chairs' exterior contour lines.

❹ I used red in shades 2 through 5 to colour the chairs, which function as the focal point of this perspective drawing.

❺ I then used grey to colour the shadows of the teacups and other objects on the table.

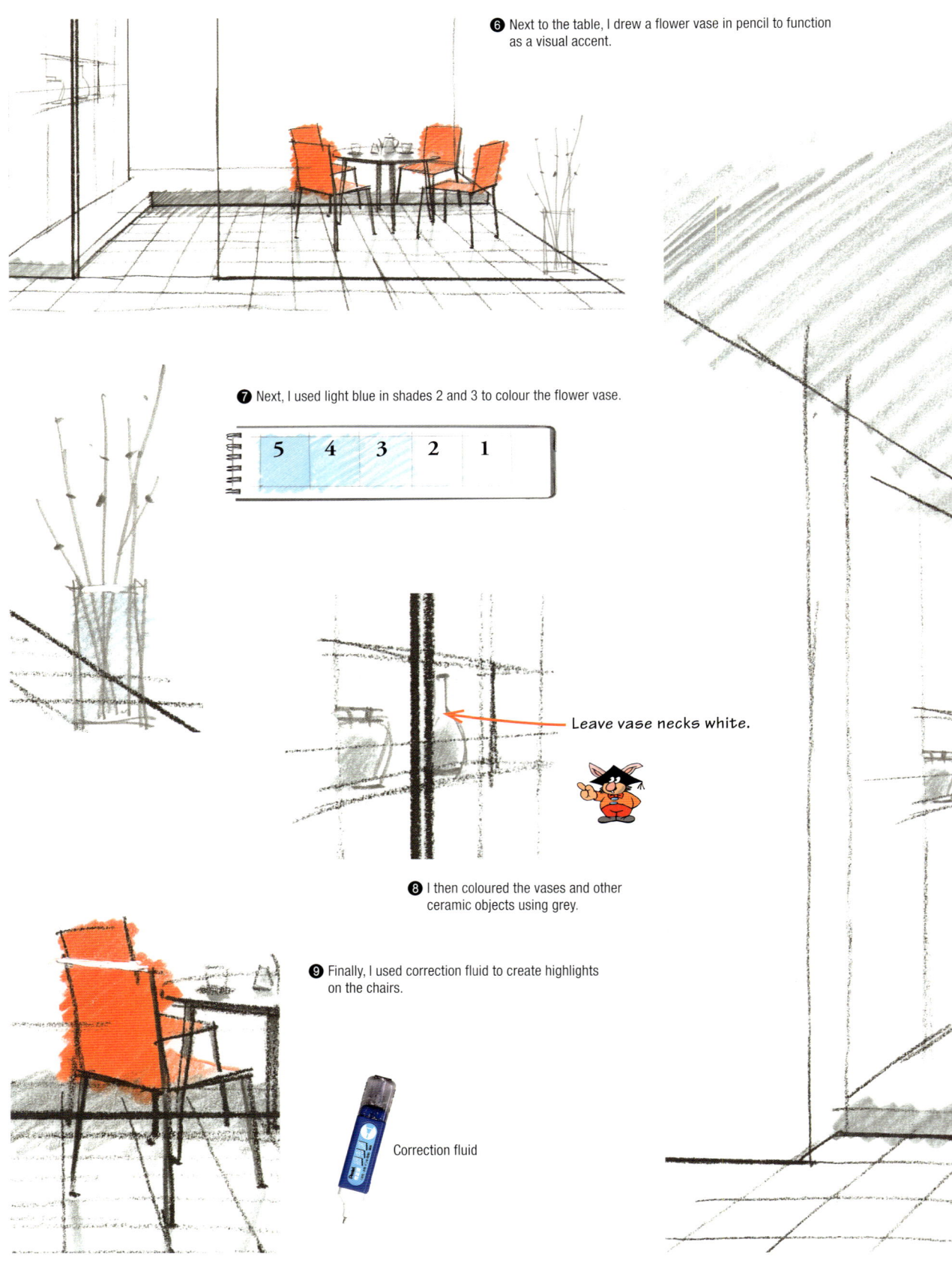

❻ Next to the table, I drew a flower vase in pencil to function as a visual accent.

❼ Next, I used light blue in shades 2 and 3 to colour the flower vase.

Leave vase necks white.

❽ I then coloured the vases and other ceramic objects using grey.

❾ Finally, I used correction fluid to create highlights on the chairs.

Correction fluid

🔟 This shows the final sketch. The chairs' red colour functions as this perspective drawing's focal point. Applying grey too heavily risks giving a composition an overly dark atmosphere, so take care to be conservative when applying grey.

Foyer with a Recessed Wall

This foyer has a recessed wall, which contains lighting. Portrayal of the indirect light from this recessed wall constitutes the focal point of this composition.

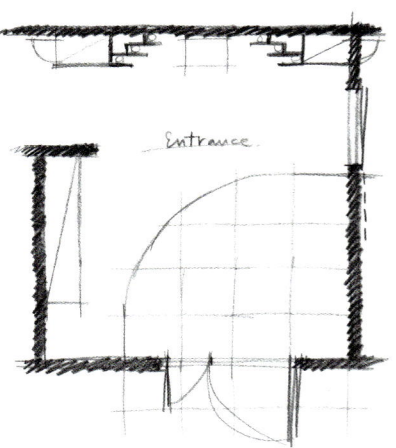

❶ I started by drawing a floor plan.

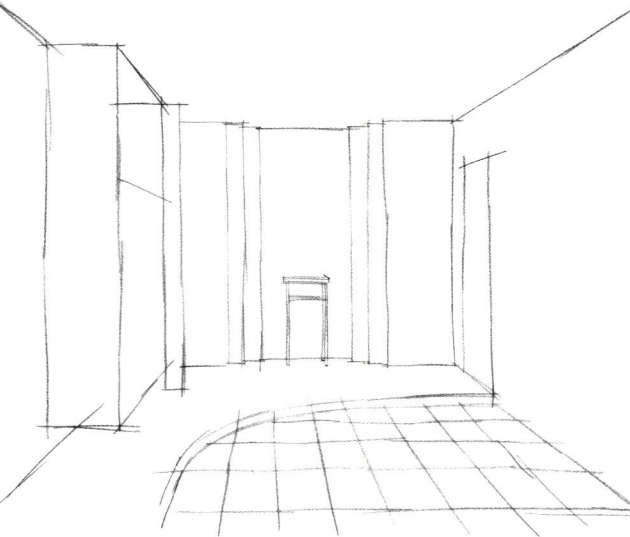

❷ Next, I produced a one-point perspective under drawing.

Leave this area uncoloured.

❸ I coloured the space using grey in shades 1 through 4 to colour this perspective sketch. Grey was really this sketch's lifeline. I particularly avoided applying grey to the indirect lighting and instead left that area uncoloured.

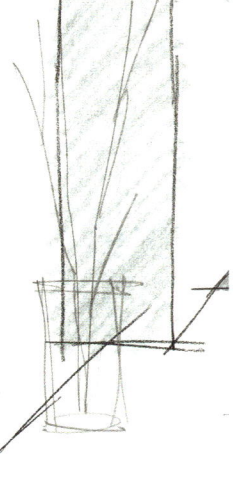

❹ I drew a flower vase in pencil in front of the foyer's cabinet.

❺ I then sketched in pencil some flowers and a flower vase on top of a stand right directly opposite entryway.

❻ After finishing the under drawing, I checked the overall visual balance.

Maintain awareness of the tops of flowers (the flowers themselves) when drawing.

❼ I coloured the leaves of the flowers in front of the entryway using dark green in shades 3 through 5. I used red in shades 4 and 5 to colour the flowers, themselves.

❽ After colouring the flowers, I checked the overall visual balance.

❾ I used a black coloured pencil in shade 5 to pull the composition together. To finish, I used correction fluid to add highlights to the center flower vase.

Correction fluid

Foyer with a Staircase

This foyer has a staircase that greets the eye as soon as the door is opened. It has a simple composition and functions solely as an entrance.

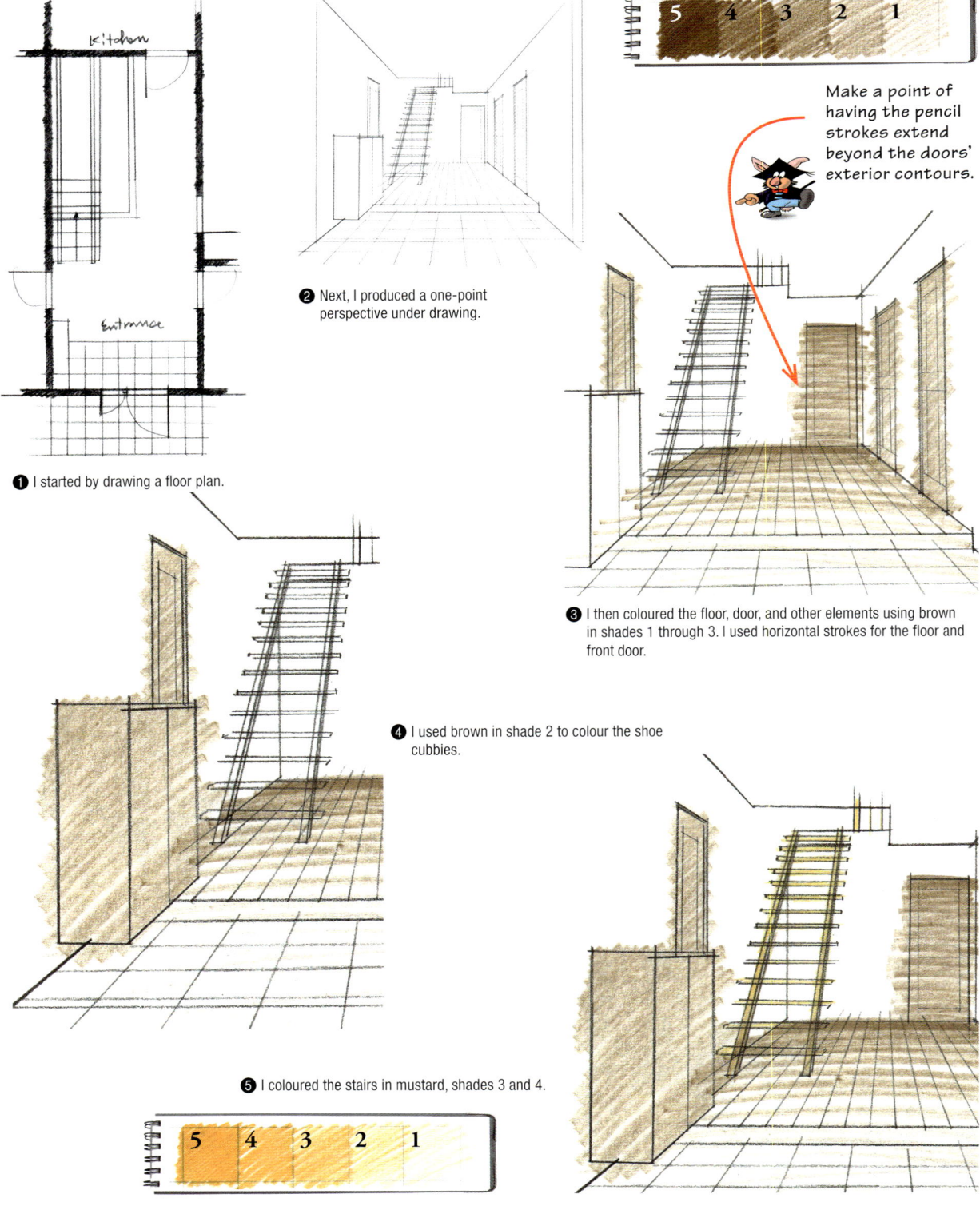

❶ I started by drawing a floor plan.

❷ Next, I produced a one-point perspective under drawing.

Make a point of having the pencil strokes extend beyond the doors' exterior contours.

❸ I then coloured the floor, door, and other elements using brown in shades 1 through 3. I used horizontal strokes for the floor and front door.

❹ I used brown in shade 2 to colour the shoe cubbies.

❺ I coloured the stairs in mustard, shades 3 and 4.

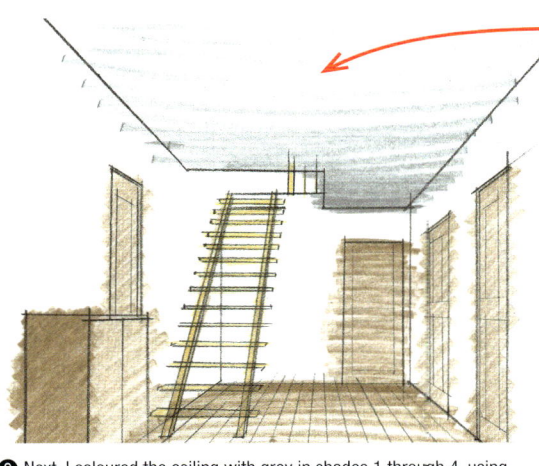

> Gradate your colours, making regions far from the picture plane darker and those close to the picture plane brighter.

❻ Next, I coloured the ceiling with grey in shades 1 through 4, using horizontal strokes.

❼ I then lightly sketched in pencil a potted plant against the facing wall and a picture frame against the left wall.

❽ I used dark green in shades 4 and 5 to colour the plant and purple in shades 4 and 5 for the plant's flowers.

❾ To finish the sketch, I double-checked the composition's overall visual balance, while adding highlights in correction fluid and enhancing some of the shadows.

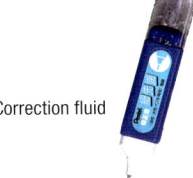

Correction fluid

Foyer with Glass Block

This is a bright entrance hall with a curved wall constructed of glass block. I positioned a chair in front of the glass block to function as an art object and a visual accent. A tree in the garden is visible from the front entrance, making the space even more comfortable.

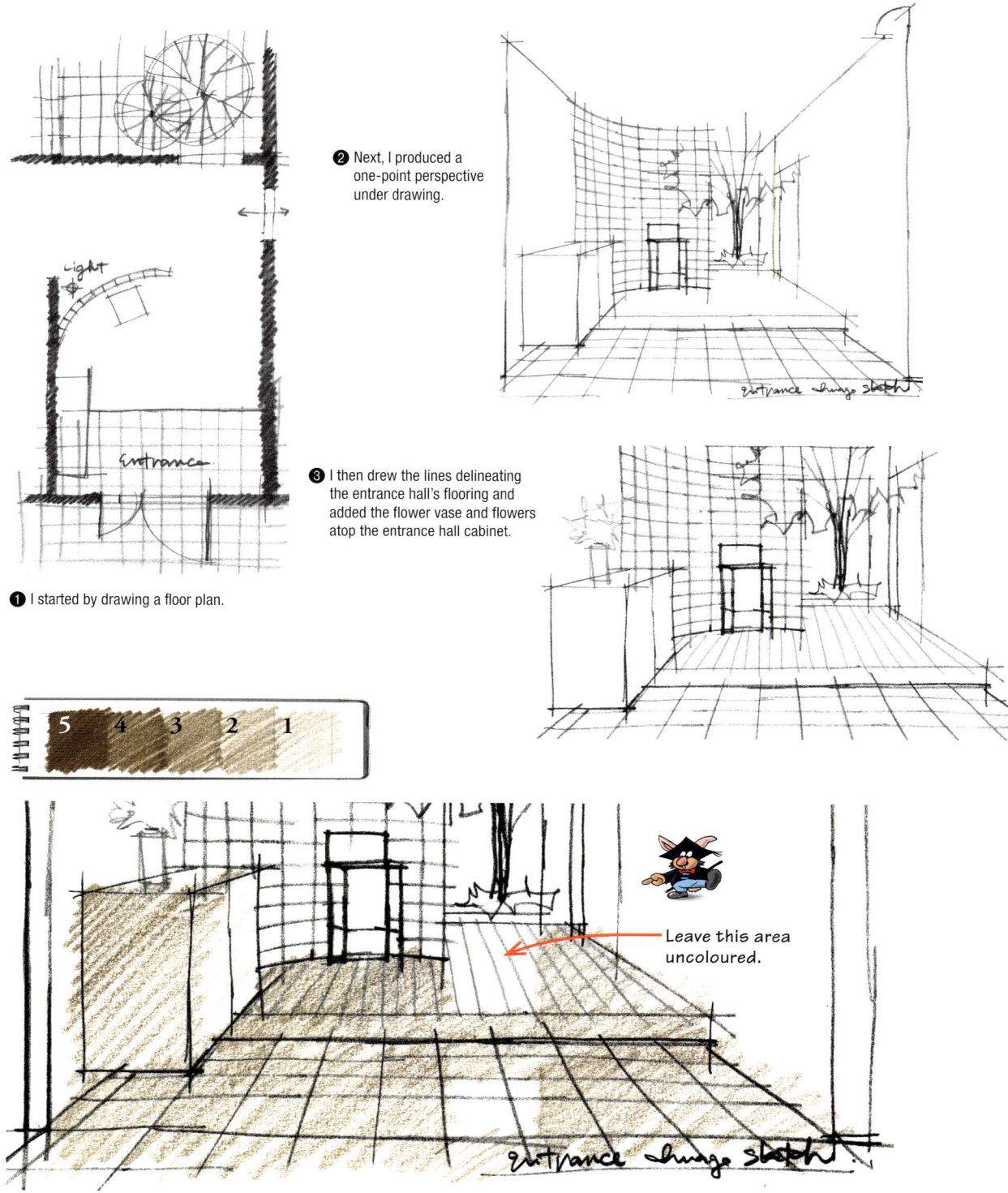

❶ I started by drawing a floor plan.

❷ Next, I produced a one-point perspective under drawing.

❸ I then drew the lines delineating the entrance hall's flooring and added the flower vase and flowers atop the entrance hall cabinet.

Leave this area uncoloured.

❹ Next, I coloured the floor and cabinet using brown in shades 1 through 3.

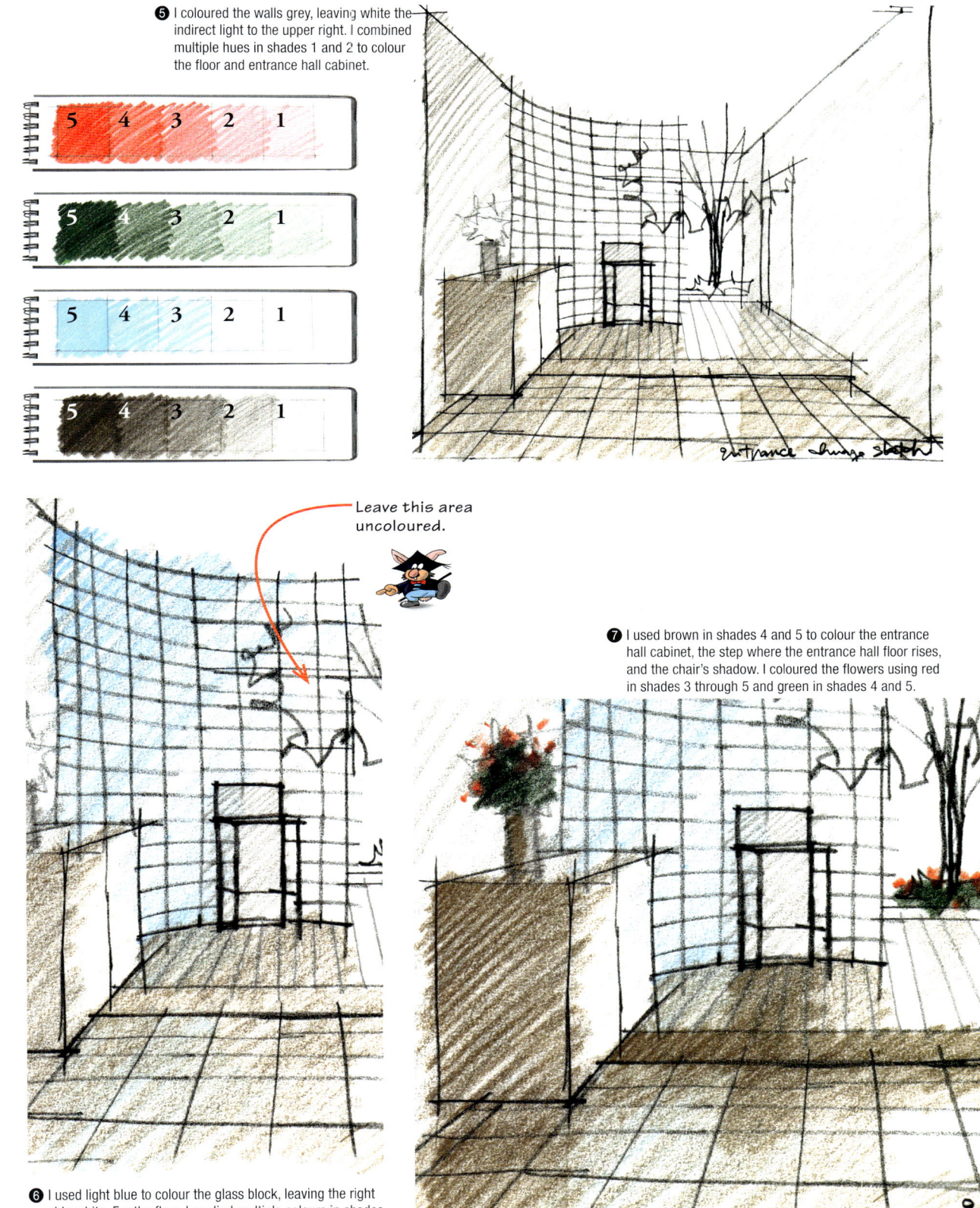

❺ I coloured the walls grey, leaving white the indirect light to the upper right. I combined multiple hues in shades 1 and 2 to colour the floor and entrance hall cabinet.

Leave this area uncoloured.

❼ I used brown in shades 4 and 5 to colour the entrance hall cabinet, the step where the entrance hall floor rises, and the chair's shadow. I coloured the flowers using red in shades 3 through 5 and green in shades 4 and 5.

❻ I used light blue to colour the glass block, leaving the right side white. For the floor, I applied multiple colours in shades 1 through 4.

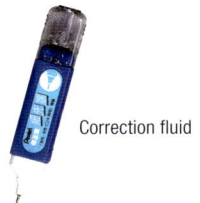

Correction fluid

❽ Finally, I added shadows in black coloured pencil in shades 1 through 5 to pull together the overall perspective sketch. I then used correction fluid to apply highlights to the greenery and cabinet top to finish.

Home Theater with *Tatami* Mats

This is a home theater/living room approximately 288 square feet in area. The resident may watch a movie while reclining on the *tatami* or may enjoy music while sitting on the sofa.

❶ I started by drawing a floor plan.

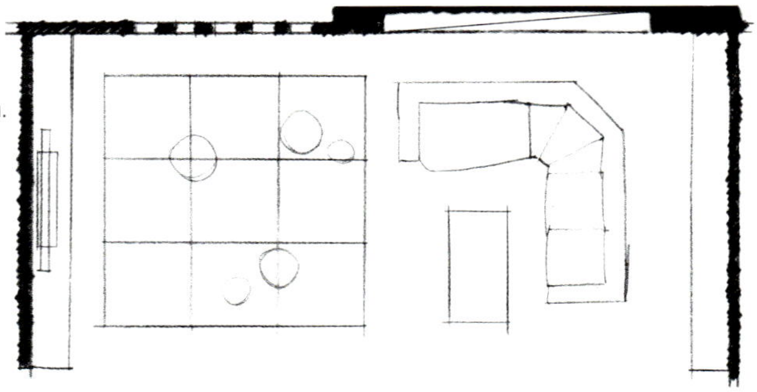

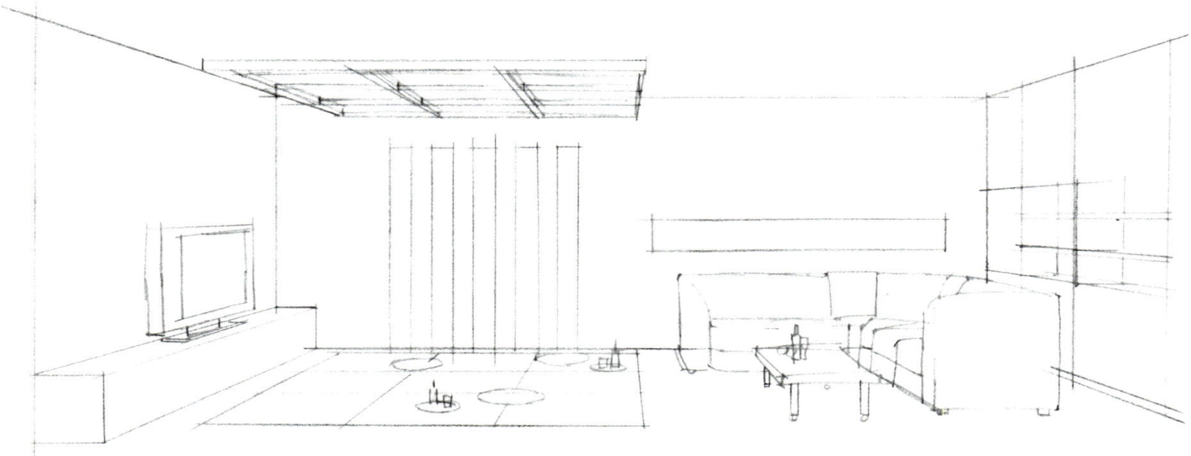

❷ Next, I produced a one-point perspective under drawing.

Quickly colour the sketch without worrying about your pencil strokes extending outside objects' exterior contour lines.

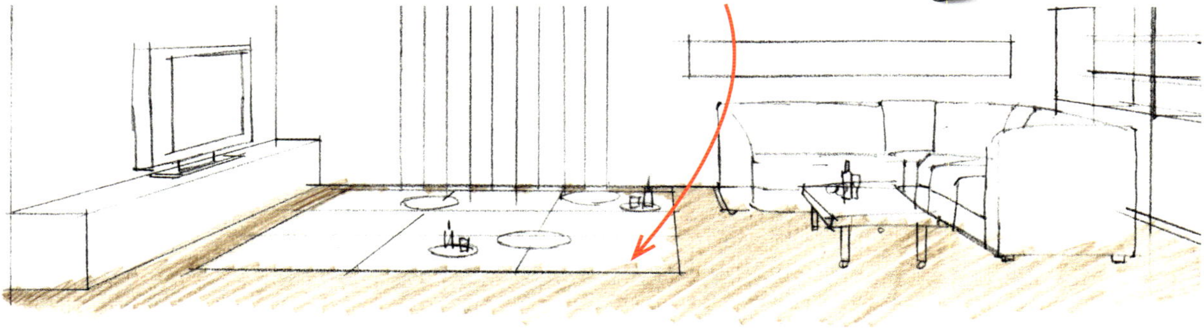

❸ I then used brown in shades 2 and 3 to colour the floor.

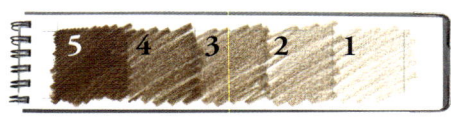

Leave this
area white.

❻ I applied red in shades 1 through 4 to the sofa, leaving the upper regions of the sofa's back and seats uncoloured.

❼ I used grey in shades 2 and 3 to colour the TV.

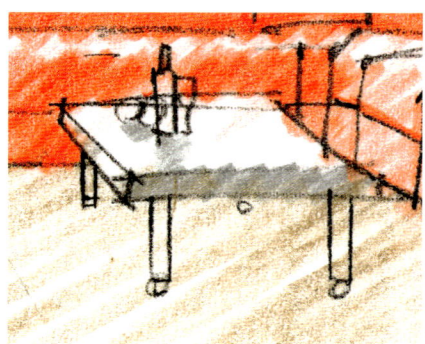

❽ I then coloured the coffee table using grey in shade 4.

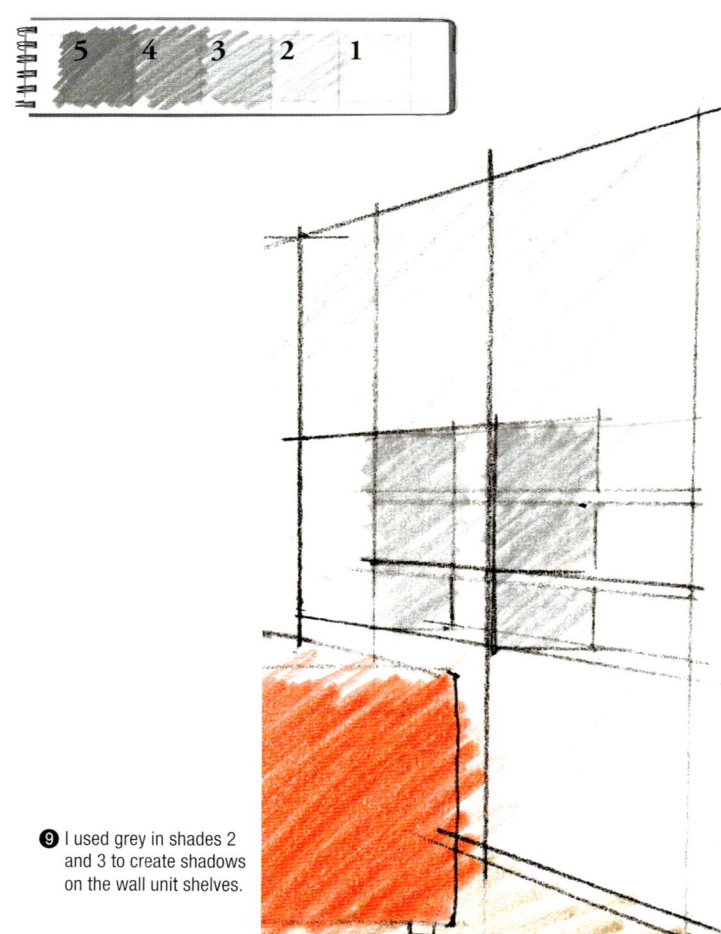

❾ I used grey in shades 2 and 3 to create shadows on the wall unit shelves.

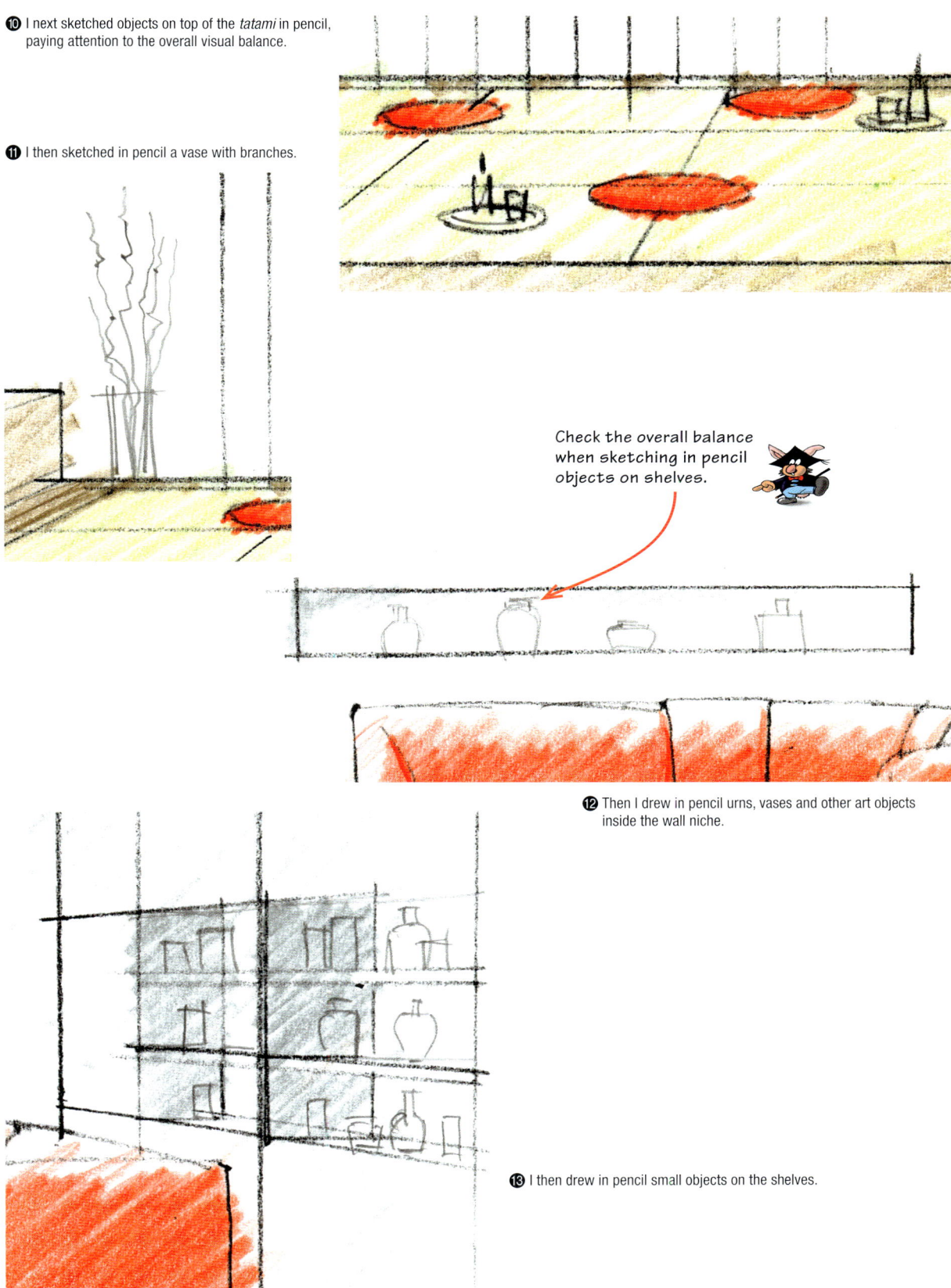

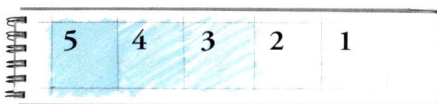

— Take care not to apply black too heavily.

⓯ Last, I combined black and brown to colour the entertainment center, reflections cast on the floor, shadows, and other areas. I used light blue in shade 2 to colour the flower vase on the floor and the wall unit.

Living Room with a Red Spiral Staircase

This sketch describes a corner living space containing a red spiral staircase. Expansive sliding glass doors are located opposite the staircase, creating a bright space.

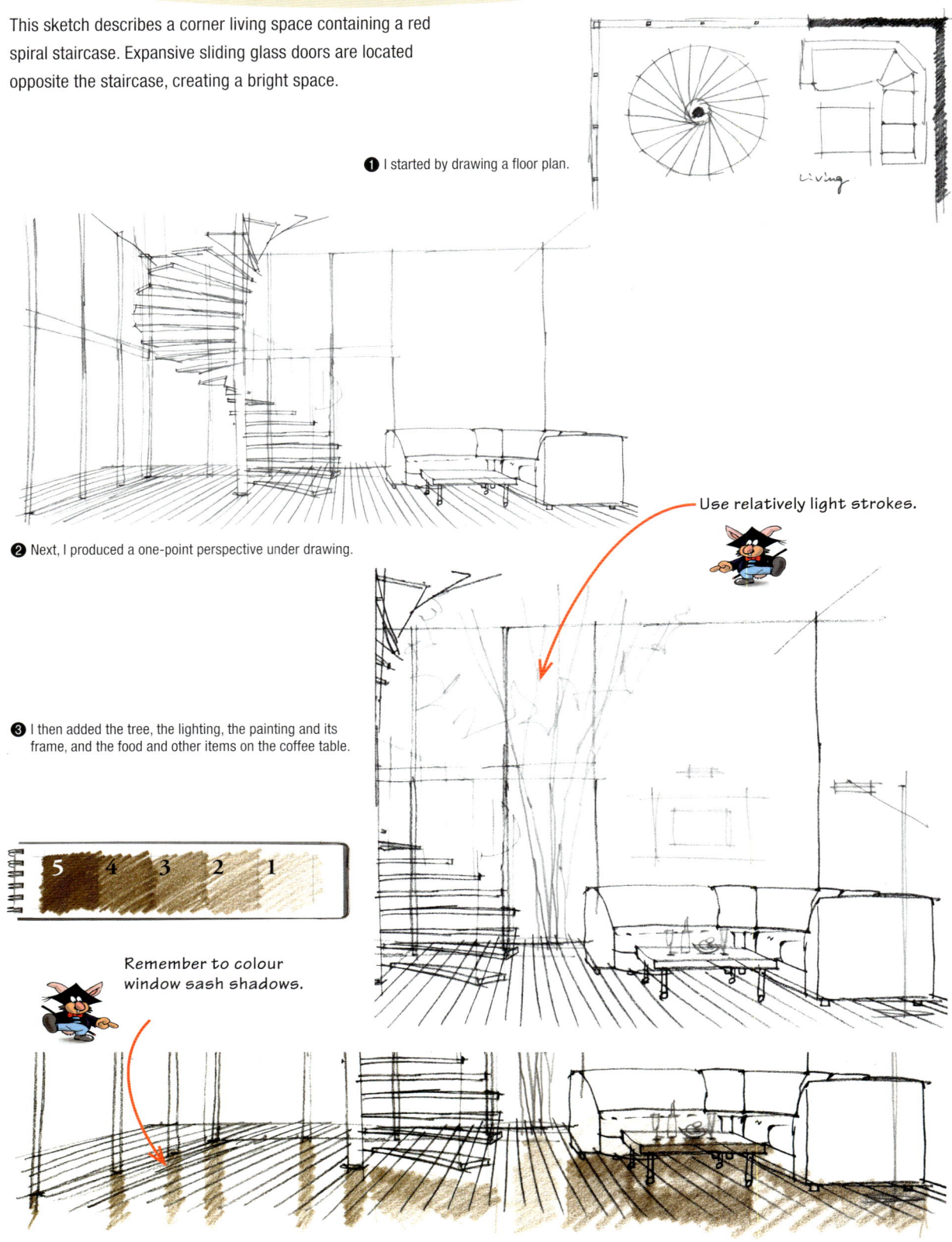

❶ I started by drawing a floor plan.

❷ Next, I produced a one-point perspective under drawing.

❸ I then added the tree, the lighting, the painting and its frame, and the food and other items on the coffee table.

Use relatively light strokes.

Remember to colour window sash shadows.

❹ Next, I coloured reflections cast on the floor using brown in shades 2 through 5.

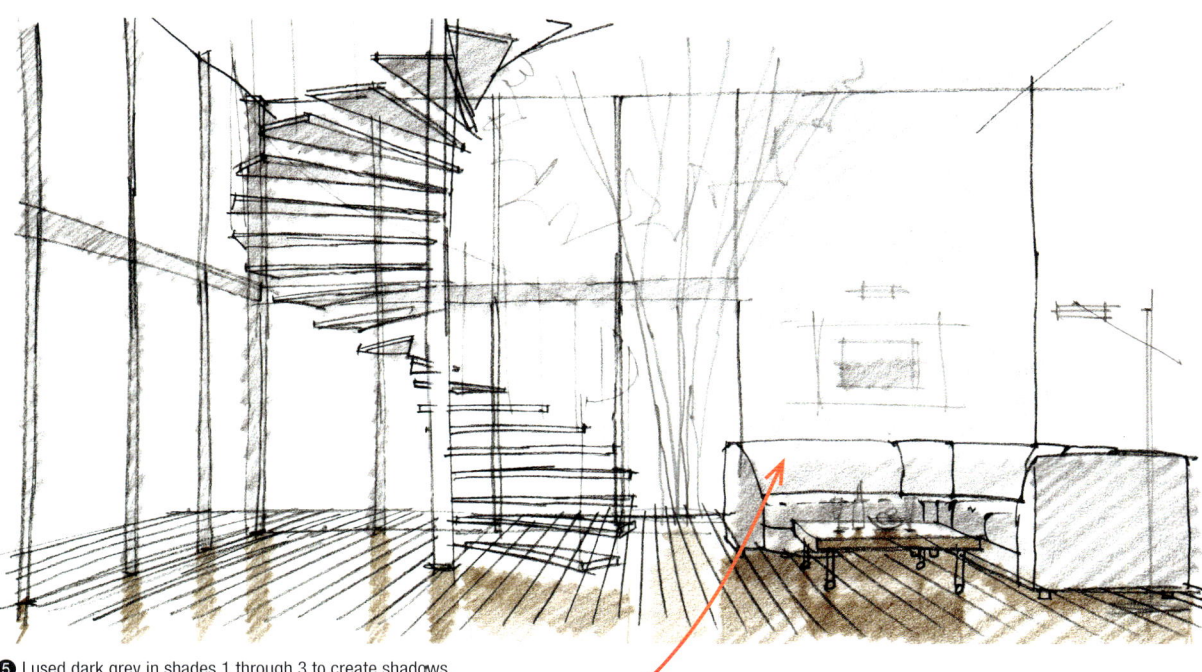

❺ I used dark grey in shades 1 through 3 to create shadows on the wall, sofa, and spiral staircase.

Make sofas appear soft.

❻ I used red in shades 2 through 5 to colour the spiral staircase and combined red with other hues to create reflections cast on the floor.

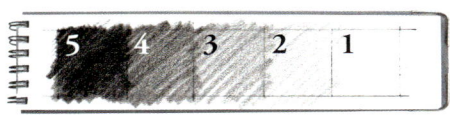
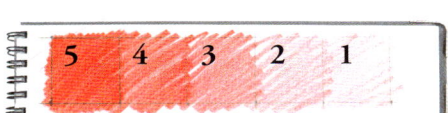

Use red on the floor as well.

Chapter III The Coloured Pencil Perspective Sketching Process

Correction fluid

❼ After sketching the curtain in pencil, I used a black coloured pencil in shades 1 through 5 to pull together this perspective sketch. I then added highlights in correction fluid to finish.

Home Theater/Living Room with a Garden View

I envisioned this as a relatively large single room subdivided by a wall unit into a bedroom and living room. I positioned a TV monitor in front of the sofa and large sliding glass doors to its side to create an open home theater/living room floor plan.

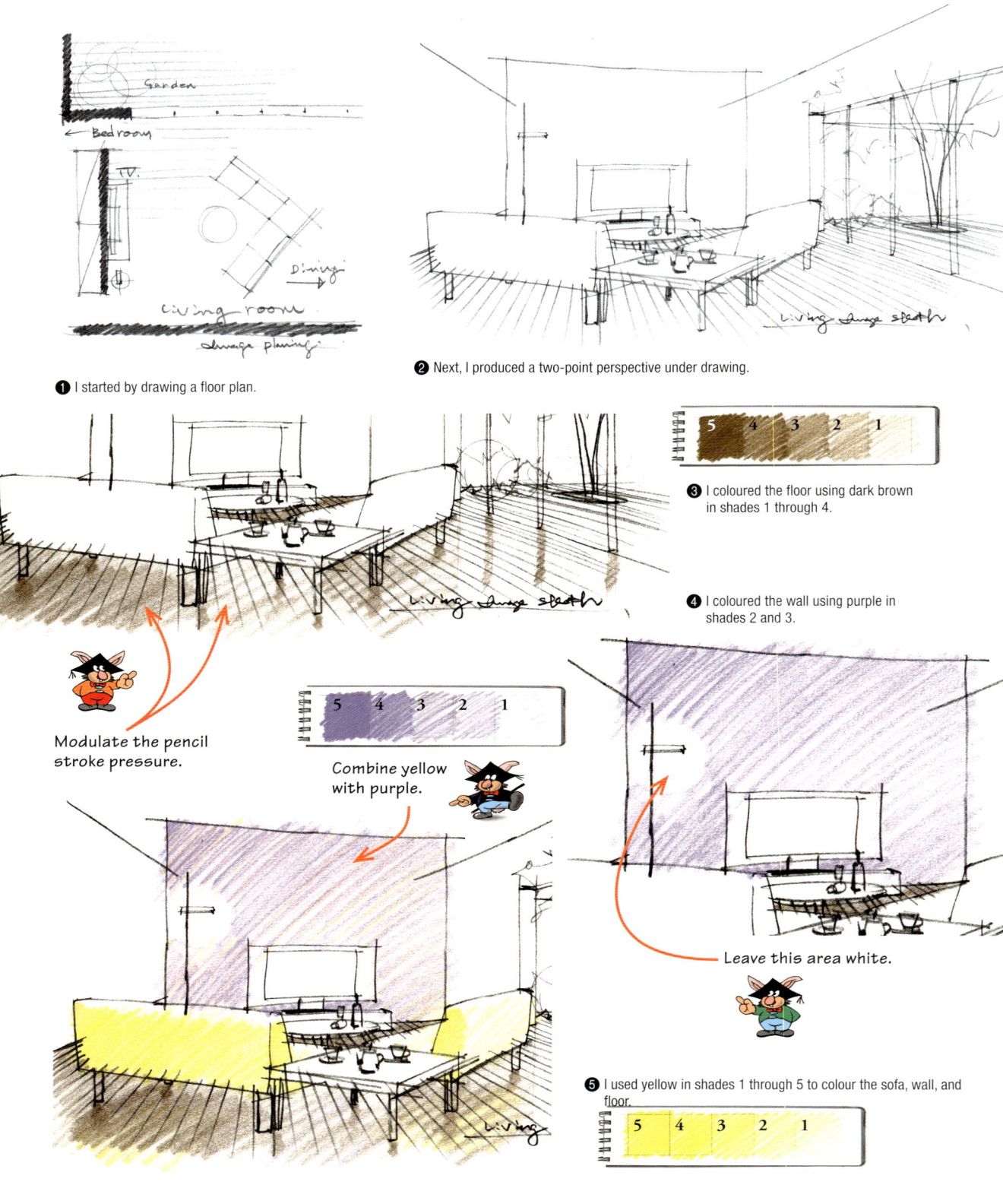

❶ I started by drawing a floor plan.

❷ Next, I produced a two-point perspective under drawing.

❸ I coloured the floor using dark brown in shades 1 through 4.

❹ I coloured the wall using purple in shades 2 and 3.

Modulate the pencil stroke pressure.

Combine yellow with purple.

Leave this area white.

❺ I used yellow in shades 1 through 5 to colour the sofa, wall, and floor.

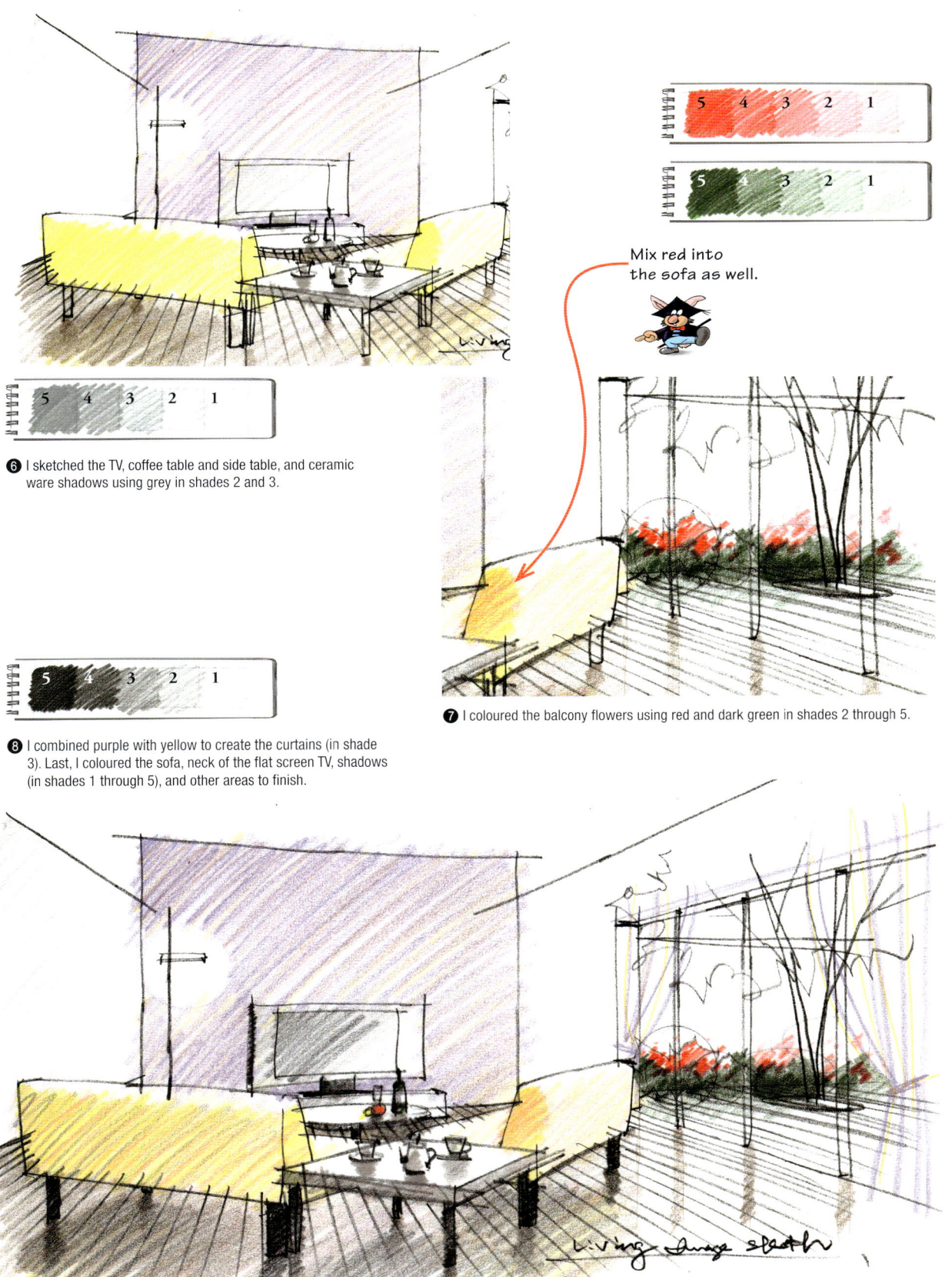

Mix red into the sofa as well.

❻ I sketched the TV, coffee table and side table, and ceramic ware shadows using grey in shades 2 and 3.

❼ I coloured the balcony flowers using red and dark green in shades 2 through 5.

❽ I combined purple with yellow to create the curtains (in shade 3). Last, I coloured the sofa, neck of the flat screen TV, shadows (in shades 1 through 5), and other areas to finish.

Living Room with Open Walls

This is a living space featuring large open walls comprising almost entirely glass windows. This composition's key point is the blue staircase next to the glass windows.

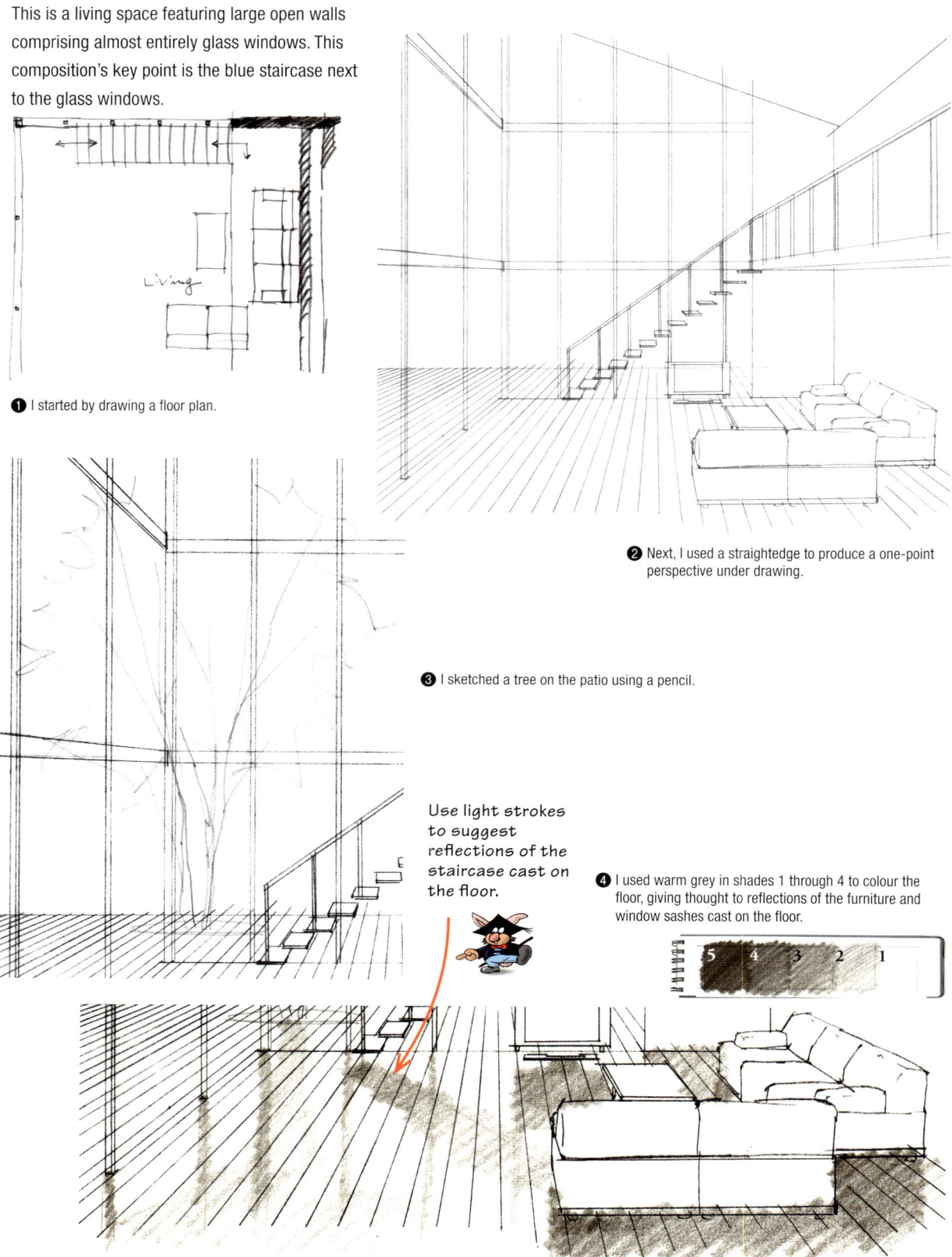

❶ I started by drawing a floor plan.

❷ Next, I used a straightedge to produce a one-point perspective under drawing.

❸ I sketched a tree on the patio using a pencil.

Use light strokes to suggest reflections of the staircase cast on the floor.

❹ I used warm grey in shades 1 through 4 to colour the floor, giving thought to reflections of the furniture and window sashes cast on the floor.

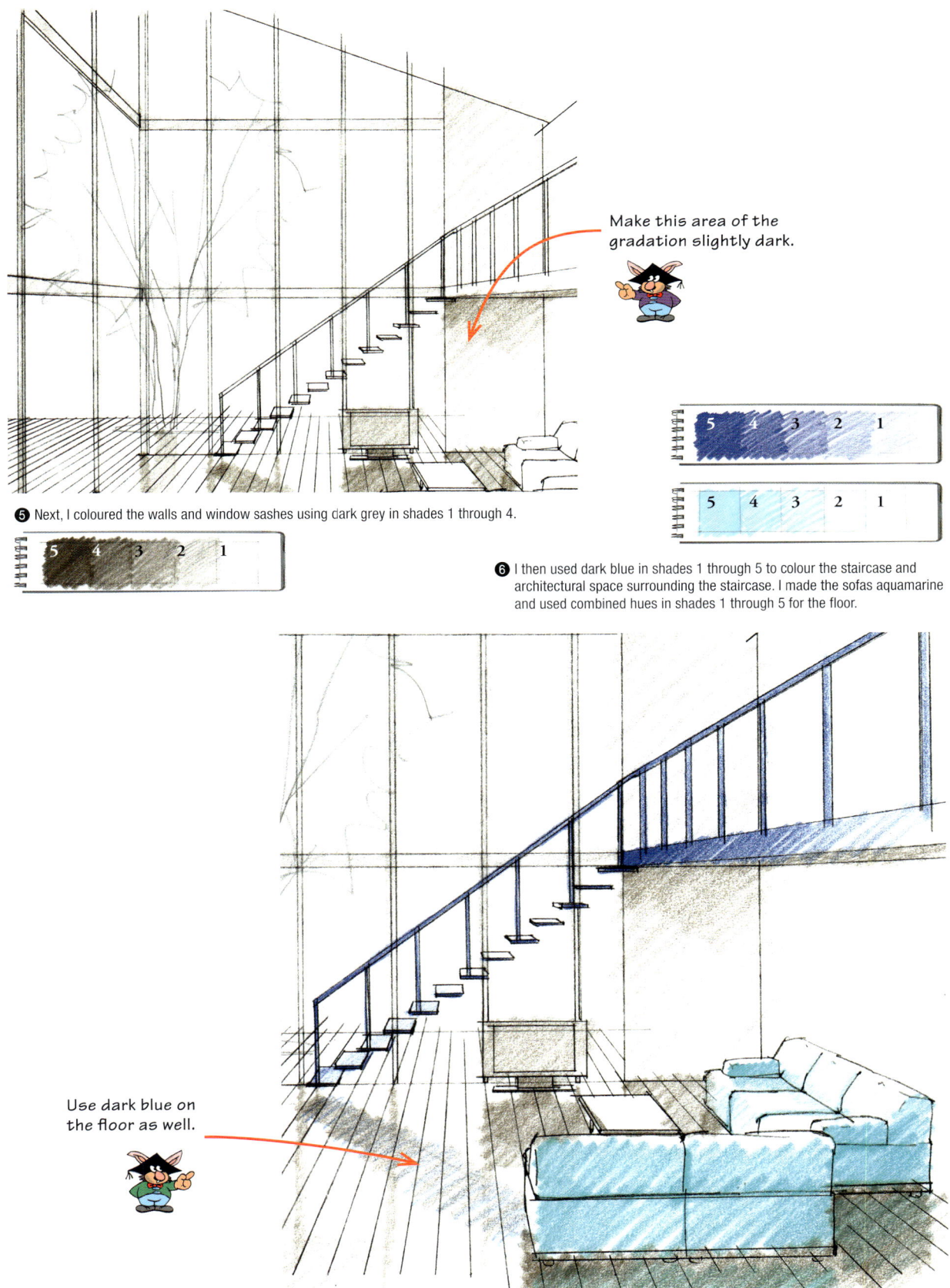

Make this area of the gradation slightly dark.

❺ Next, I coloured the walls and window sashes using dark grey in shades 1 through 4.

❻ I then used dark blue in shades 1 through 5 to colour the staircase and architectural space surrounding the staircase. I made the sofas aquamarine and used combined hues in shades 1 through 5 for the floor.

Use dark blue on the floor as well.

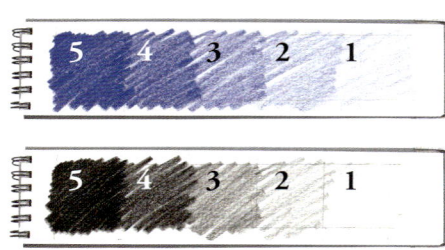

⑦ Last, I added curtain using grey (in shade 3) and went back over the sofa with dark blue (in shades 1 through 3). I sketched in the food and other items on the coffee table and then coloured them to finish. In order to enhance the interior space's impact, I omitted giving colour to the tree in the exterior garden.

Home Theater/Living Room with a Yellow Sofa

This is a cozy home theater/living room, consisting simply of a yellow sofa and a large TV.

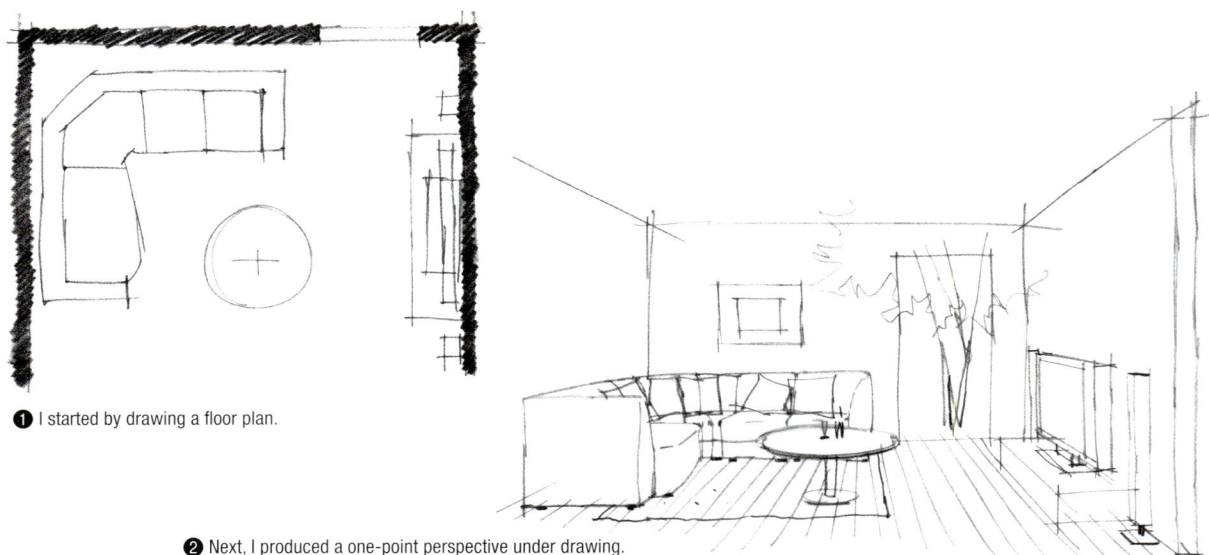

❶ I started by drawing a floor plan.

❷ Next, I produced a one-point perspective under drawing.

When duplicating this sketch, go ahead and colour the entertainment unit while you have the warm grey pencil in your hand.

❸ I then coloured the floor using a warm grey in shades 1 through 3, while maintaining awareness of those areas I would leave uncoloured to accentuate reflections on the floor.

❹ I also coloured the walls, the TV and other items in warm grey shades 1 through 3.

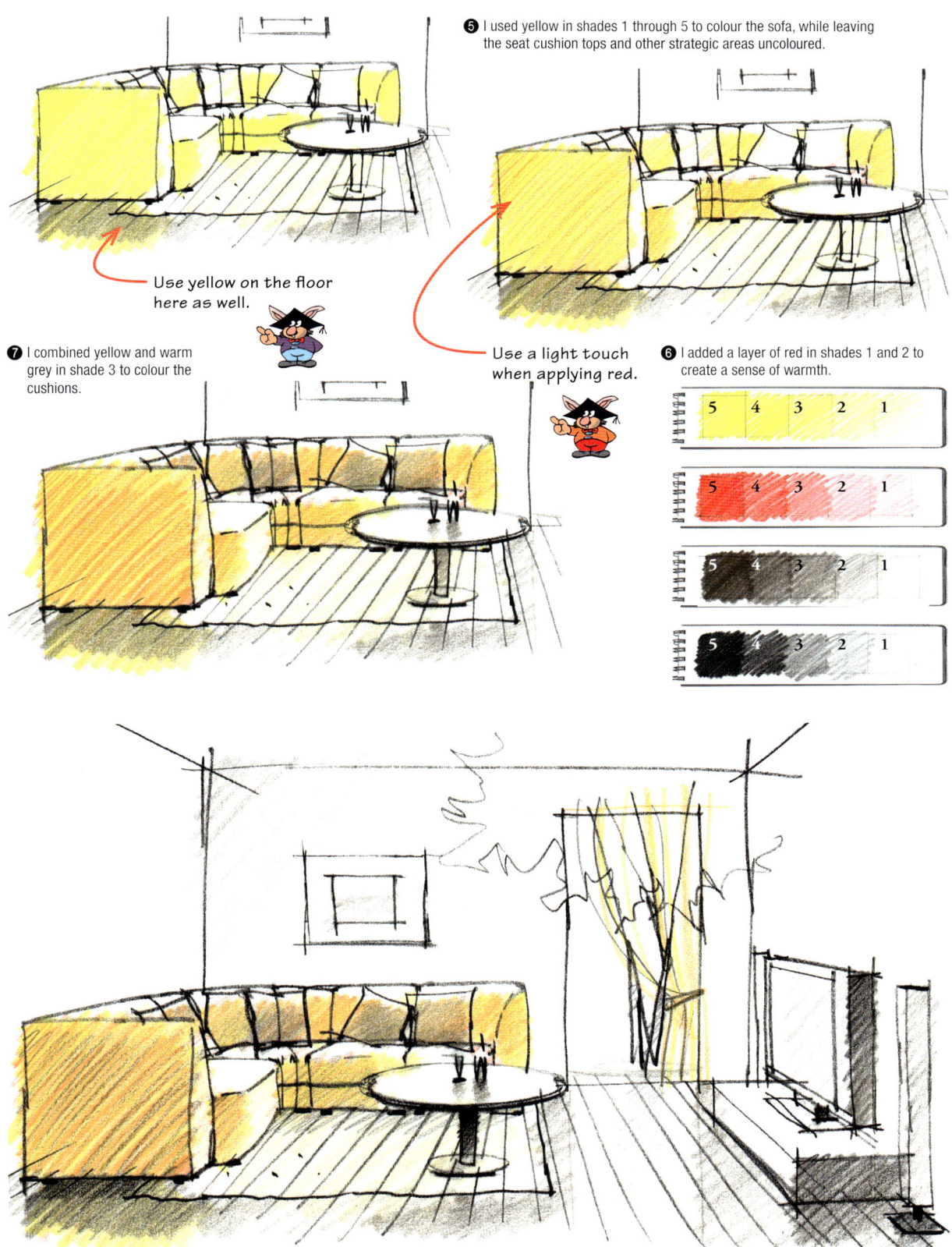

Living Room/Kitchen Space with an Atrium

The star of this floor plan is the tiny atrium positioned at its center. While there is not much to the atrium, it does effectively offer a change in atmosphere to the resident. Opposite the atrium, I positioned a large window, which allows a view of the outside garden. The walls to the right and left of this large window are slotted, and each slot functions as a visual accent.

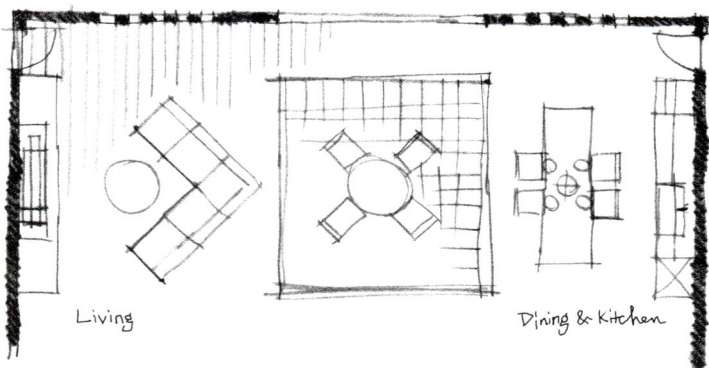

❶ I started by drawing a floor plan.

❷ Next, I produced a one-point perspective under drawing.

❸ I then coloured the floor using dark brown in shades 1 through 4.

❹ I used grey in shades 1 through 3 to colour the wall unit and the atrium chairs.

Apply colour lightly to the walls.

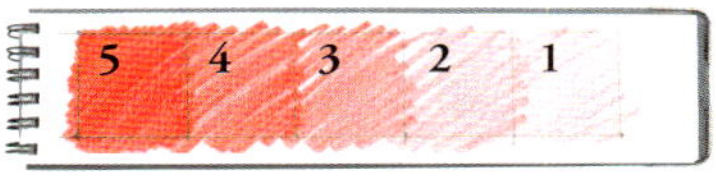

❺ Next, I coloured the sofa, kitchen chairs, and kitchen cabinets using red in shades 1 through 5.

Modulate the hue's saturation when colouring the cabinet doors.

Use a heavy application of yellow to create shadows underneath the dishes.

❼ I used red and dark green in shades 4 and 5 to colour the food.

❻ I then used mustard in shades 2 through 4 to colour the dining room table.

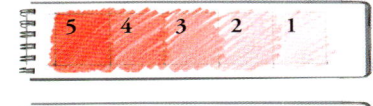

Use light strokes to colour the tree's foliage

❽ I applied dark green in shades 4 and 5 to the tree.

9 I touched up shadows over the entire composition using a black coloured pencil (in shades 1 through 4). I added a few beer glasses atop the atrium table to finish.

Room with a Purple Sofa

This shows a living room with a sofa at its focal point. For this sketch, I used a light touch and mixed colours to obtain a palette with depth.

❶ First I used a grey coloured pencil in shades 3 and 4 to produce an under drawing.

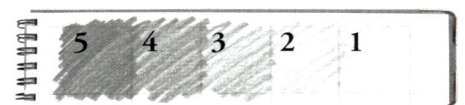

❷ I coloured the entire floor using brown in shades 1 through 4.

❸ I used light blue in shades 1 through 4 to colour the sofa and reflections of the sofa cast onto the floor. The trick was to leave bright areas uncoloured.

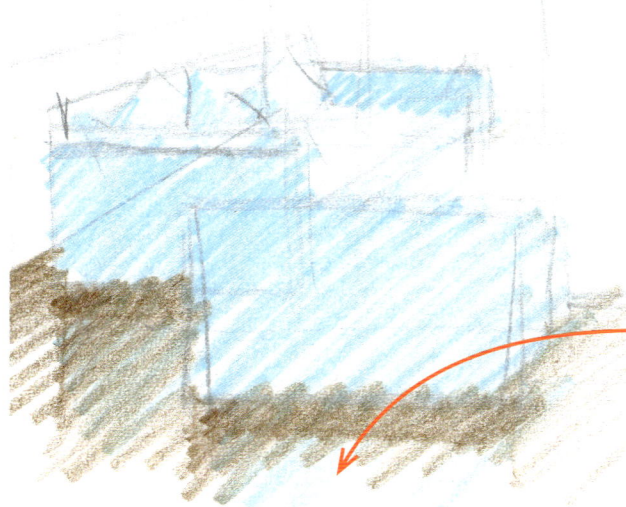

Use light blue applied in light strokes to create reflections cast onto the floor.

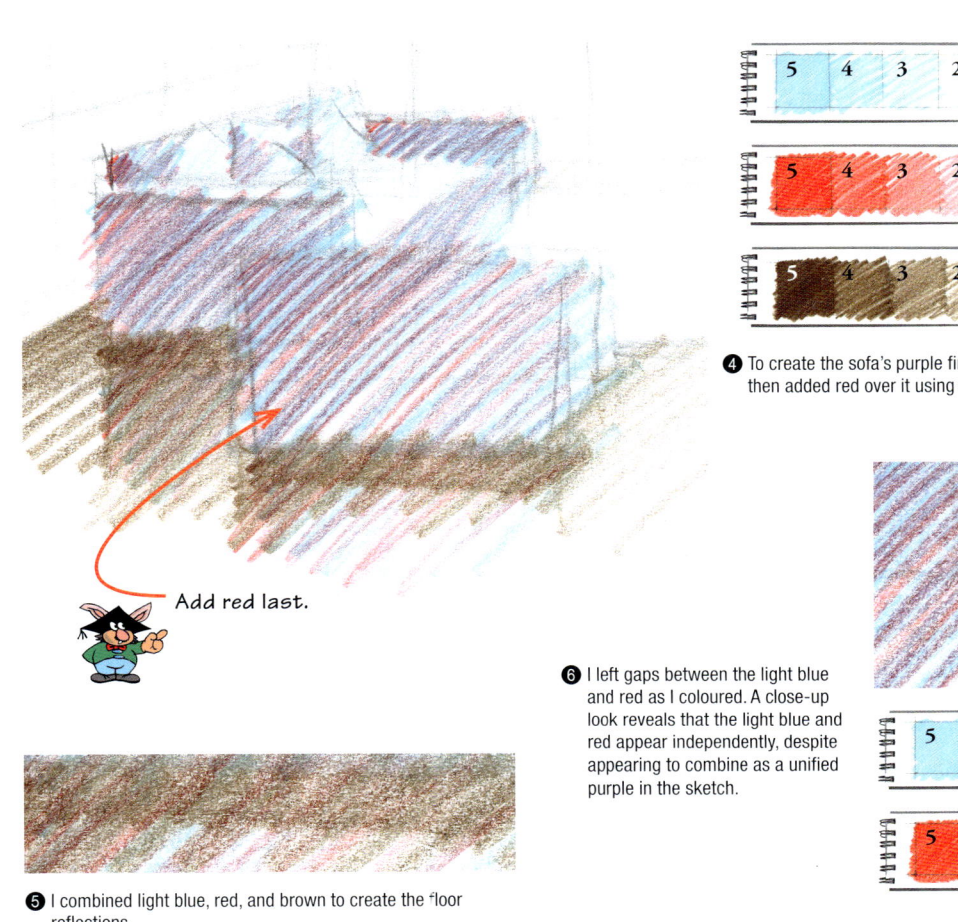

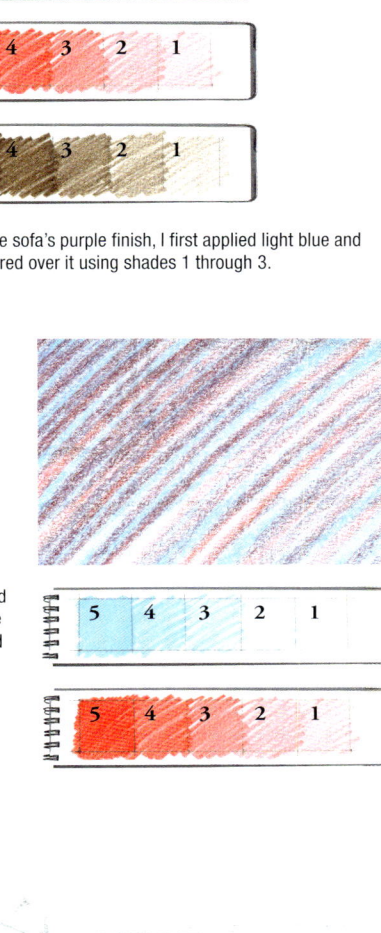

4 To create the sofa's purple finish, I first applied light blue and then added red over it using shades 1 through 3.

Add red last.

5 I combined light blue, red, and brown to create the floor reflections.

6 I left gaps between the light blue and red as I coloured. A close-up look reveals that the light blue and red appear independently, despite appearing to combine as a unified purple in the sketch.

7 The key is to apply the light blue and then red in light strokes.

8 I used grey in shades 1 through 3 to colour the living room's wall unit to finish.

Living /Dining Space with a Red Sofa

The red on the living area sofa and dining area chairs play the star visual roles in this sketch. The minute amount of colour applied to the floor gives the composition a fresh, clean look.

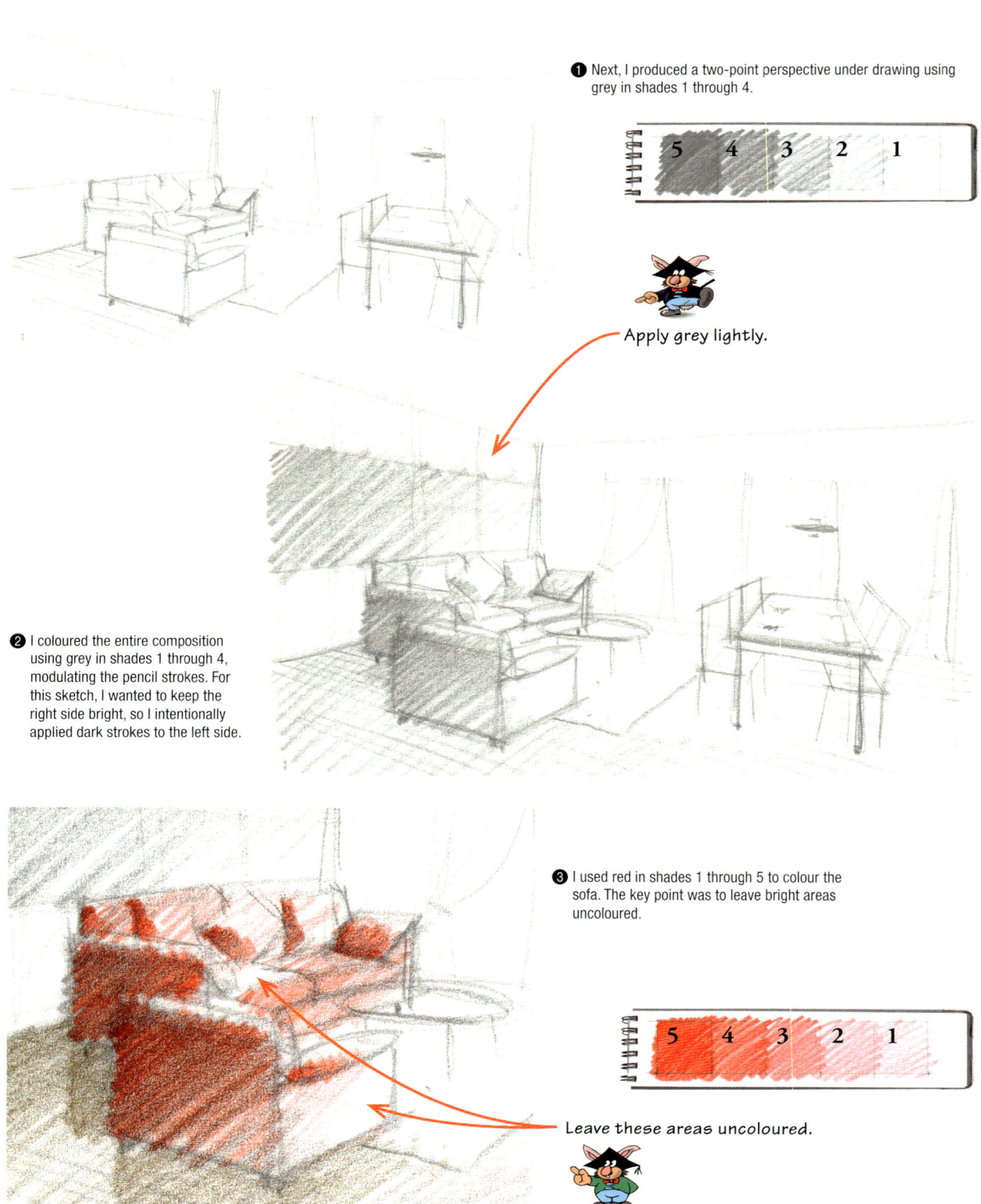

❶ Next, I produced a two-point perspective under drawing using grey in shades 1 through 4.

Apply grey lightly.

❷ I coloured the entire composition using grey in shades 1 through 4, modulating the pencil strokes. For this sketch, I wanted to keep the right side bright, so I intentionally applied dark strokes to the left side.

❸ I used red in shades 1 through 5 to colour the sofa. The key point was to leave bright areas uncoloured.

Leave these areas uncoloured.

④ Next, I coloured the chairs using red in shades 1 through 4. I then added yellow in shades 1 through 4 to the sofa over the red, which created a warm atmosphere. I coloured the floor using brown in shades 1 through 3, while giving thought to reflections cast onto the floor.

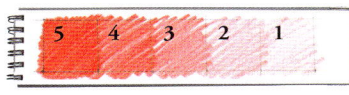
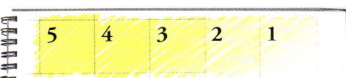

 Colour sofa reflections onto the floor in the manner shown above.

⑤ I then used a black coloured pencil in shades 1 through 5 to create shadows as well as the coffee cups and other ceramic ware atop the table.

Apply black lightly.

⑥ Next, I added food and flowers to the dining area table, using dark green in shades 4 and 5. For the flowers, I used red in shades 4 and 5.

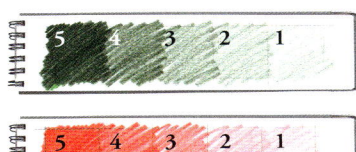

Remember to add reflections of food cast by objects onto tabletops.

❼ Since the red of the sofa and dining area chairs functions as this composition's primary visual accent, I applied the other colours in muted tones. I used grey contour lines in shades 1 and 2 to make the sliding glass doors appear bright, keeping my strokes as light as possible.

Blue L-shaped Kitchen Cabinets

This is an open kitchen/dining room floor plan, consisting of a round table positioned in front of blue kitchen cabinets and counter that form an "L". Rather than sketch the foreground round table and chairs in their entirety, instead I opted to draw attention to the kitchen cabinets and counter.

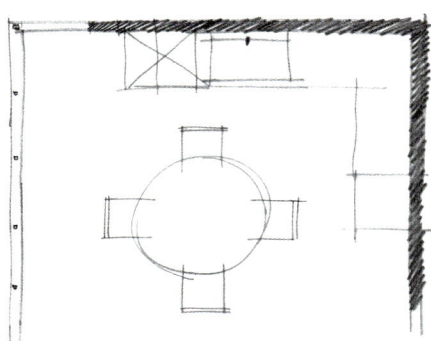

❶ I started by drawing a floor plan.

❷ I used grey in shade 3 to sketch an under drawing.

❸ Next, using brown in shade 3, I sketched the exterior contours of reflections of the kitchen cabinets cast onto the floor.

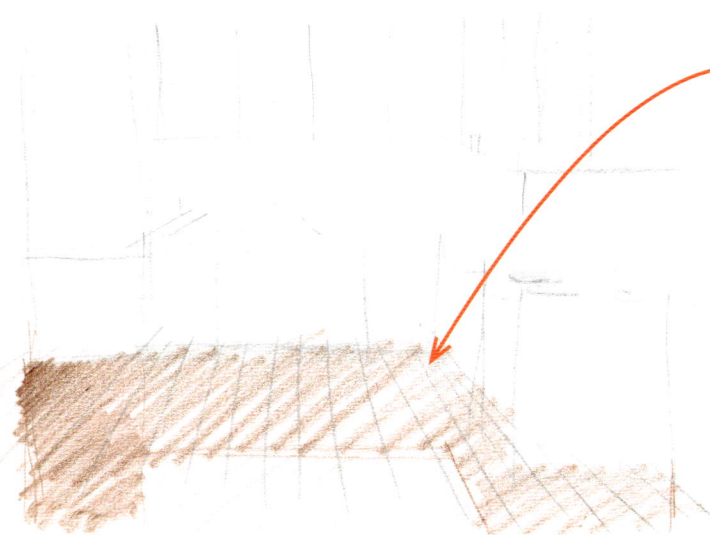

Reflections of the kitchen cabinets cast onto the floor should look like this.

❹ I then coloured the floor using brown in shades 2 and 3, not particularly worrying if the pencil strokes extended somewhat outside of boundaries and exterior contours.

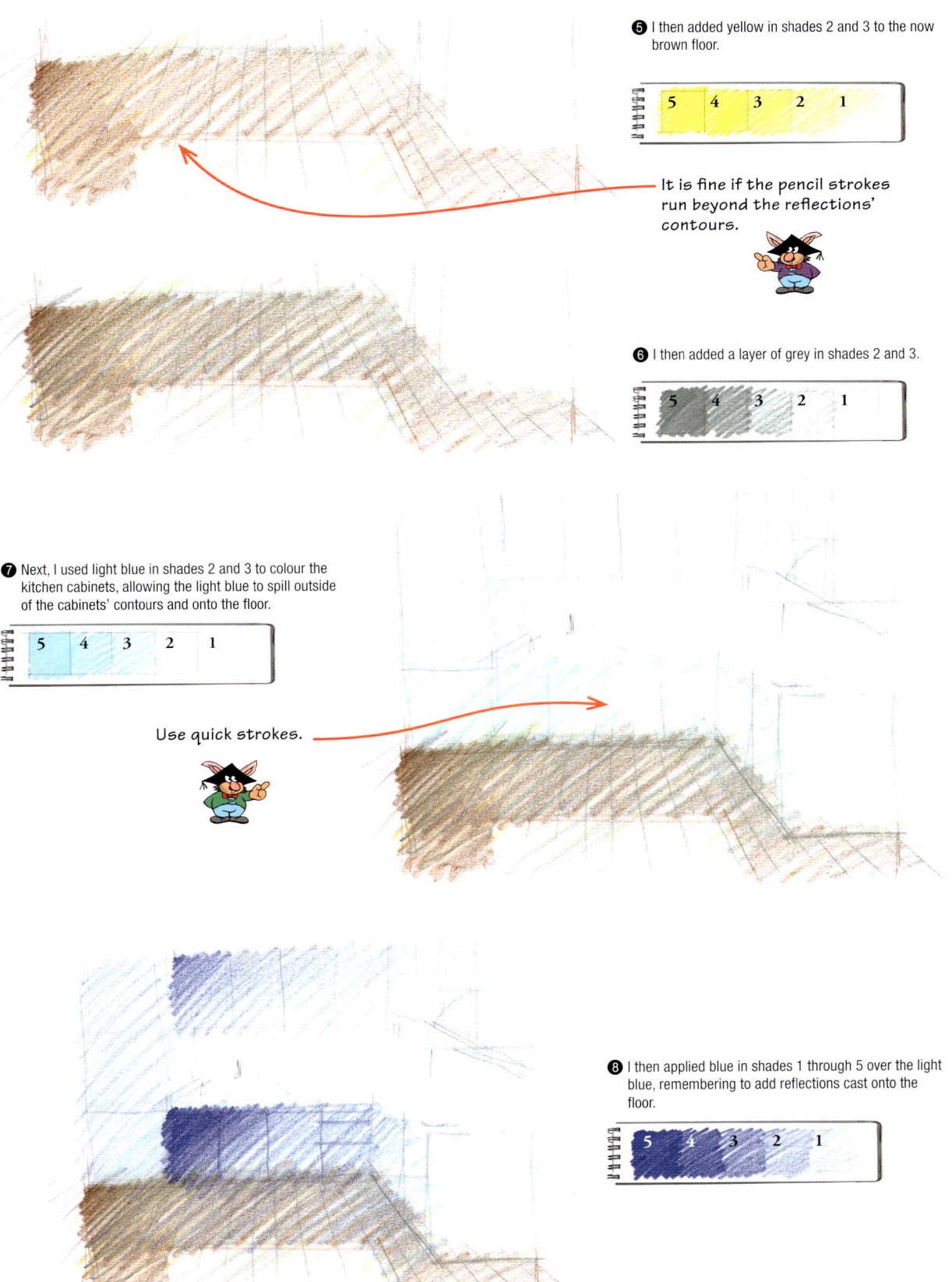

❺ I then added yellow in shades 2 and 3 to the now brown floor.

It is fine if the pencil strokes run beyond the reflections' contours.

❻ I then added a layer of grey in shades 2 and 3.

❼ Next, I used light blue in shades 2 and 3 to colour the kitchen cabinets, allowing the light blue to spill outside of the cabinets' contours and onto the floor.

Use quick strokes.

❽ I then applied blue in shades 1 through 5 over the light blue, remembering to add reflections cast onto the floor.

9 I applied black coloured pencil in shades 2 through 4 to create shadows for the range hood and cabinet bases.

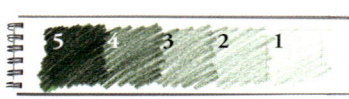

13 Next, I added flowers to the tabletop and food on the plates using dark green in shades 3 through 5 and red in shades 4 and 5.

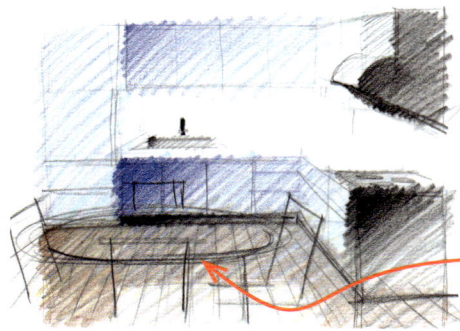

10 Then, using a black coloured pencil in shades 3 and 4, I sketched the kitchen table and chairs in front of the cabinets, omitting the chair legs. Note the proportioning of the ellipse used to create the table.

Consider proportioning when drawing ellipses for tabletops and the like.

11 I used red in shades 2 through 5 to create the chairs.

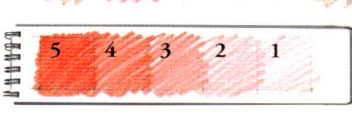

Apply coloured pencil lightly to chairs' undersides.

12 I used a black coloured pencil (in shades 4 and 5) to colour the back of this foreground chair.

⑭ This is how the sketch appeared after I had finished applying coloured pencils.

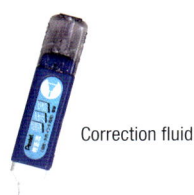

Correction fluid

⑮ Finally, I added highlights in correction fluid to complete the perspective sketch. (Keep use of correction fluid to a minimum.)

Kitchen with a Red Island

This is a kitchen that includes a dining area and a red island in the foreground, which functions as a visual accent. While I did make all other colours as muted as possible, I also mixed brown, grey, yellow, and other hues together to colour the floor in order to give the sketch warmth.

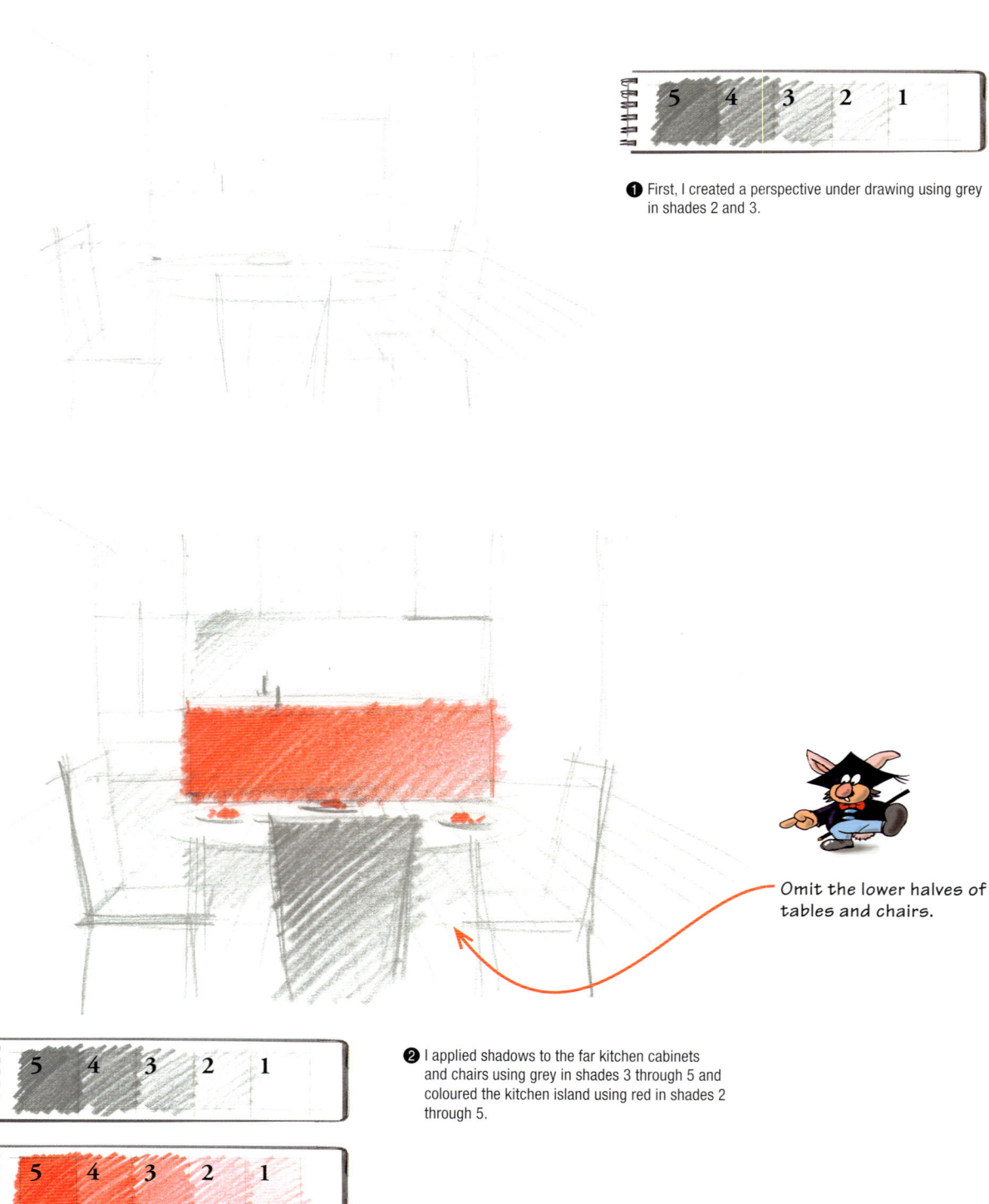

❶ First, I created a perspective under drawing using grey in shades 2 and 3.

❷ I applied shadows to the far kitchen cabinets and chairs using grey in shades 3 through 5 and coloured the kitchen island using red in shades 2 through 5.

Omit the lower halves of tables and chairs.

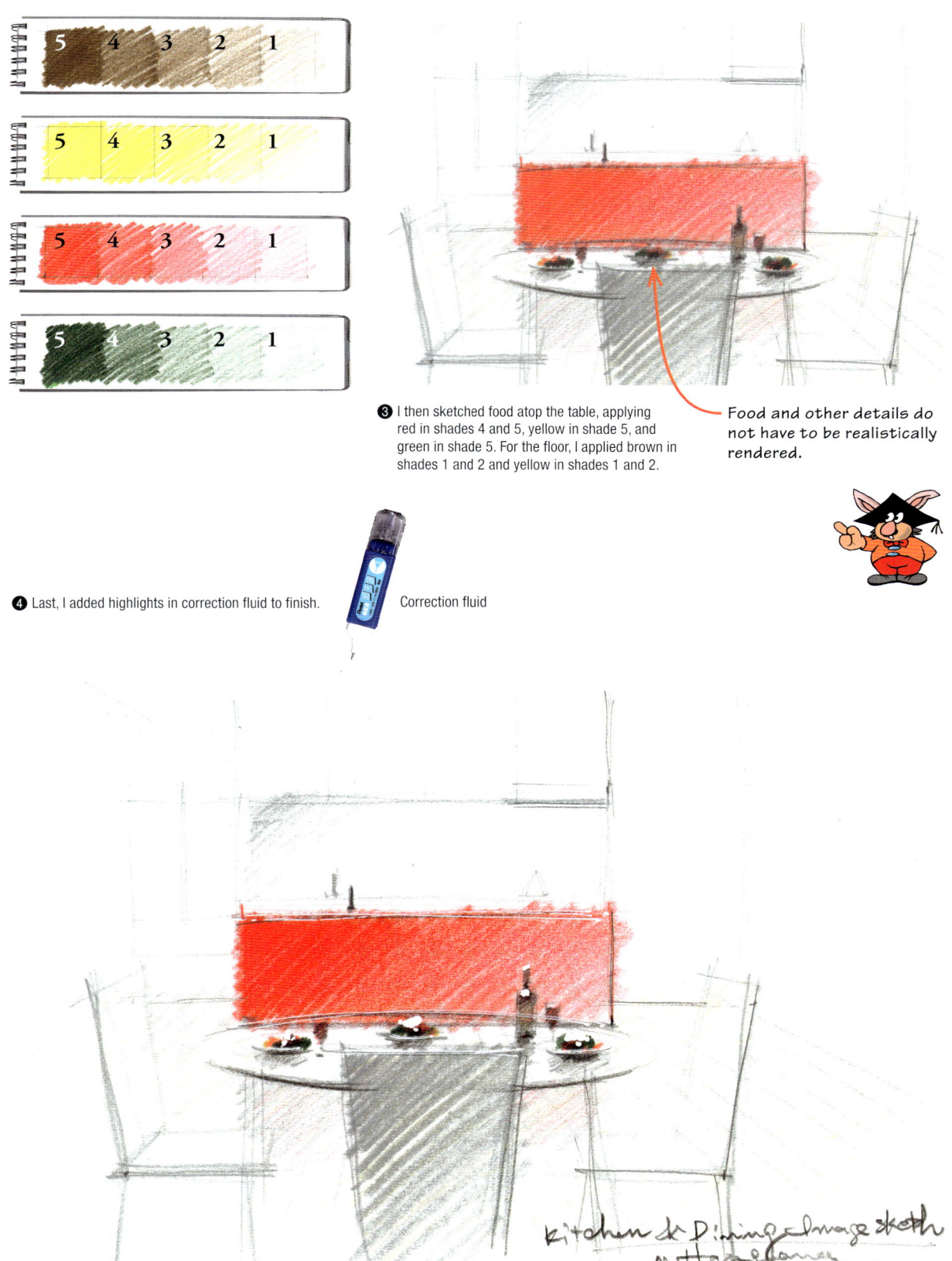

❸ I then sketched food atop the table, applying red in shades 4 and 5, yellow in shade 5, and green in shade 5. For the floor, I applied brown in shades 1 and 2 and yellow in shades 1 and 2.

Food and other details do not have to be realistically rendered.

❹ Last, I added highlights in correction fluid to finish.

Correction fluid

Ample 288 Square Foot Living /Dining /Kitchen/Home Theater Space

This is a living/dining/kitchen space that is approximately 288 square feet in area and contains a home theater. This one room contains multiple lifestyle functions unified within a single space.

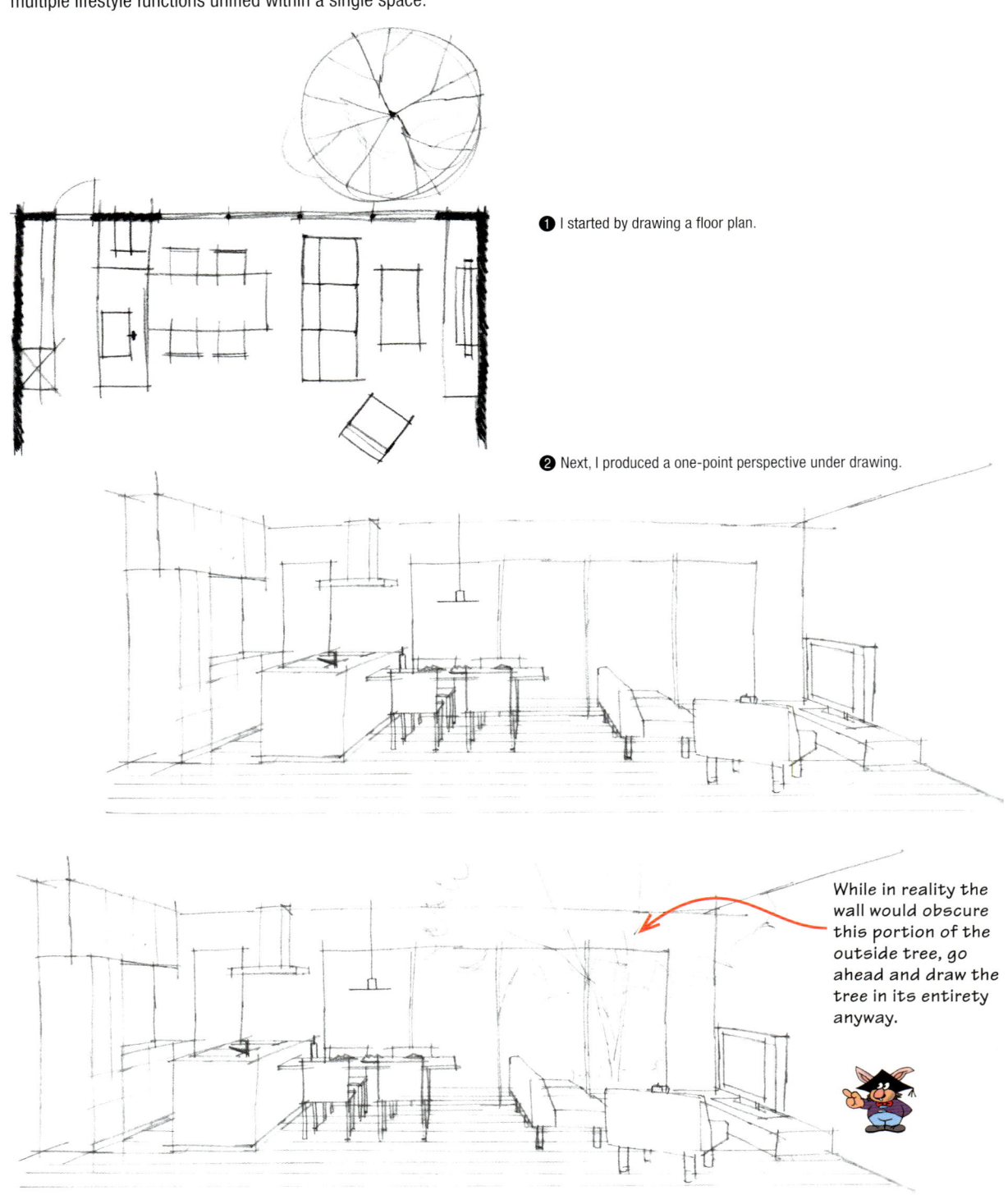

❶ I started by drawing a floor plan.

❷ Next, I produced a one-point perspective under drawing.

While in reality the wall would obscure this portion of the outside tree, go ahead and draw the tree in its entirety anyway.

❸ I then sketched the tree outside the sliding glass doors lightly in pencil.

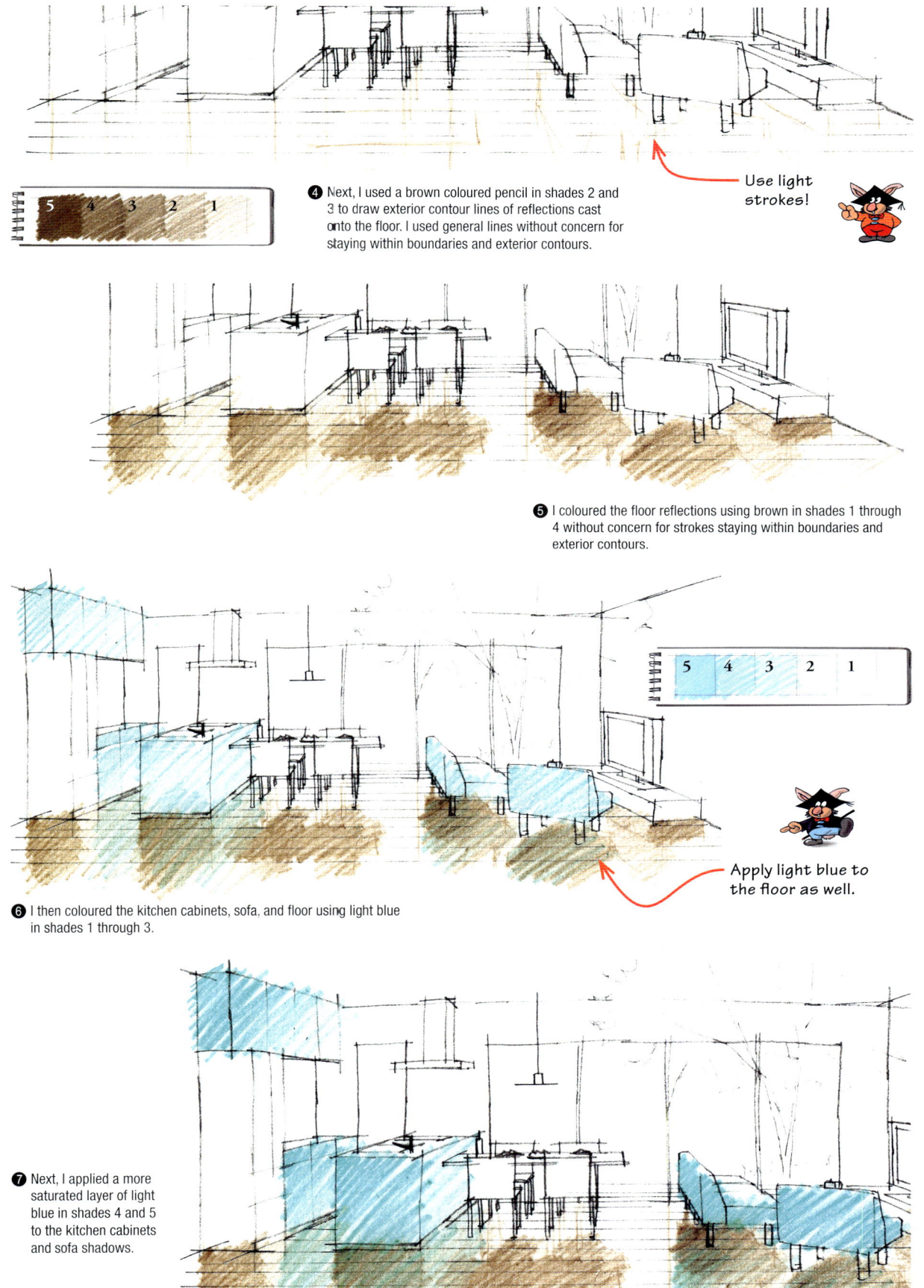

④ Next, I used a brown coloured pencil in shades 2 and 3 to draw exterior contour lines of reflections cast onto the floor. I used general lines without concern for staying within boundaries and exterior contours.

Use light strokes!

⑤ I coloured the floor reflections using brown in shades 1 through 4 without concern for strokes staying within boundaries and exterior contours.

⑥ I then coloured the kitchen cabinets, sofa, and floor using light blue in shades 1 through 3.

Apply light blue to the floor as well.

⑦ Next, I applied a more saturated layer of light blue in shades 4 and 5 to the kitchen cabinets and sofa shadows.

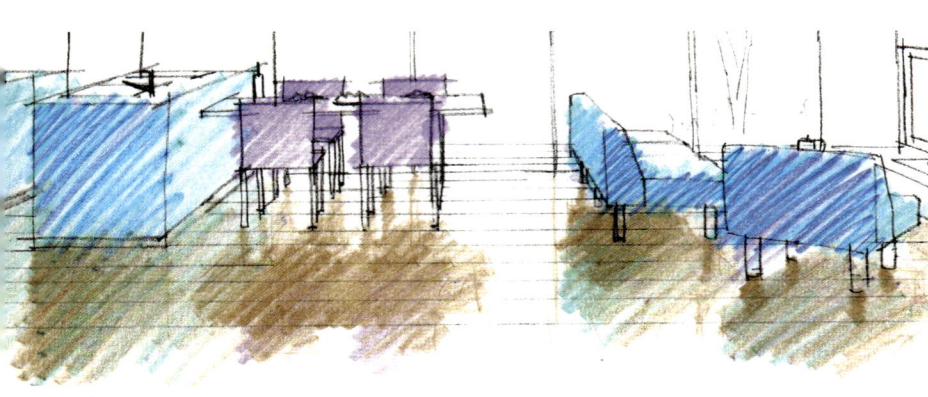

❽ I used dark blue in shades 4 and 5 and purple in shade 3 to colour the backs of the loveseat and sofa. I used brown in shades 4 and 5 to create reflections of the furniture's legs cast onto the floor.

Add purple to the floor.

❾ I applied purple in shades 3 and 4 to the dining room chairs and the floor.

❿ Note the appearance of uncoloured patches on the floor. When sketching a space with backlighting, only apply colour to areas where objects cast reflections onto the floor, as shown in this sketch.

Correction fluid

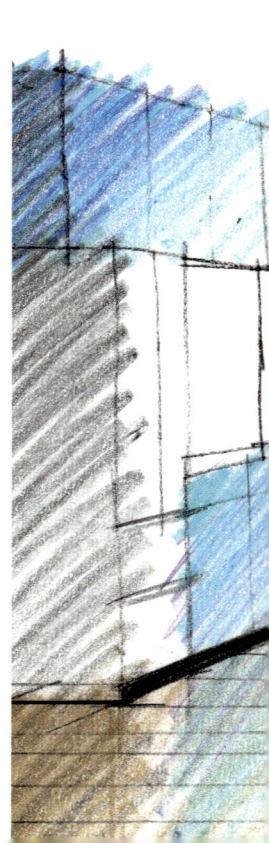

⓫ I then created shadows for the kitchen cabinets and other fixtures using grey in shades 2 through 5.

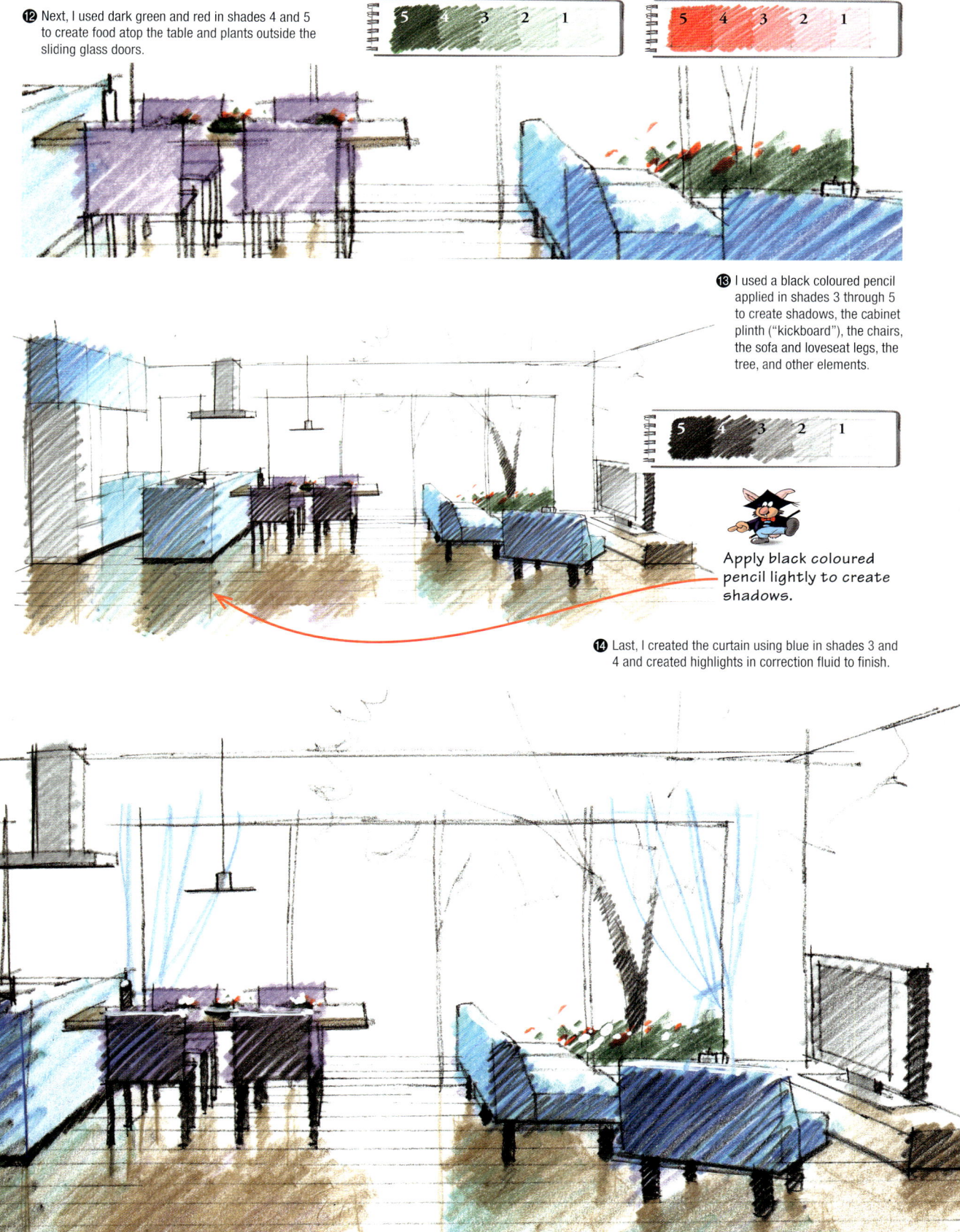

⓬ Next, I used dark green and red in shades 4 and 5 to create food atop the table and plants outside the sliding glass doors.

⓭ I used a black coloured pencil applied in shades 3 through 5 to create shadows, the cabinet plinth ("kickboard"), the chairs, the sofa and loveseat legs, the tree, and other elements.

Apply black coloured pencil lightly to create shadows.

⓮ Last, I created the curtain using blue in shades 3 and 4 and created highlights in correction fluid to finish.

Spacious 288 Square Foot Dining Room/Kitchen

This presentation was for a spacious dining room/kitchen space. I made the kitchen counter wide so that it could be used both to prepare food and to eat. I positioned bar chairs at the counter.

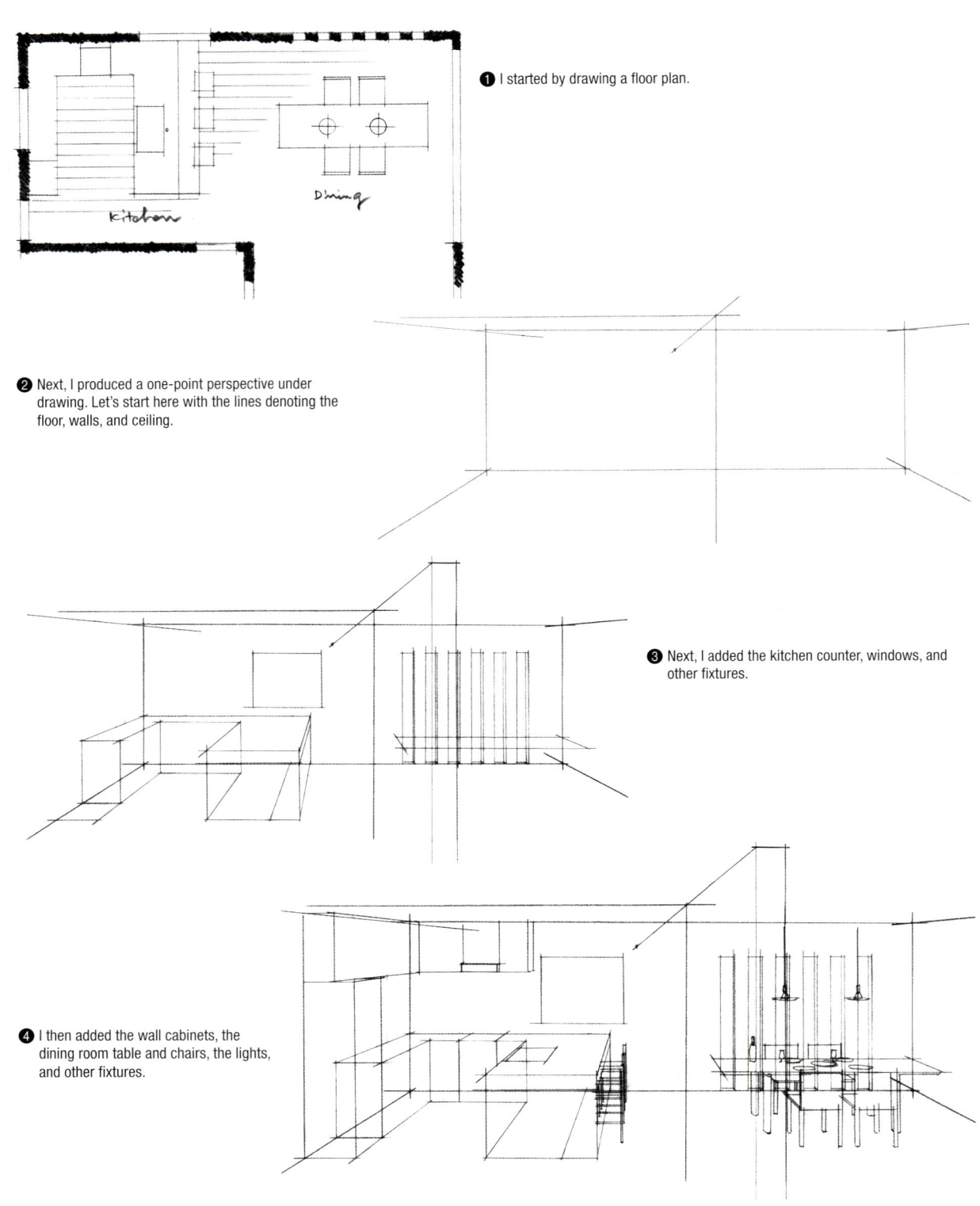

❶ I started by drawing a floor plan.

❷ Next, I produced a one-point perspective under drawing. Let's start here with the lines denoting the floor, walls, and ceiling.

❸ Next, I added the kitchen counter, windows, and other fixtures.

❹ I then added the wall cabinets, the dining room table and chairs, the lights, and other fixtures.

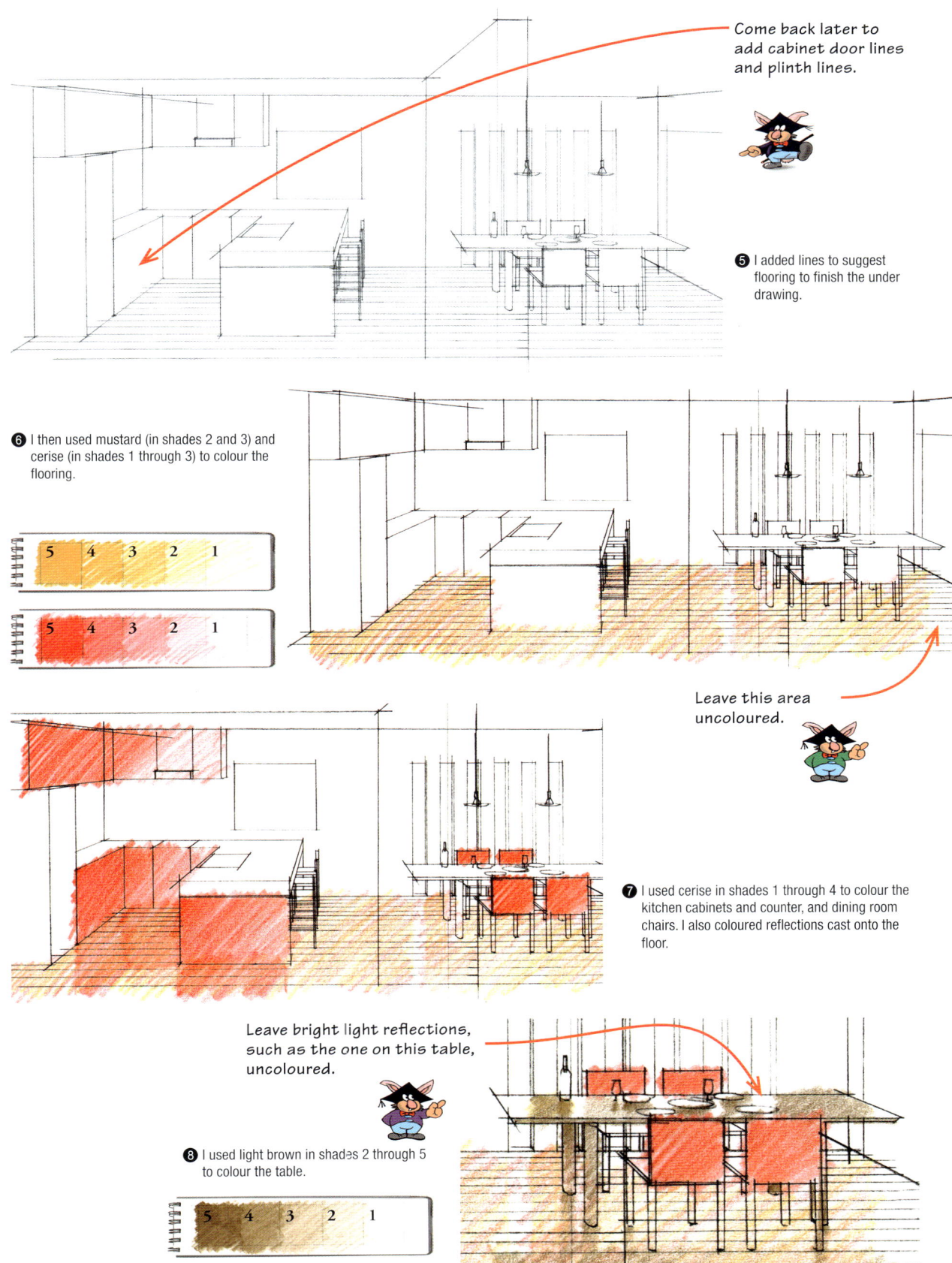

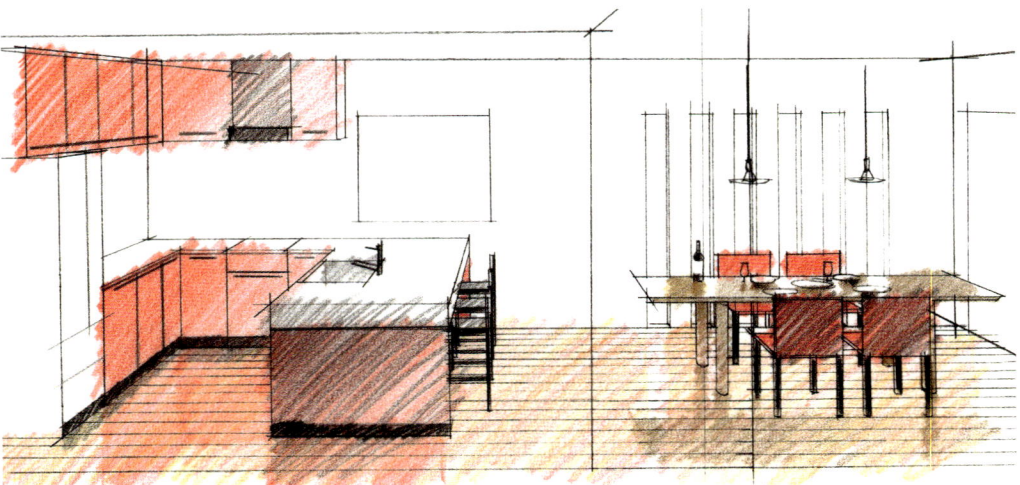

9 Next, I used a black coloured pencil in shades 1 through 5 to draw lines for the kitchen counter doors, the plinth, the counter's shadows, the range hood, the chair legs, and other assorted shadows.

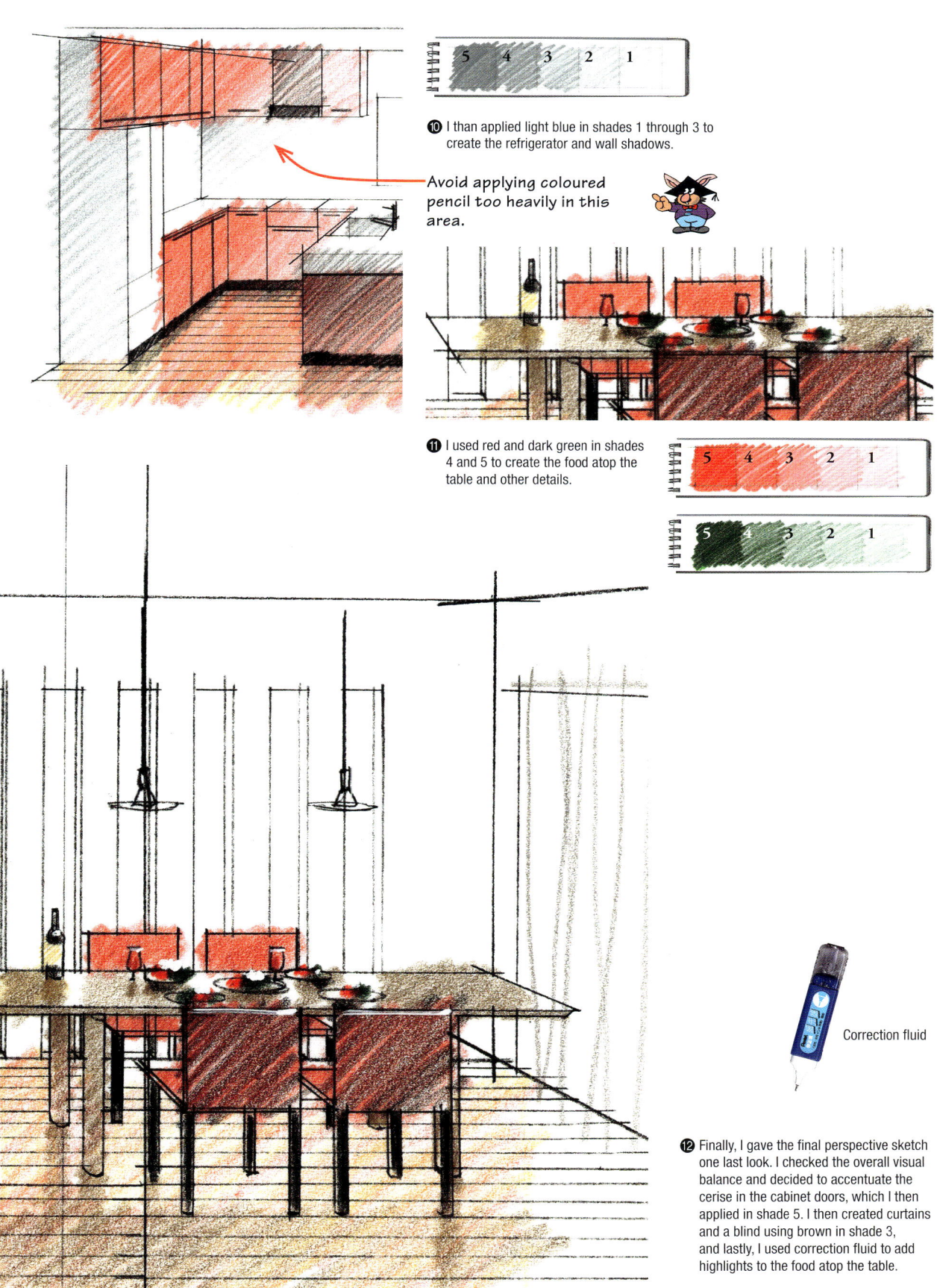

⑩ I than applied light blue in shades 1 through 3 to create the refrigerator and wall shadows.

Avoid applying coloured pencil too heavily in this area.

⑪ I used red and dark green in shades 4 and 5 to create the food atop the table and other details.

Correction fluid

⑫ Finally, I gave the final perspective sketch one last look. I checked the overall visual balance and decided to accentuate the cerise in the cabinet doors, which I then applied in shade 5. I then created curtains and a blind using brown in shade 3, and lastly, I used correction fluid to add highlights to the food atop the table.

Kitchen/Dining Room Featuring a Long Table

The dining room table is long enough to extend through the open wall and into the courtyard. The kitchen section of the table is not particularly long. However, the table serves to connect the courtyard to the house's interior, psychologically dissolving the table's interior section's smallness. I intended for the table's courtyard section to be used for barbecues and other outdoor functions during clement weather.

❶ I started by drawing a floor plan.

❷ Next, I produced a two-point perspective under drawing, setting the vanishing points low in the composition.

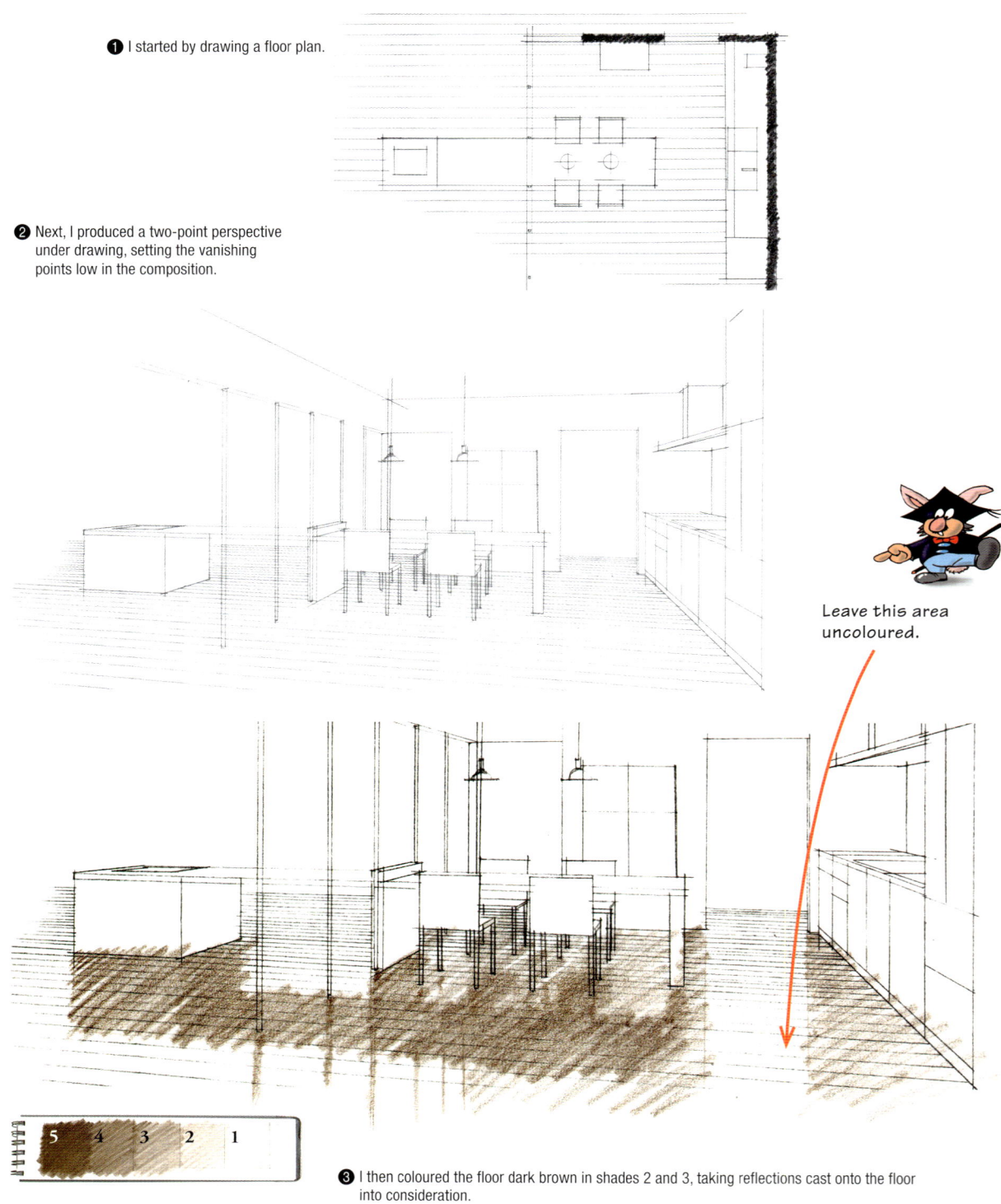

Leave this area uncoloured.

❸ I then coloured the floor dark brown in shades 2 and 3, taking reflections cast onto the floor into consideration.

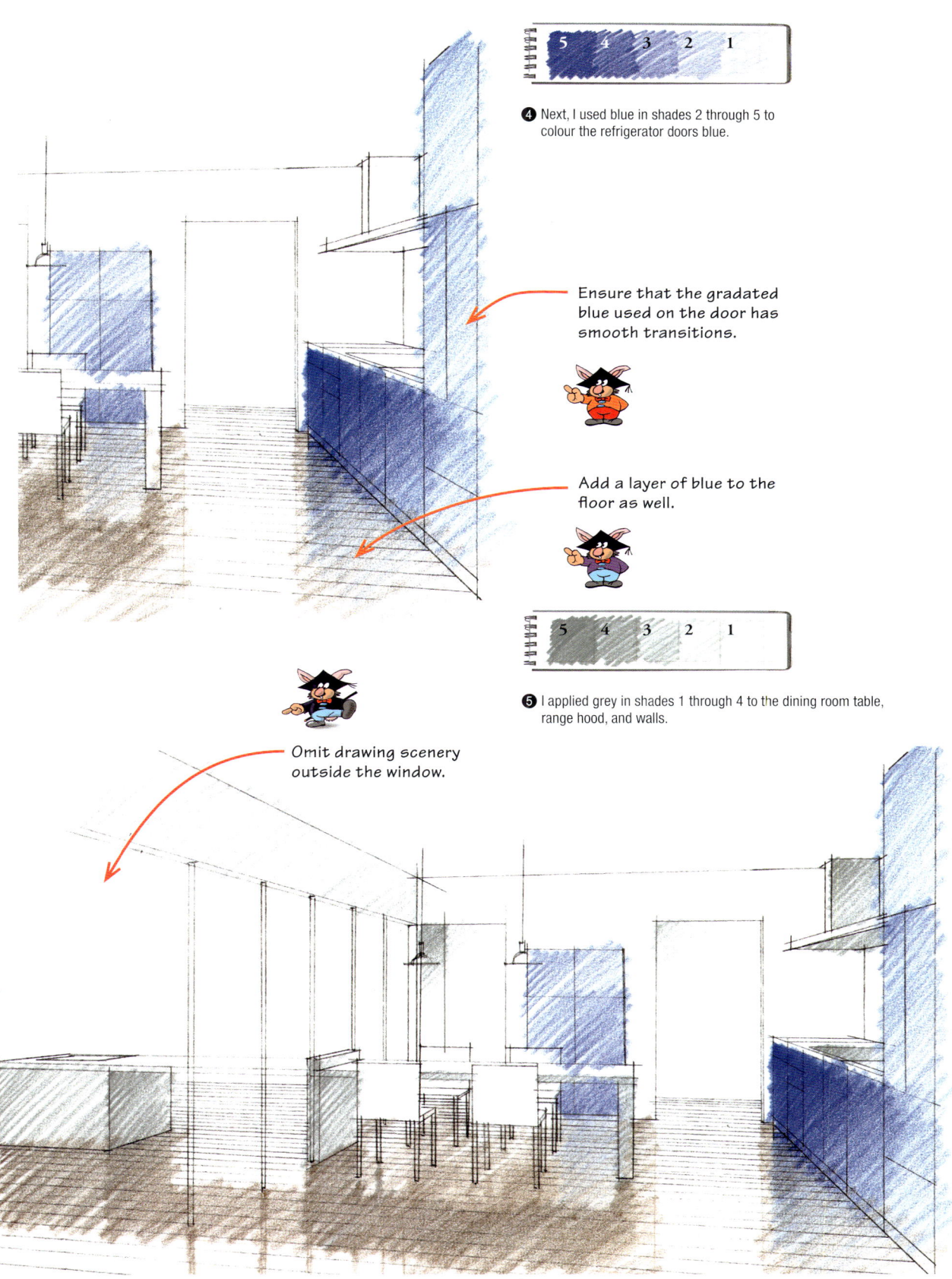

❹ Next, I used blue in shades 2 through 5 to colour the refrigerator doors blue.

Ensure that the gradated blue used on the door has smooth transitions.

Add a layer of blue to the floor as well.

❺ I applied grey in shades 1 through 4 to the dining room table, range hood, and walls.

Omit drawing scenery outside the window.

❻ I used aquamarine in shades 2 through 4 to colour the chairs and then applied red and dark green in shades 4 and 5 to create the fruit. To create the beer, I used mustard in shade 5.

Apply saturated colour to the fruit.

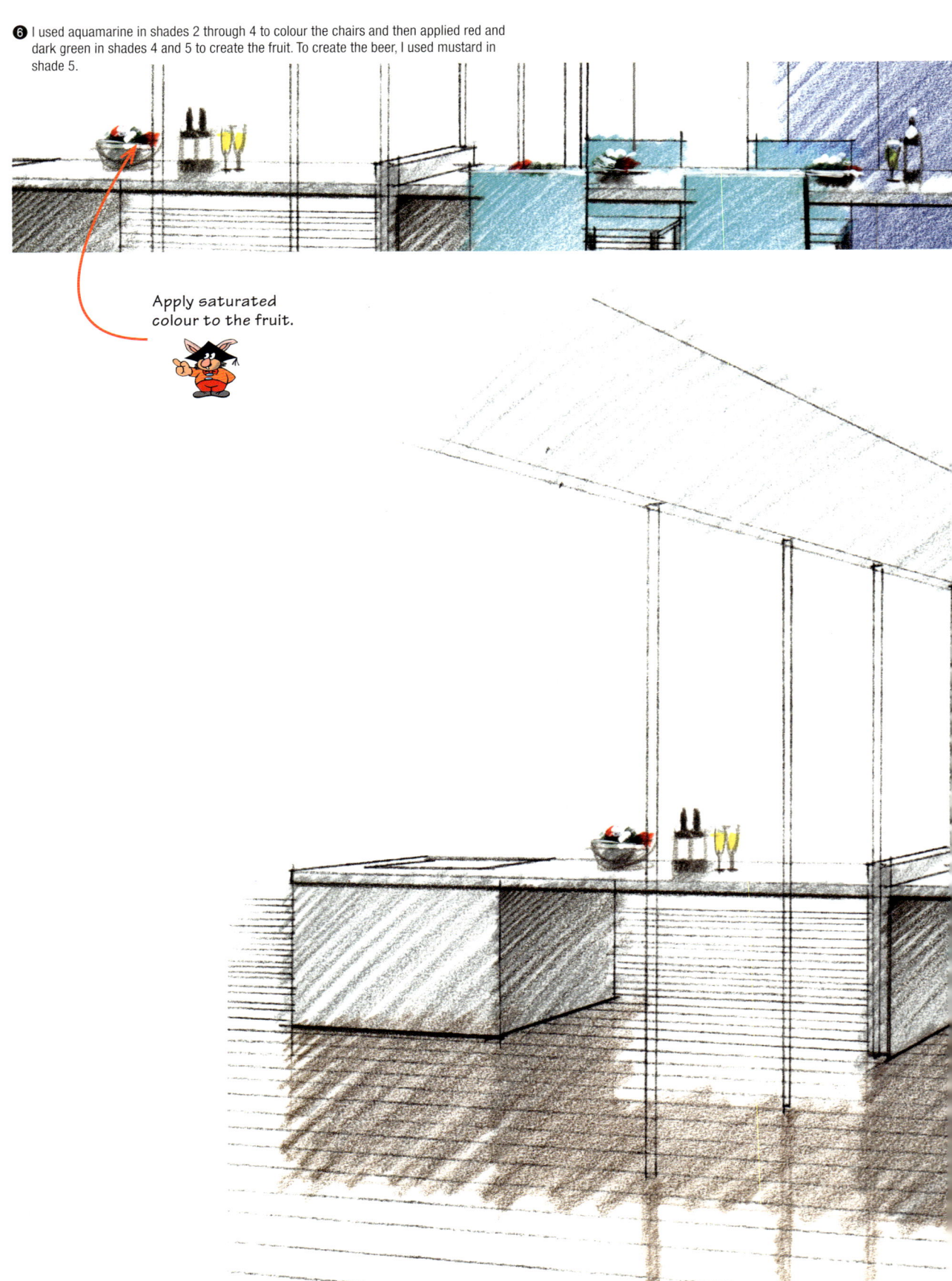

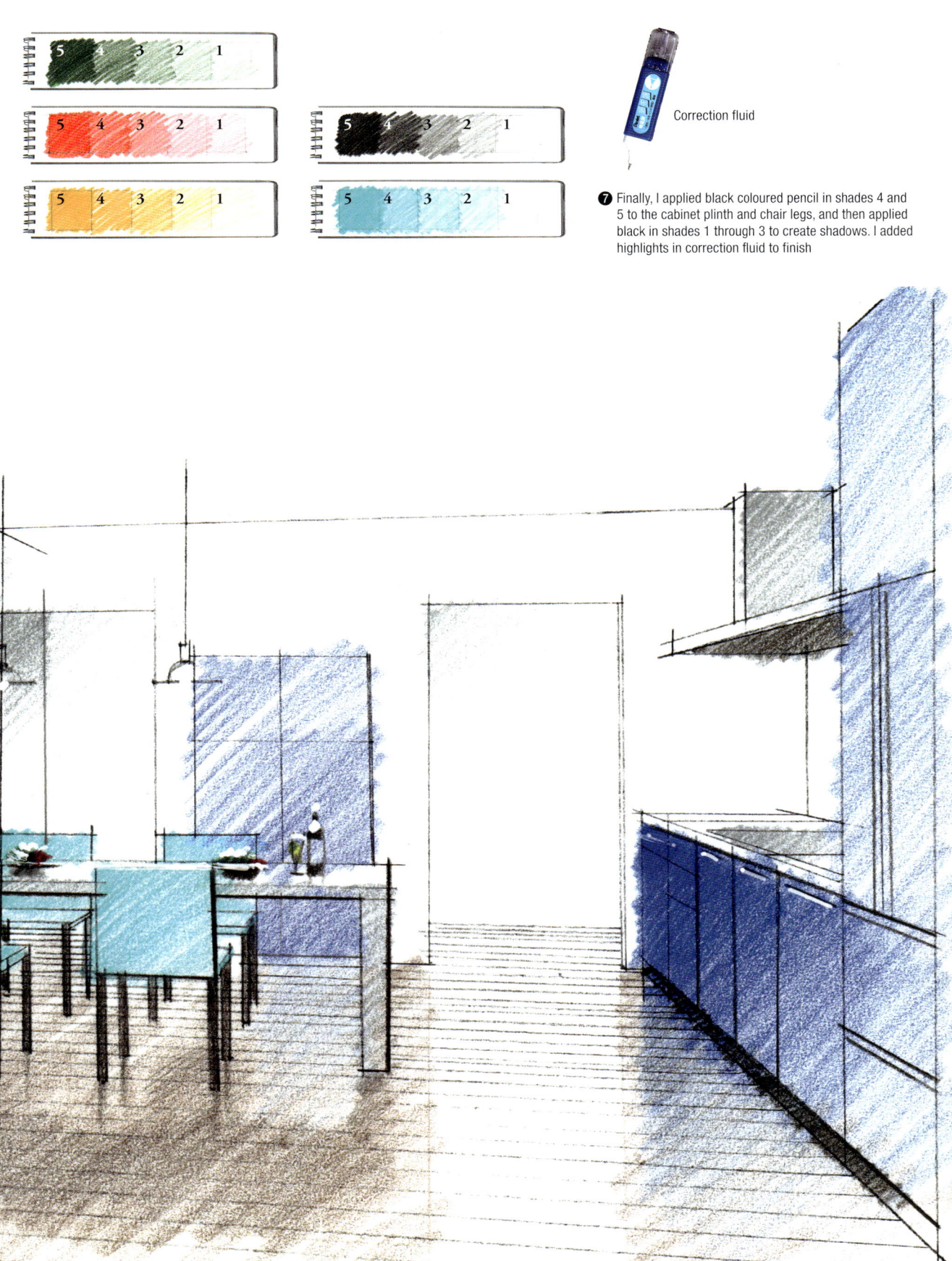

Correction fluid

❼ Finally, I applied black coloured pencil in shades 4 and 5 to the cabinet plinth and chair legs, and then applied black in shades 1 through 3 to create shadows. I added highlights in correction fluid to finish

Subdued Kitchen with a Table and Earthen Floor

The earthen floor comprises terracotta tiles. The space includes a table for dining in addition to a generous counter and ample cabinets.

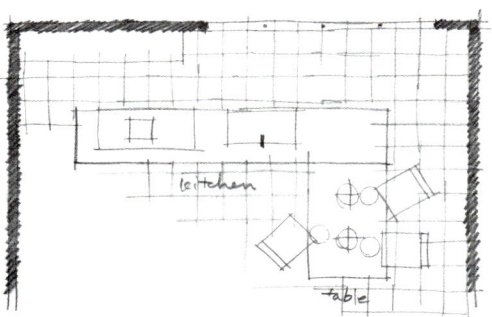

❶ I started by drawing a floor plan.

❷ Next, I sketched a one-point perspective under drawing freehand, without using a straightedge.

❸ I then coloured the cabinets and the floor using dark brown in shades 1 through 4, modulating the pencil's stroke pressure.

Apply colour lightly to the cabinet doors.

❹ Next, I coloured the sides of the cabinets and counter using light brown in shades 1 through 3.

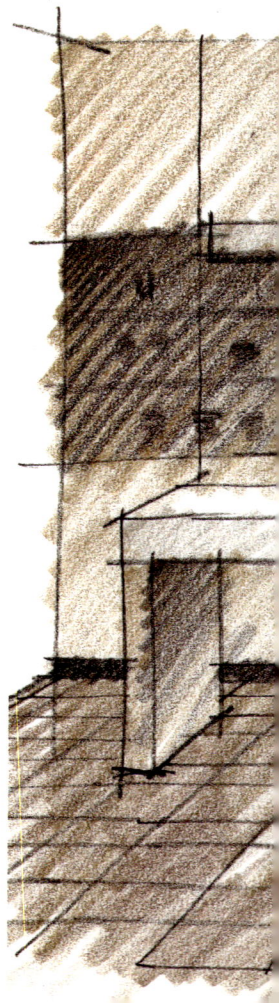

5 I added warm grey in shades 1 through 3 to create shadows on the counter and range hood.

6 I then applied red in shades 1 through 5 to the chairs.

The key is to modulate the pencil's pressure.

7 I coloured the food red and dark green, both in shades 4 and 5. I then used a black coloured pencil in shades 1 through 5 to add shadows to the cabinet plinth, the chairs' legs, the cabinets, and other fixtures. I applied black in shades 3 and 4 to create the dishes inside the cabinets. I added the curtains using light brown in shade 3.

Kitchen with a Large, Tranquil Tree Visible from Outside

This kitchen features cabinets attached to one wall and an island. The island is physically fused with a table into one unit. Large sliding glass windows offer a view of a soul-soothing tree outside the house.

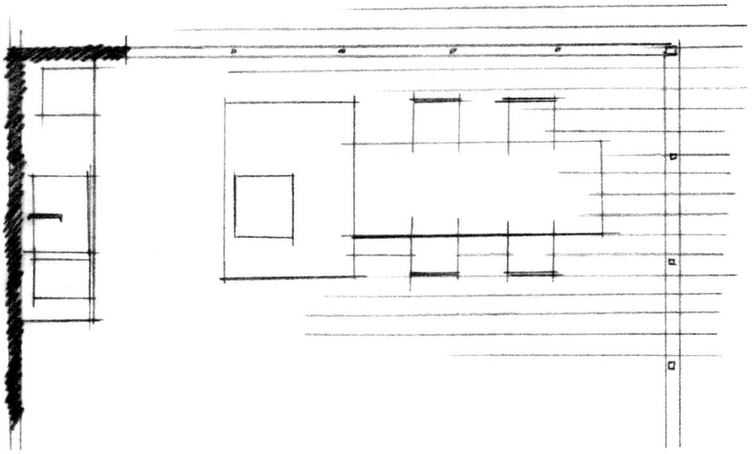

❶ I started by drawing a floor plan.

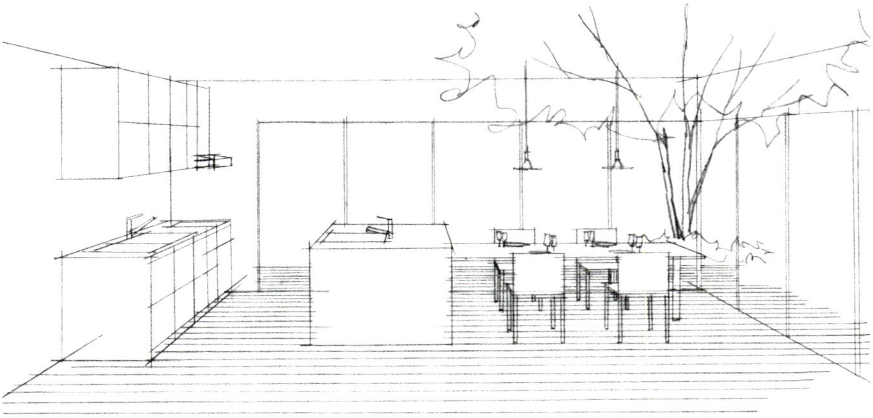

❷ Next, I produced a one-point perspective under drawing.

Remember to include shadows underneath tables.

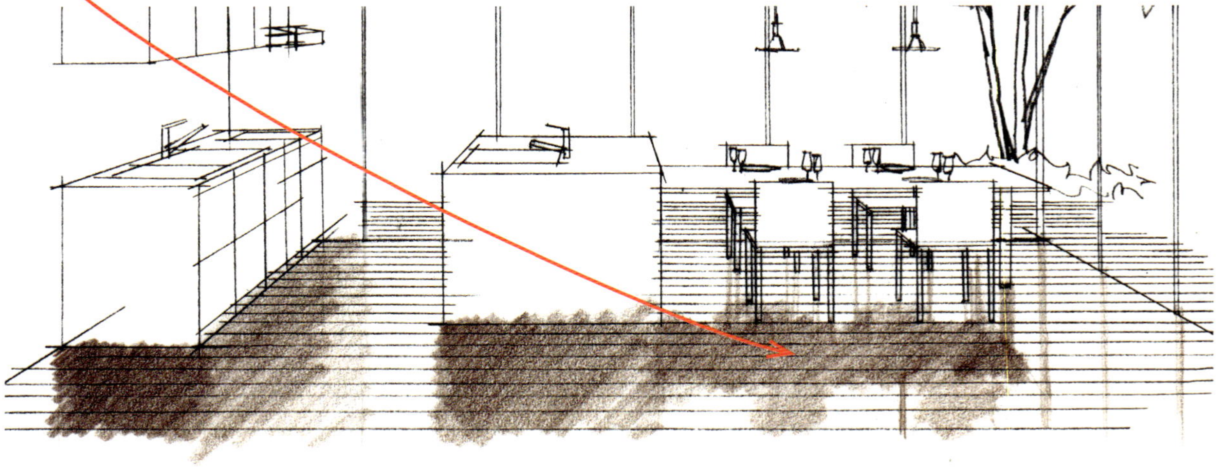

❸ I applied dark brown in shades 1 through 4 to the floor, maintaining awareness of floor reflections.

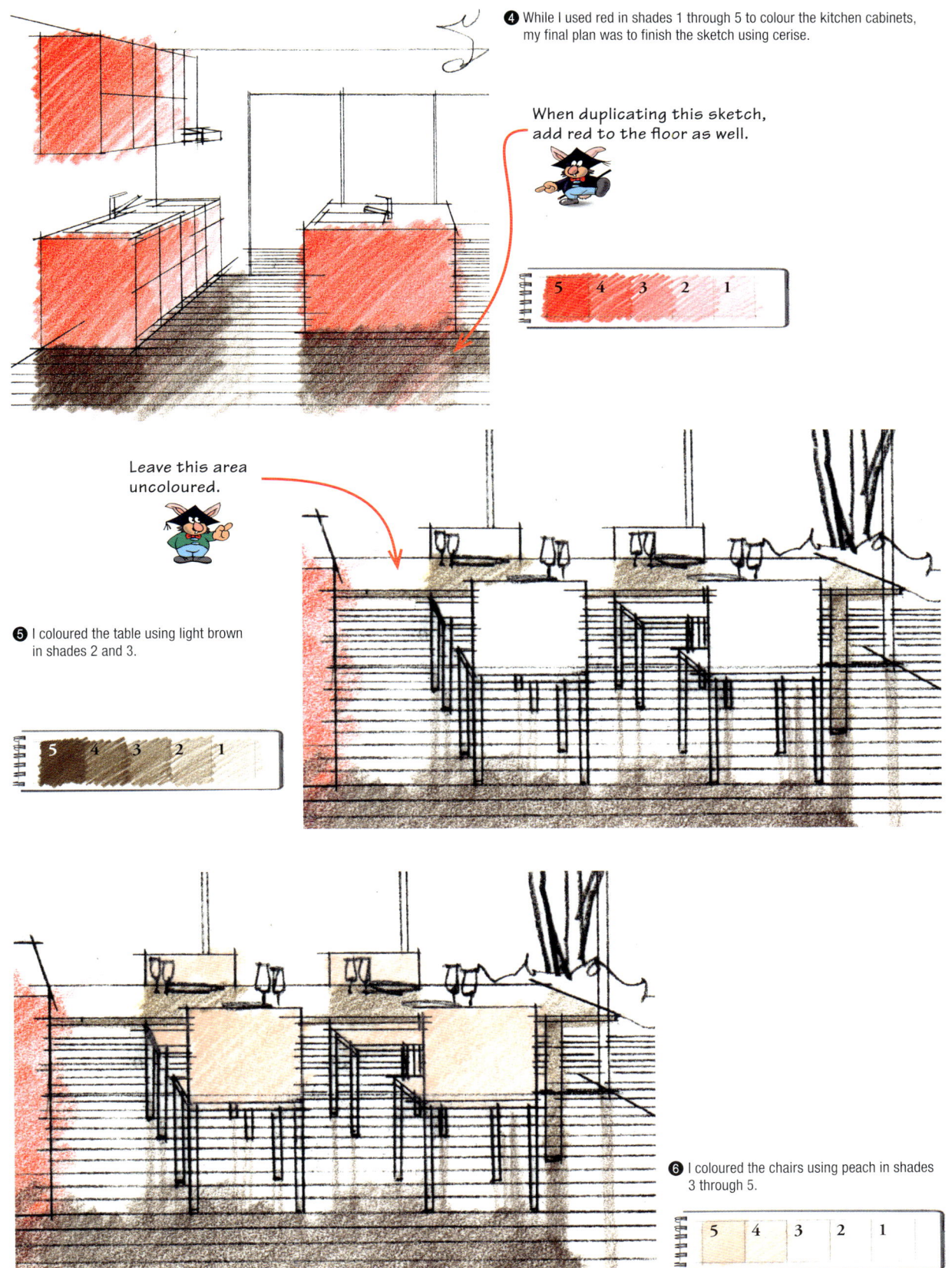

❹ While I used red in shades 1 through 5 to colour the kitchen cabinets, my final plan was to finish the sketch using cerise.

When duplicating this sketch, add red to the floor as well.

Leave this area uncoloured.

❺ I coloured the table using light brown in shades 2 and 3.

❻ I coloured the chairs using peach in shades 3 through 5.

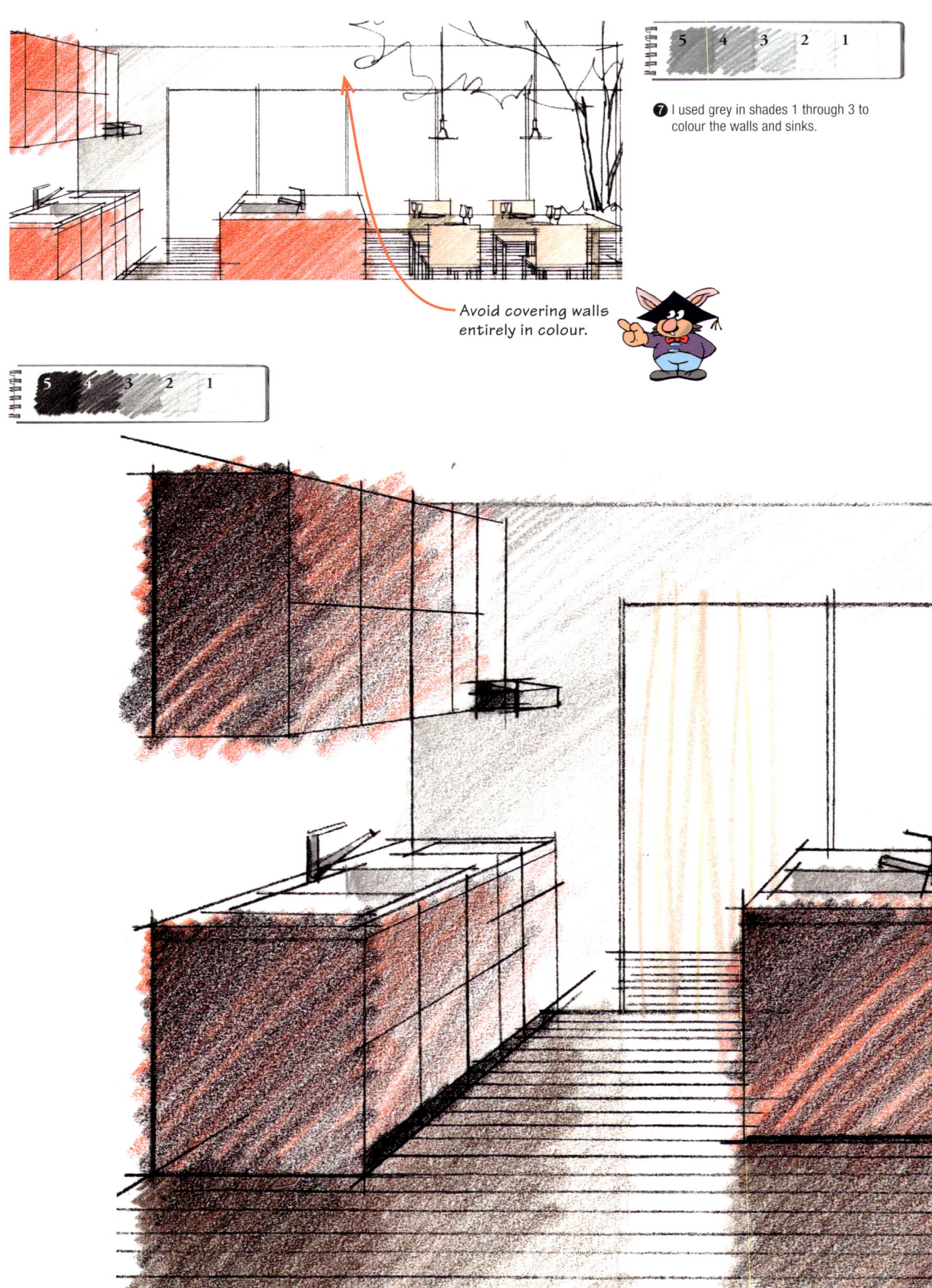

❼ I used grey in shades 1 through 3 to colour the walls and sinks.

Avoid covering walls entirely in colour.

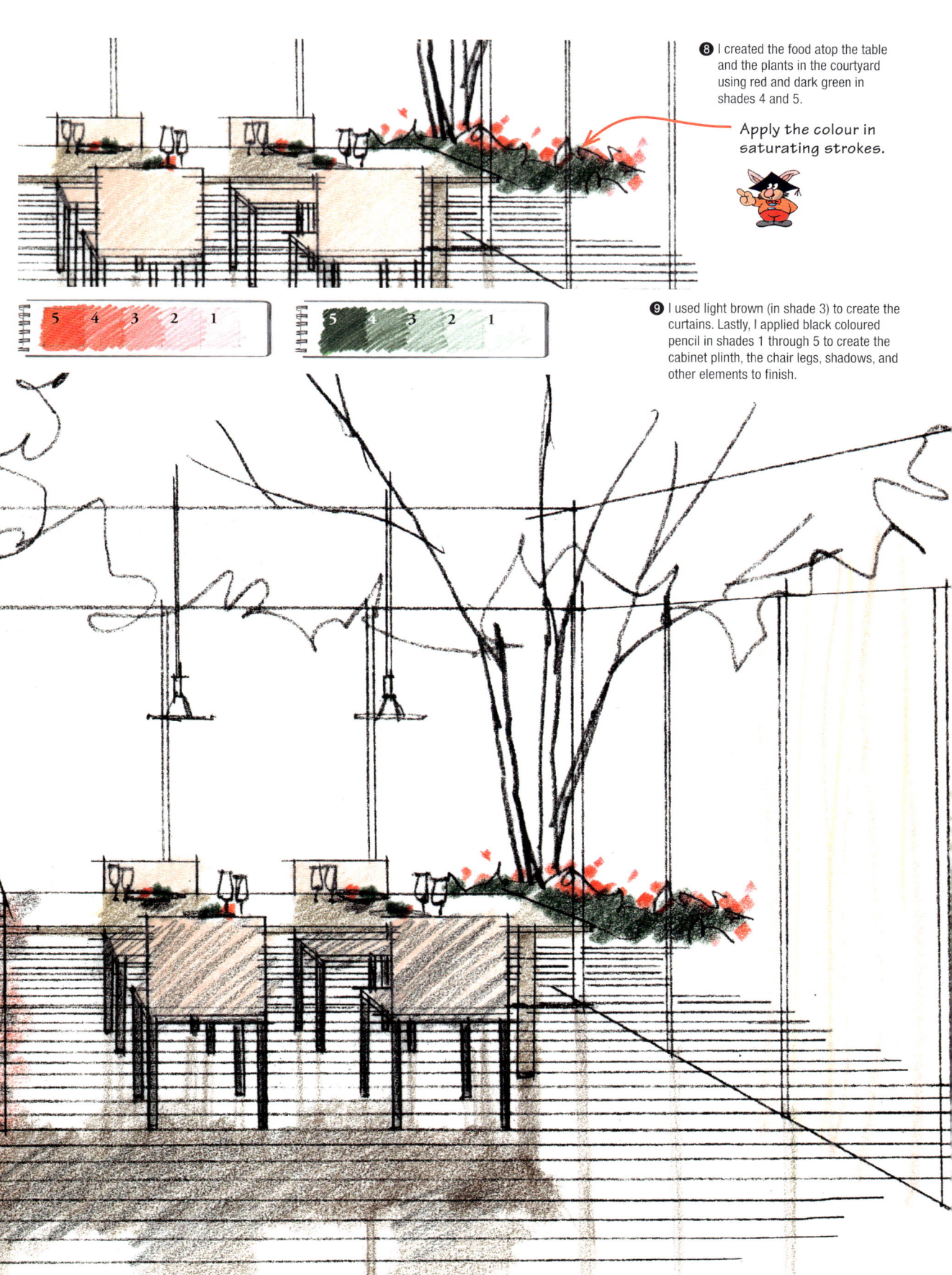

❽ I created the food atop the table and the plants in the courtyard using red and dark green in shades 4 and 5.

Apply the colour in saturating strokes.

❾ I used light brown (in shade 3) to create the curtains. Lastly, I applied black coloured pencil in shades 1 through 5 to create the cabinet plinth, the chair legs, shadows, and other elements to finish.

Embraced by Nature: A Bedroom with a Garden View

This is a bright, airy bedroom. Opening the bedroom curtains reveals a patio, which enables the resident to sip tea or enjoy a meal surrounded by flowers and trees.

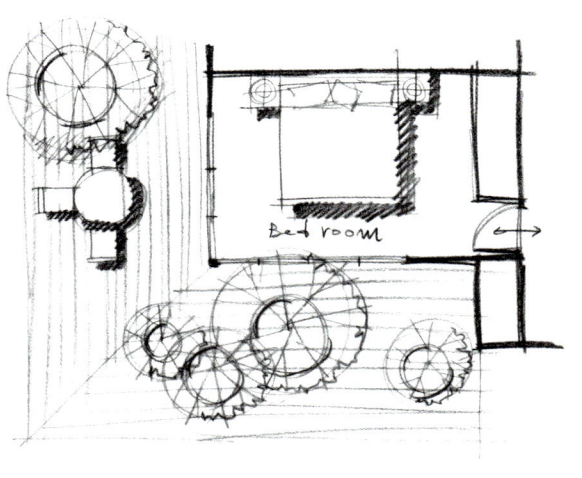

❶ I started by drawing a floor plan.

❷ Next, I produced a one-point perspective under drawing using a regular pencil. I positioned the point-of-view (vanishing point) above the ceiling to allow view of the bed's upper surface.

❸ I then coloured the floor using brown in moderately light strokes in shades 1 through 3. I also used brown in shade 1 to colour the bed's front.

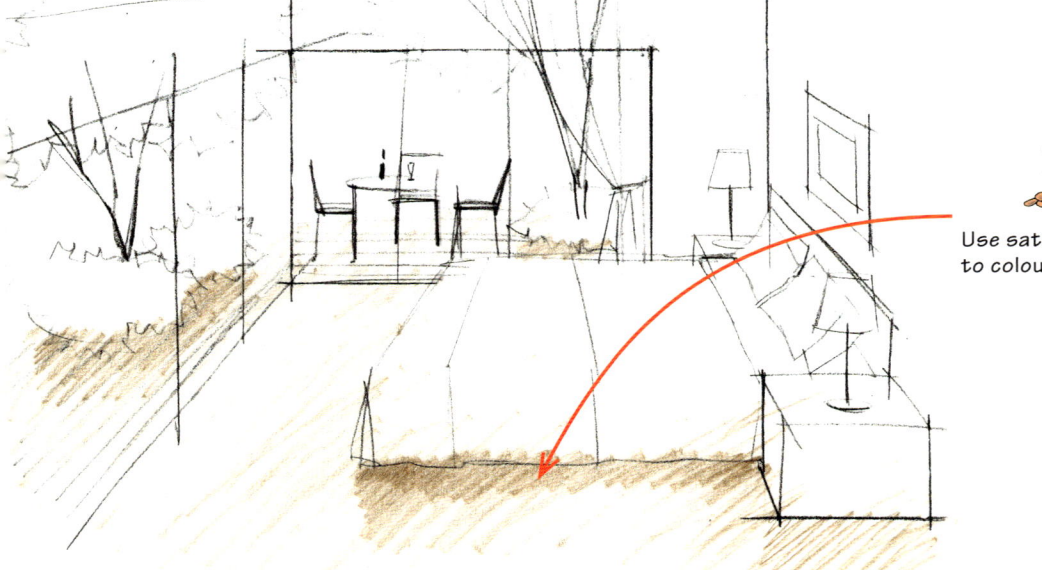

Use saturated strokes to colour this area.

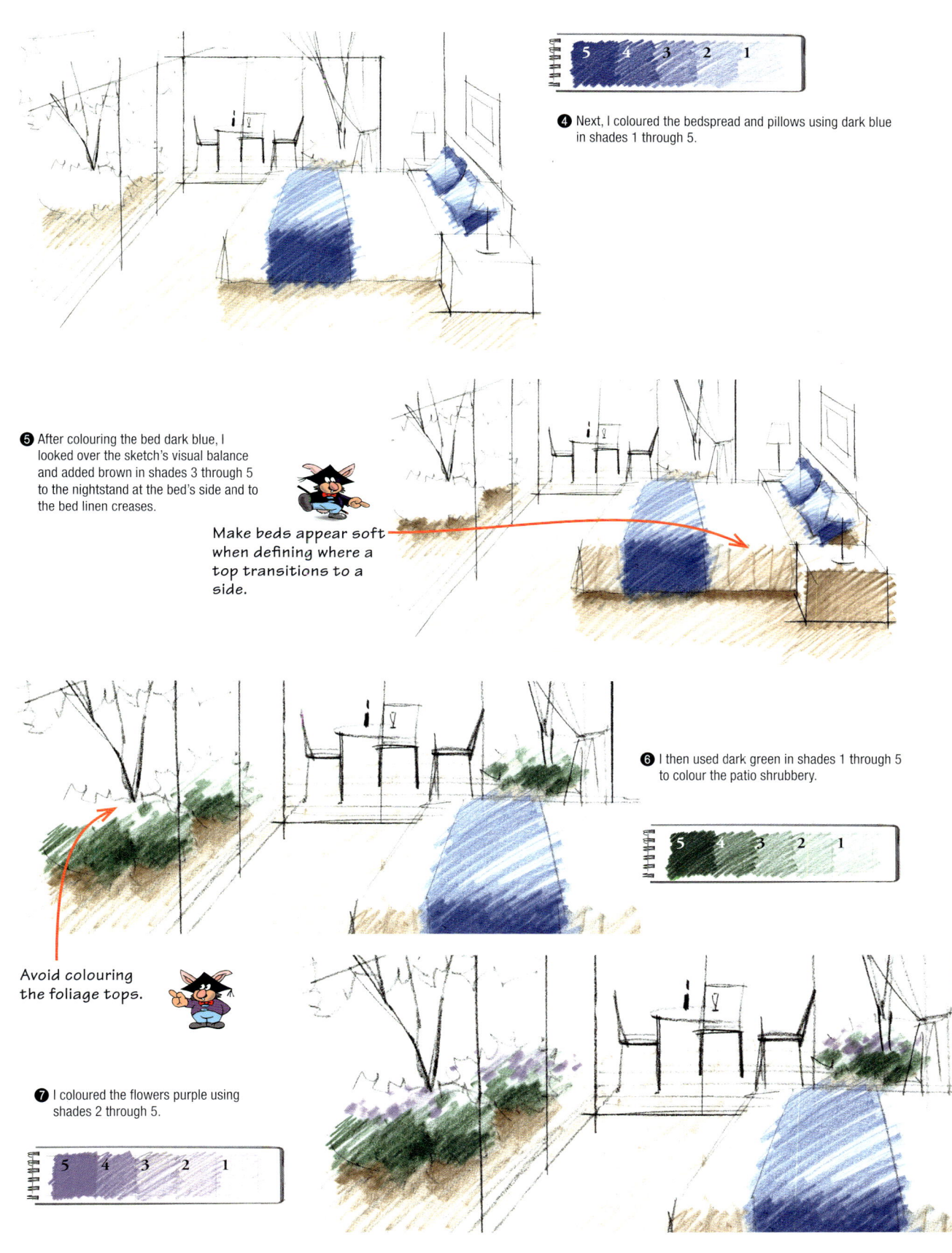

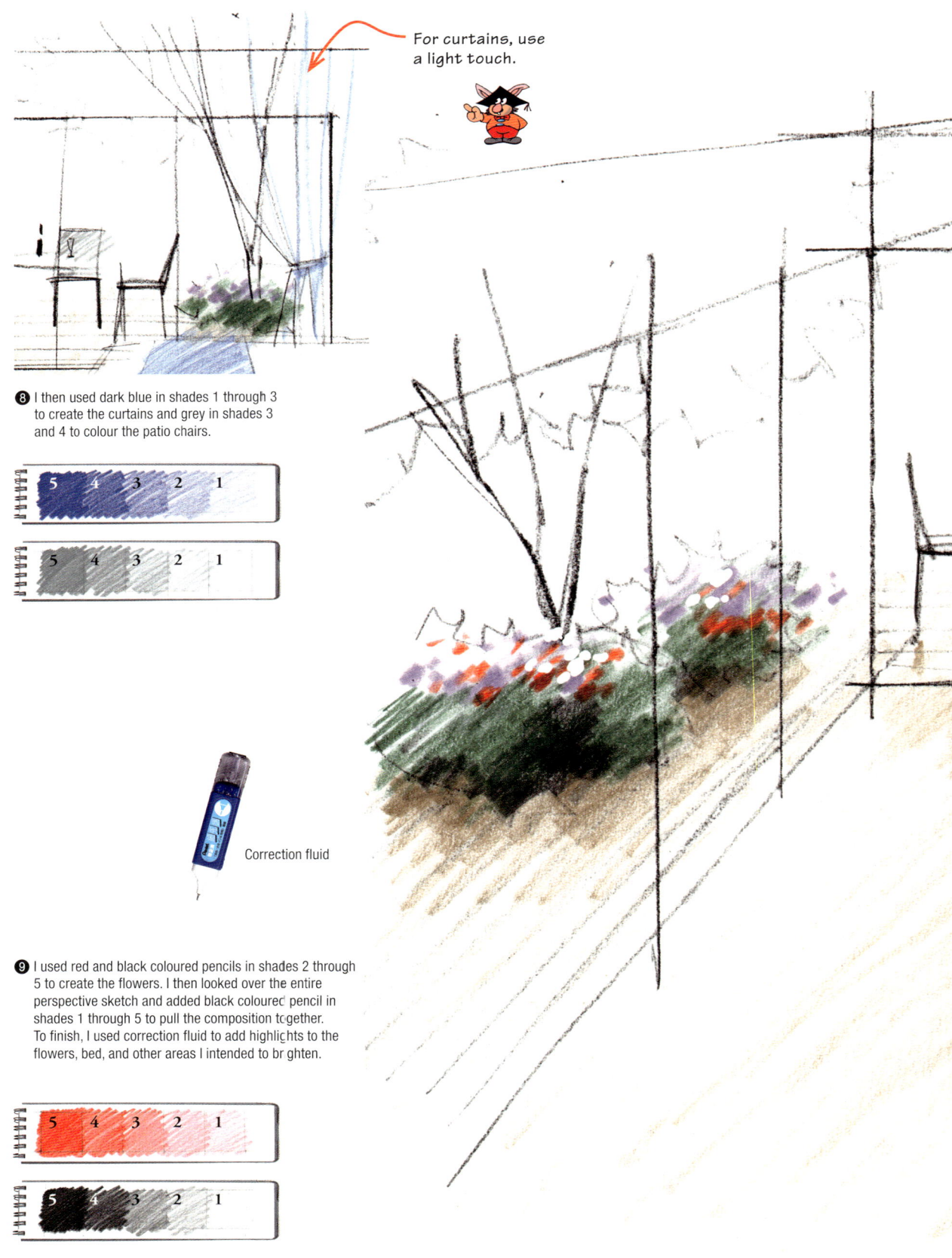

For curtains, use a light touch.

❽ I then used dark blue in shades 1 through 3 to create the curtains and grey in shades 3 and 4 to colour the patio chairs.

Correction fluid

❾ I used red and black coloured pencils in shades 2 through 5 to create the flowers. I then looked over the entire perspective sketch and added black coloured pencil in shades 1 through 5 to pull the composition together. To finish, I used correction fluid to add highlights to the flowers, bed, and other areas I intended to brighten.

Eye-catching Bedroom/Bathroom

I positioned a spacious, open bathroom next to the bedroom. The bathroom contains a chaise lounge, creating a resort atmosphere. I sketched the composition in monochrome to give the overall space a chic look.

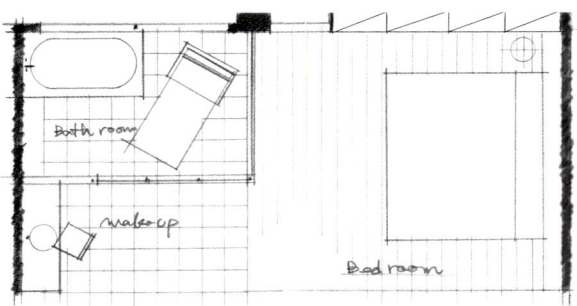

❶ I started by drawing a floor plan.

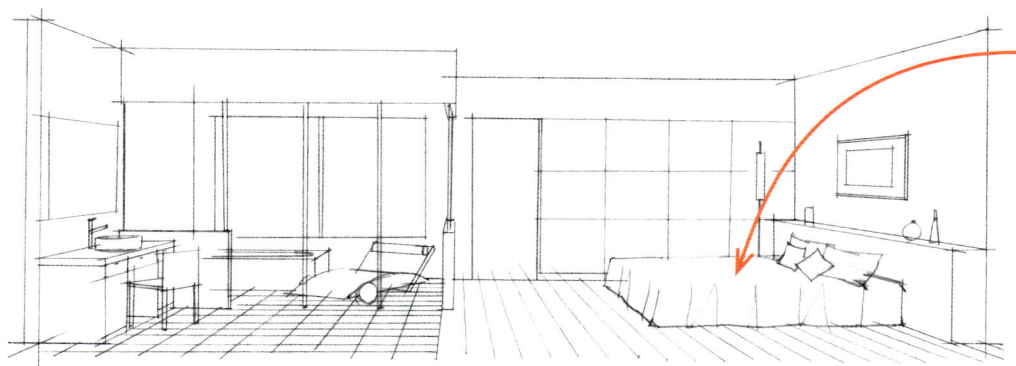

Omit drawing a line to define where the bed's top meets its side. This will make the bed appear soft.

❷ Next, I produced a one-point perspective under drawing using a regular pencil and a straightedge.

❻ This shows the completed sketch. The black applied to the bed (creating shadows and the illusion of a soft solid object) constitutes a key point.

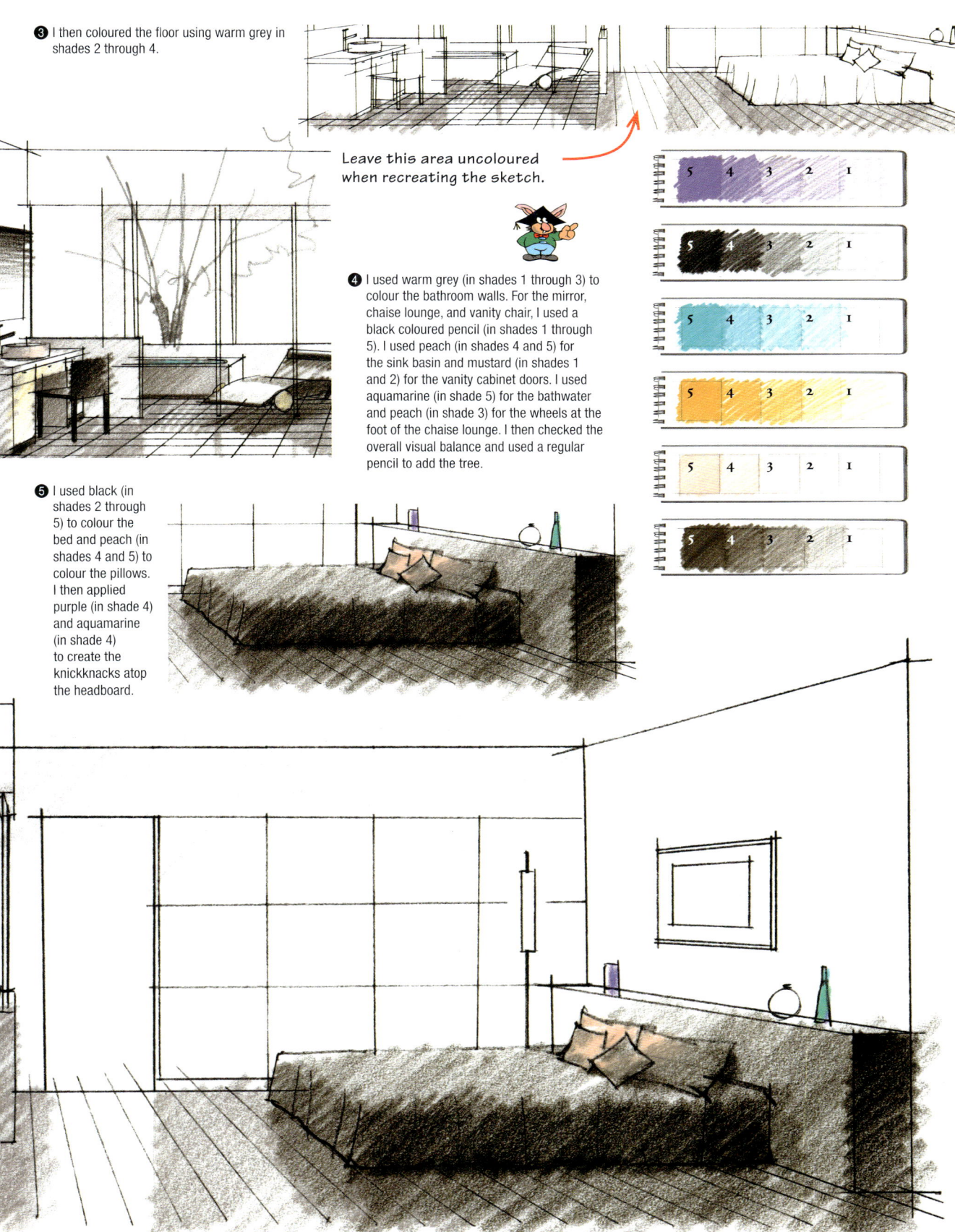

Fantasy Theater Bedroom

The beds' headboards are adjustable. A table lies between the two beds, allowing the residents to enjoy a snack while watching a favorite movie.

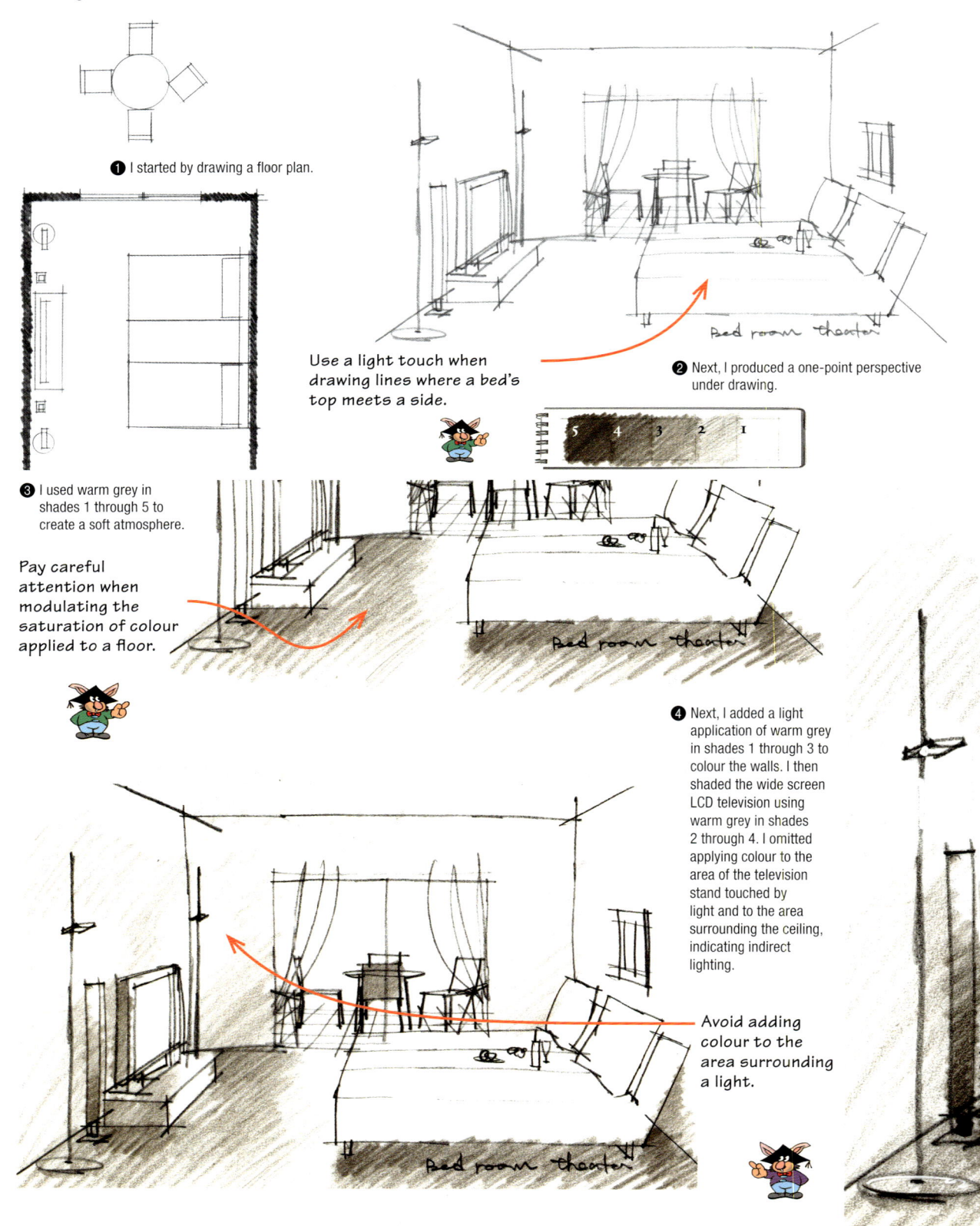

❶ I started by drawing a floor plan.

❷ Next, I produced a one-point perspective under drawing.

Use a light touch when drawing lines where a bed's top meets a side.

❸ I used warm grey in shades 1 through 5 to create a soft atmosphere.

Pay careful attention when modulating the saturation of colour applied to a floor.

❹ Next, I added a light application of warm grey in shades 1 through 3 to colour the walls. I then shaded the wide screen LCD television using warm grey in shades 2 through 4. I omitted applying colour to the area of the television stand touched by light and to the area surrounding the ceiling, indicating indirect lighting.

Avoid adding colour to the area surrounding a light.

Use a light touch when colouring pillows.

5 I then used brown in shades 1 through 5 to shade the bed and the wide screen LCD TV's stand.

6 I created the curtains using brown.

For curtains, use coloured pencils to sketch the contours of draping folds rather than to "colour" the curtains.

Correction fluid

7 I then used red and mustard (both in shade 5) to create the food atop the table between the two beds. I applied black coloured pencil in shades 4 and 5 to those areas I intended to tighten up visually and in shades 1 through 3 to create pale shadows. Finally, I added highlights using correction fluid to finish.

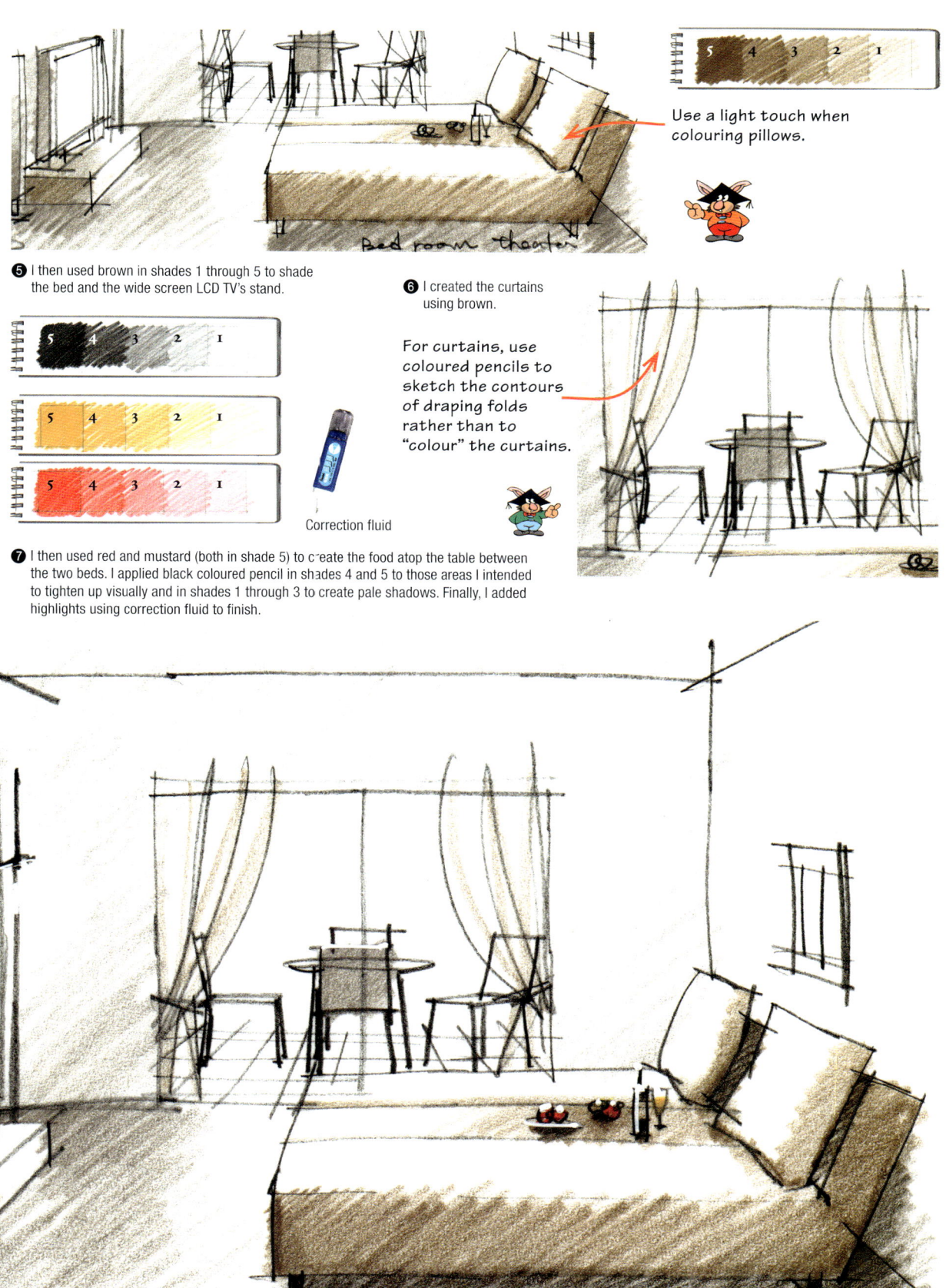

Room with an *Irori*: Trendy Japanese *Tatami* Mat Room

This 8-*tatami* mat room (approximately 144 square feet) contains a sunken hearth called ar "*irori*," which enables the resident to heat a kettle or grill a fish while gazing at the garden's pond. A "*sagarikabe*," which is a header wall, somewhat restricts the inhabitant's view, creating a calming atmosphere.

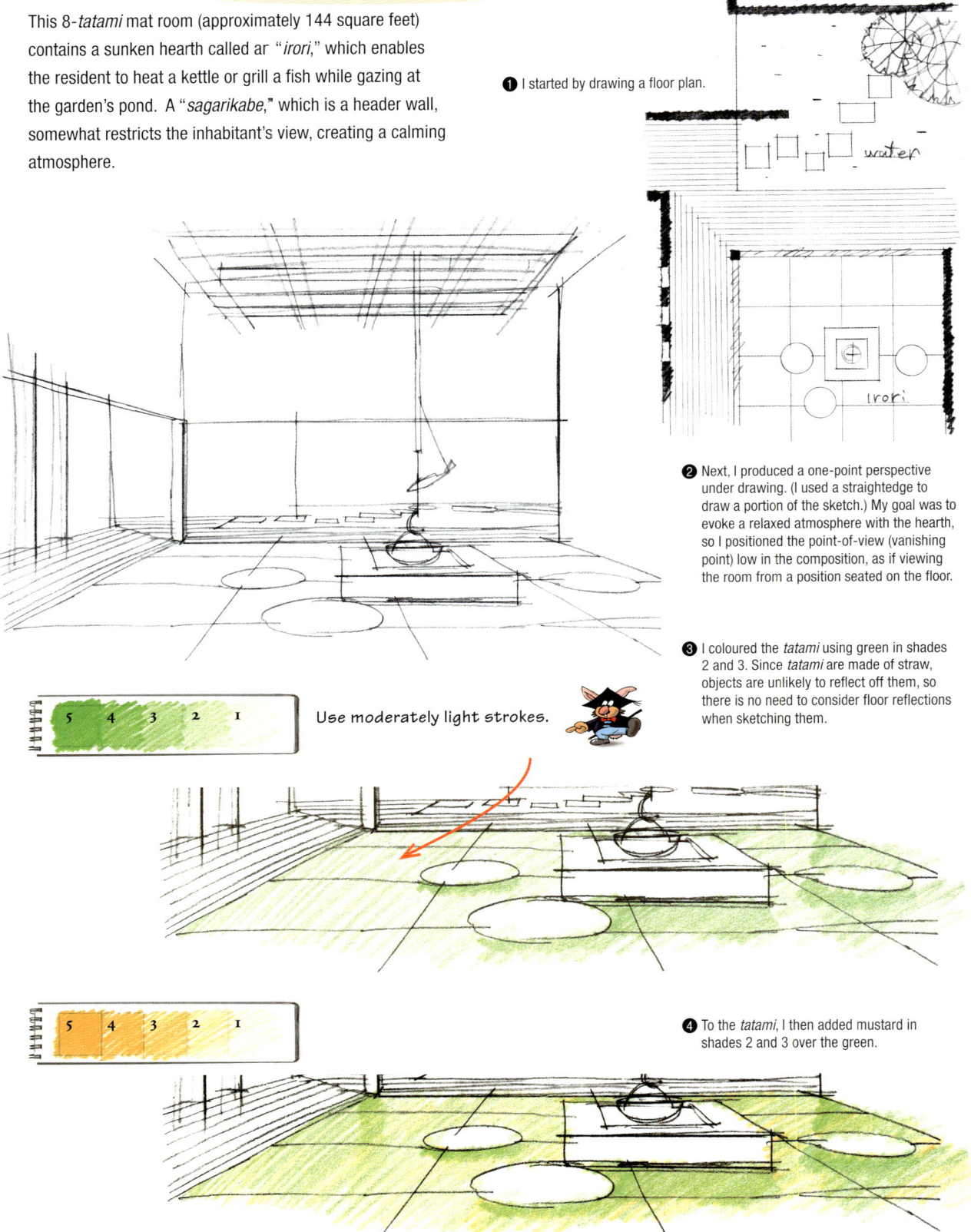

❶ I started by drawing a floor plan.

❷ Next, I produced a one-point perspective under drawing. (I used a straightedge to draw a portion of the sketch.) My goal was to evoke a relaxed atmosphere with the hearth, so I positioned the point-of-view (vanishing point) low in the composition, as if viewing the room from a position seated on the floor.

❸ I coloured the *tatami* using green in shades 2 and 3. Since *tatami* are made of straw, objects are unlikely to reflect off them, so there is no need to consider floor reflections when sketching them.

Use moderately light strokes.

❹ To the *tatami*, I then added mustard in shades 2 and 3 over the green.

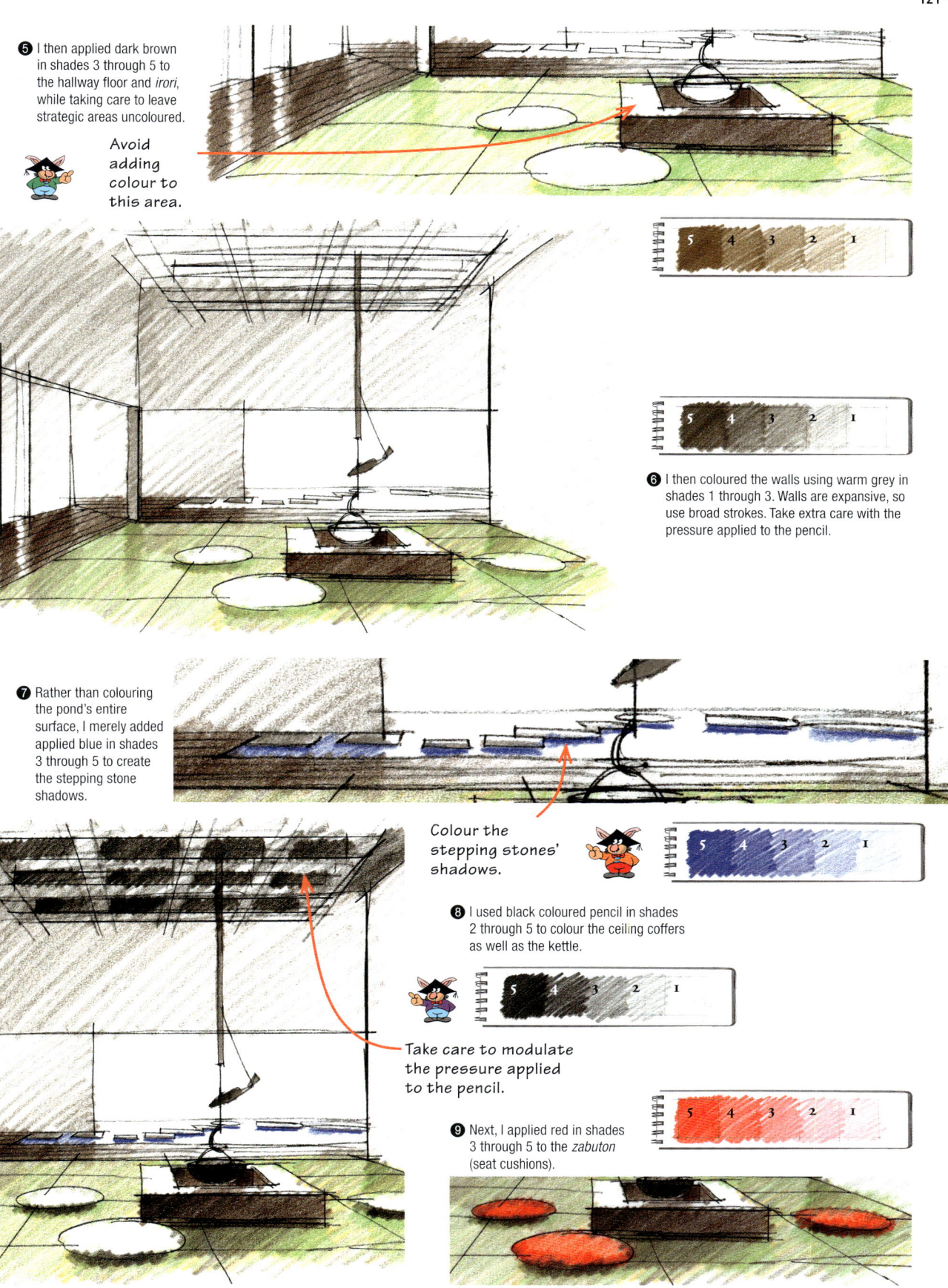

⑩ I then added the tree in pencil, while considering the proportioning of the pond to the tree

⑪ I used dark green and red in shades 3 though 5 to create the grass and flowers.

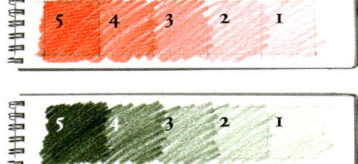

⑬ This shows the final sketch. Applying colour too heavily makes a space appear dark and gloomy, so modulating pencil pressure when colouring the walls constituted a key point in this composition.

Correction fluid

❷ I then briskly applied correction fluid to the flowers, the kettle, the water's surface, and other very bright areas.

Giving an Asian Flair to a Living Room/Office Space

I unified this space by giving it an Asian look. The resident may use this space for work as well as for reclining on the sofa and gazing at the garden. This space evokes the impression of a resort hotel merged with an office.

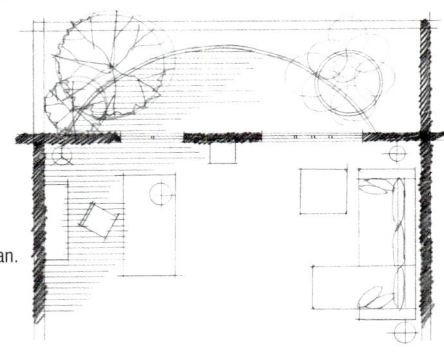

❶ I started by drawing a floor plan.

❷ Next, I produced a one-point perspective under drawing. (I used a straightedge.) From the start, my client had expressed a wish for the room to have an Asian flair, so I included plants, furniture, and lighting at this stage of the sketch.

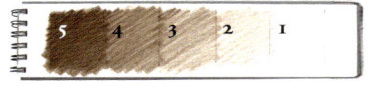

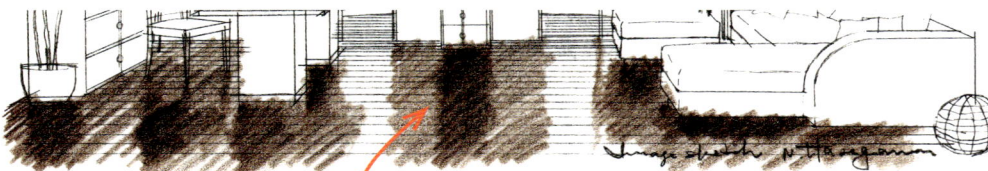

❸ I used dark brown in shades 2 through 5 to colour the floor, leaving uncoloured areas where objects cast reflections onto the floor.

Modulate the stroke pressure you use.

❹ I then applied dark brown in shades 2 through 5 to the furniture.

Leave areas touched by light uncoloured.

❼ Next, I used red in shades 3 through 5 to colour the flowers and throw pillows. I then applied black coloured pencil in shades 3 through 5 to pull together the shadows, the window sash, and other compositional elements. Lastly, I used correction fluid to the lighting and to create highlights.

❺ I applied warm grey to the walls, sofa, chairs, plant pots, and the like. I used shades 1 through 3 for the floor and 2 through 4 for the sofa and other objects.

Leave uncoloured those areas touched by light.

❻ I then applied yellow-brown in shades 1 through 4 to the furniture, light fixtures, and other furnishings.

Correction fluid

The Ultimate Bath Space: Bedroom with an Outdoor Bath

Here, I gave the garden a circular outdoor bath so the resident could relax while gazing at the moon or bathing in light filtering through tree leaves. My concept was to recreate the feeling of a resort hotel with an outdoor bath.

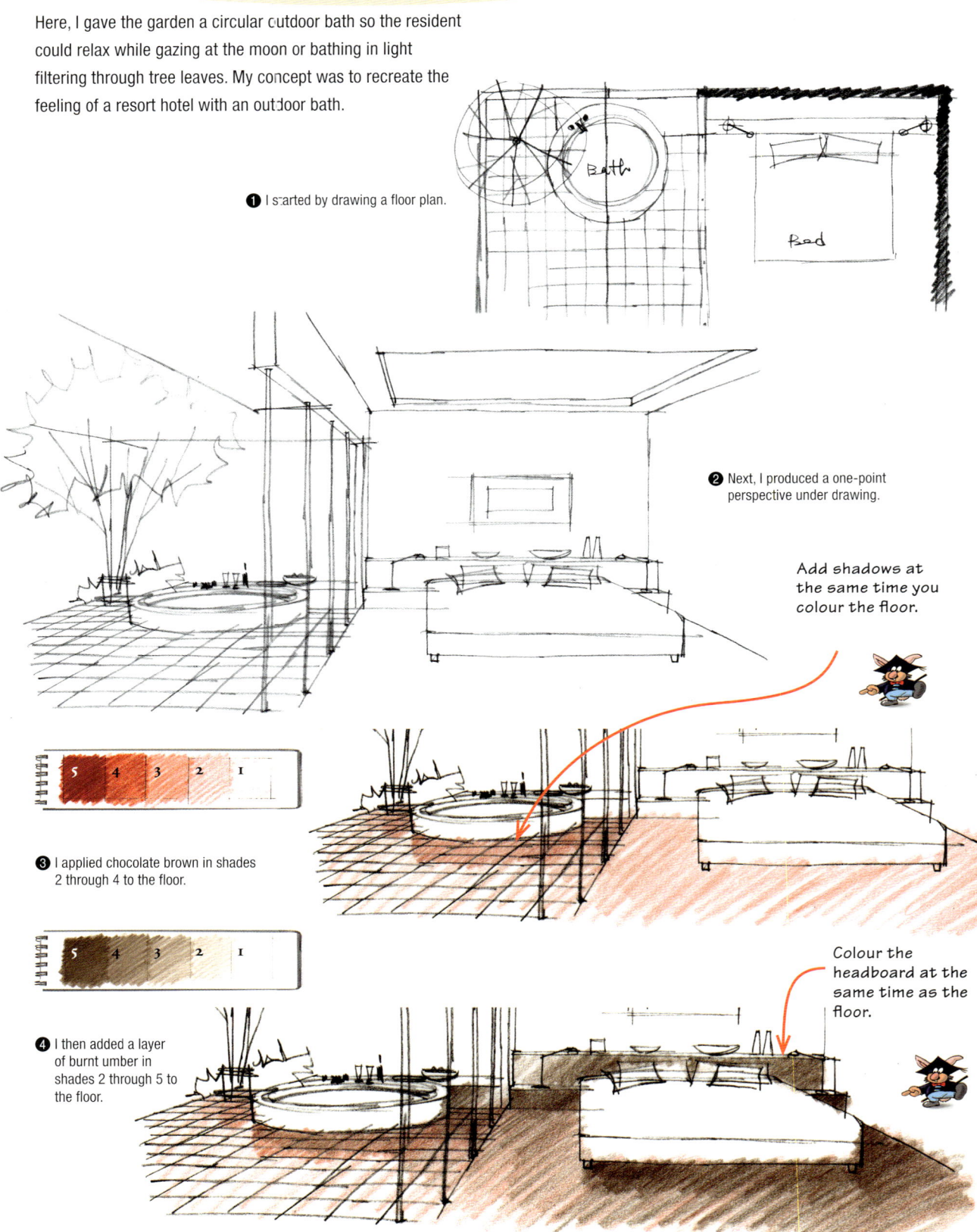

❶ I started by drawing a floor plan.

❷ Next, I produced a one-point perspective under drawing.

Add shadows at the same time you colour the floor.

❸ I applied chocolate brown in shades 2 through 4 to the floor.

❹ I then added a layer of burnt umber in shades 2 through 5 to the floor.

Colour the headboard at the same time as the floor.

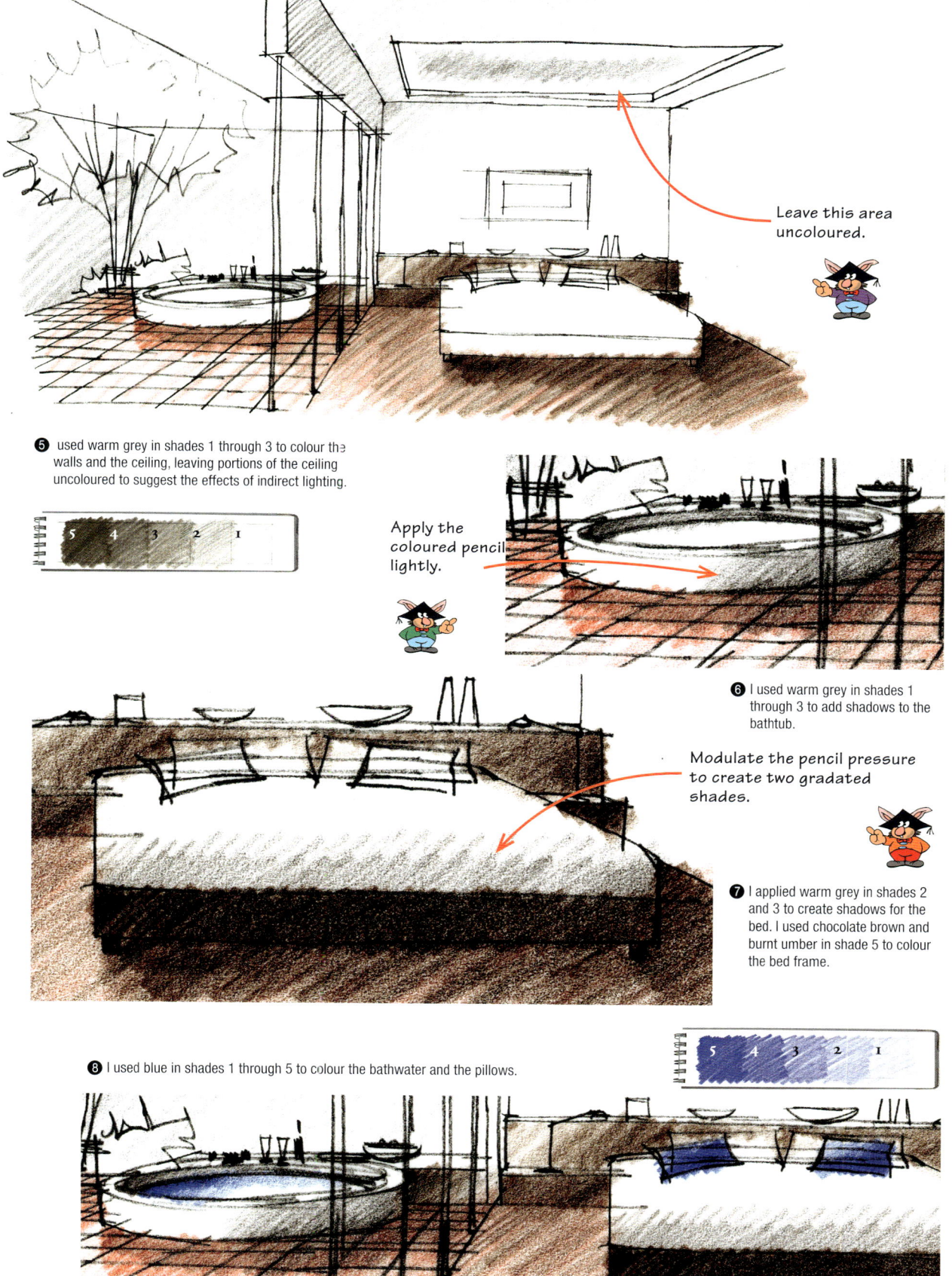

❺ used warm grey in shades 1 through 3 to colour the walls and the ceiling, leaving portions of the ceiling uncoloured to suggest the effects of indirect lighting.

Leave this area uncoloured.

Apply the coloured pencil lightly.

❻ I used warm grey in shades 1 through 3 to add shadows to the bathtub.

Modulate the pencil pressure to create two gradated shades.

❼ I applied warm grey in shades 2 and 3 to create shadows for the bed. I used chocolate brown and burnt umber in shade 5 to colour the bed frame.

❽ I used blue in shades 1 through 5 to colour the bathwater and the pillows.

128 ▶ Chapter III The Coloured Pencil Perspective Sketching Process

❿ I used purple and aquamarine in shades 4 and 5 to colour the knickknacks atop the headboard.

❾ I used red and dark green in shades 4 and 5 to create the grass and flowers.

⓬ To finish the sketch, I sketched the blinds using a regular pencil and then used a black coloured pencil (in shades 1 through 5) to create shadows, pulling the composition together.

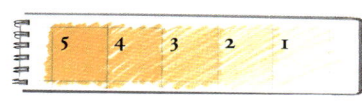

⑪ I applied mustard in shade 5 to create the detailed items (beer and fruit) around the bath and then used correction fluid to add highlights.

Correction fluid

Washroom/Toilet/Bath: Pipelines Unified in One Space

This floor plan features all plumbing aligned side by side. The washroom with a relatively spacious vanity top lies at the floor plan's focus. The bathroom occupies the space to the right, while to the toilet occupies the space to the left. I used this floor plan to discuss with the client adding a washing machine that would be hidden behind a door.

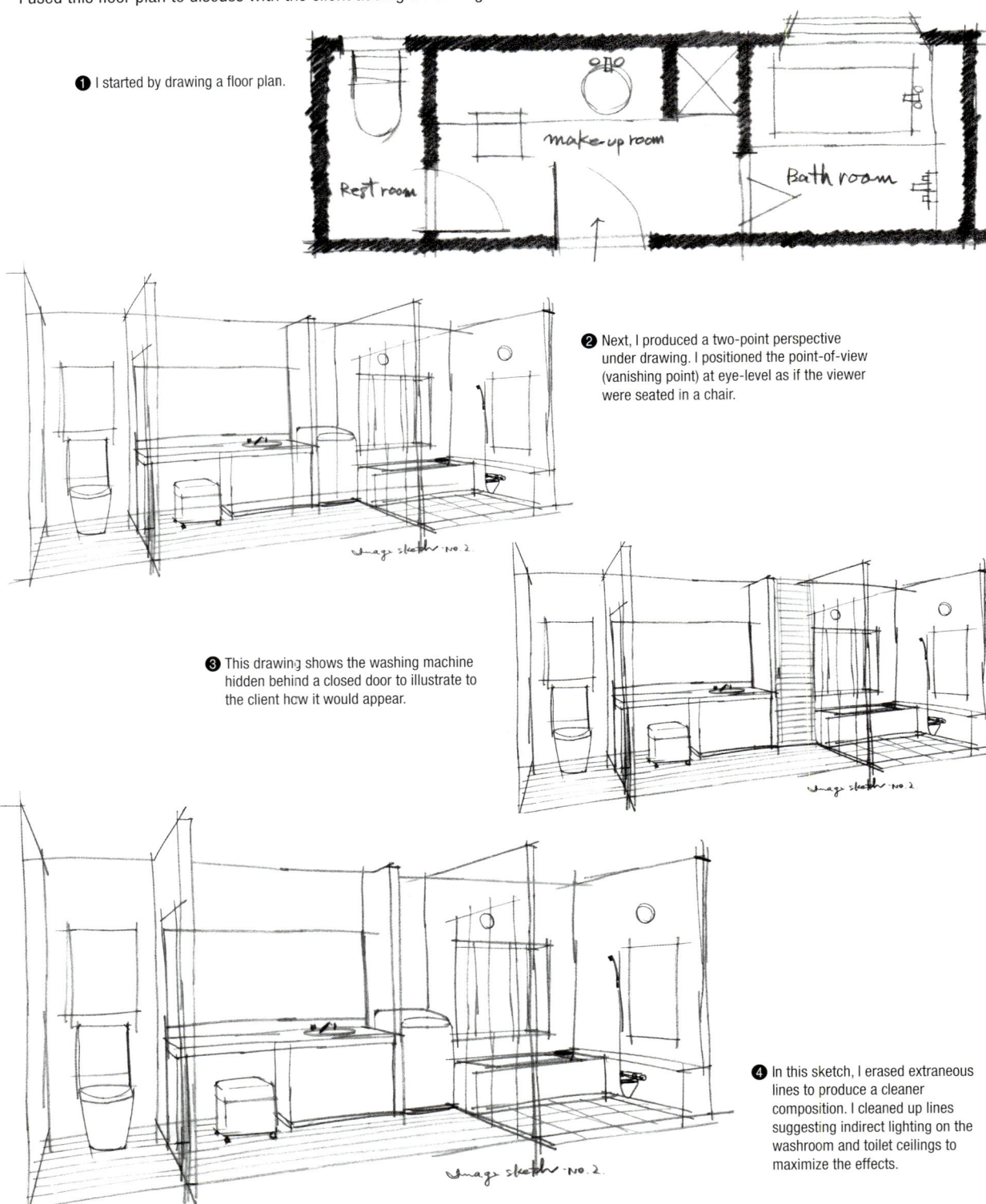

❶ I started by drawing a floor plan.

❷ Next, I produced a two-point perspective under drawing. I positioned the point-of-view (vanishing point) at eye-level as if the viewer were seated in a chair.

❸ This drawing shows the washing machine hidden behind a closed door to illustrate to the client how it would appear.

❹ In this sketch, I erased extraneous lines to produce a cleaner composition. I cleaned up lines suggesting indirect lighting on the washroom and toilet ceilings to maximize the effects.

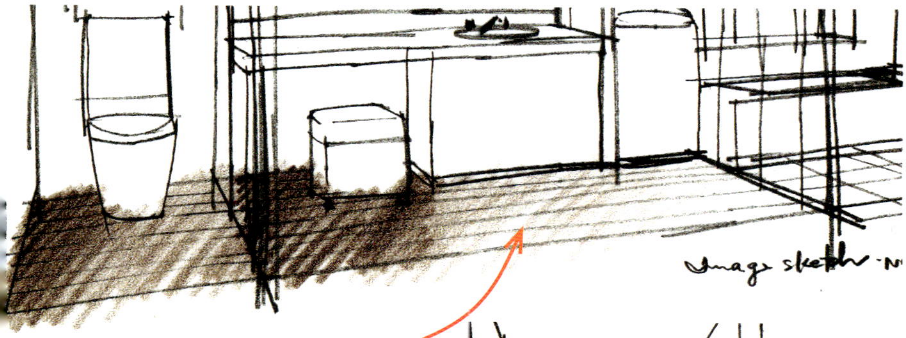

5 I coloured the floor using burnt umber in shades 1 through 4. The bathroom located to the floor plan's right has a large bay window, so I intentionally coloured the floors of the toilet and washroom lighter toward the upper right.

Avoid allowing the colour to become too dark.

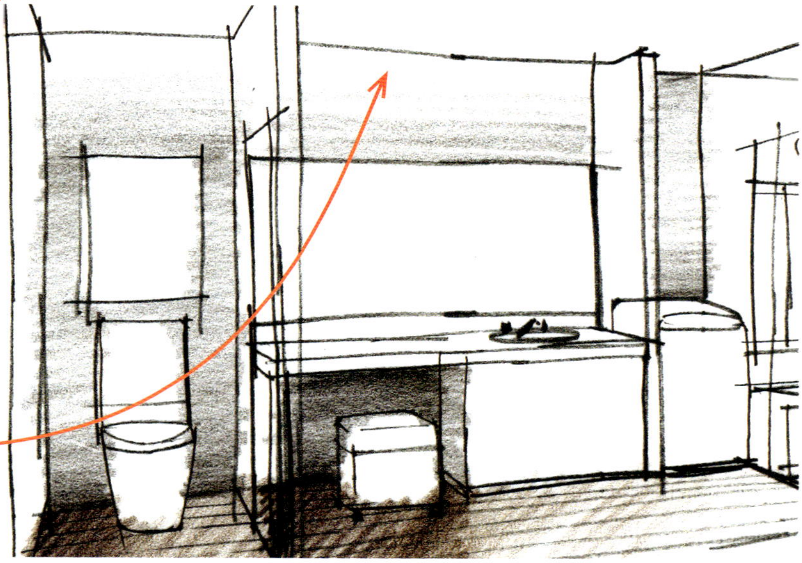

6 I used warm grey in shades 1 through 4 to colour the walls of the toilet, washroom, and washing machine closet. To suggest indirect lighting between the walls and ceiling, I applied warm grey using horizontal strokes rather than hatching at a 45° angle.

Leave this area uncoloured.

7 I applied warm grey in shades 1 through 4 to create shadows for the toilet, washroom vanity seat, and bathtub.

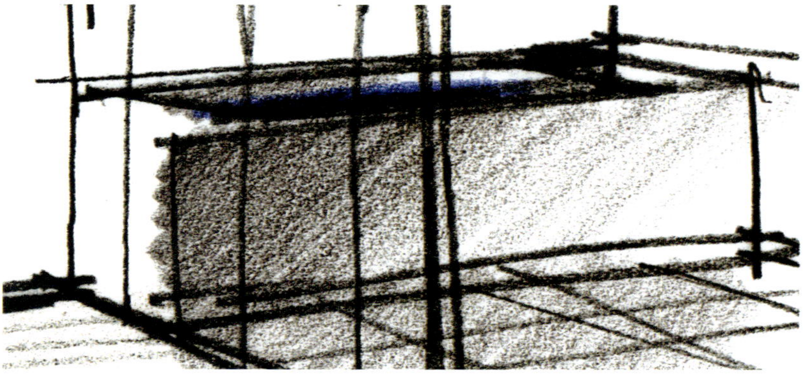

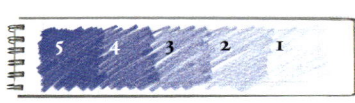

8 I used blue in shade 5 to colour the bathwater.

Chapter III The Coloured Pencil Perspective Sketching Process

9 I applied black coloured pencil in gradated shades (shades 5 through 1) to create the washroom and bathroom mirror, using rapid strokes and moving from top to bottom.

Start by applying saturated black strokes and then move downward.

Leave this area uncoloured.

10 I used a lightly applied, gradated layer of yellow to enhance the appearance of indirect lighting on the walls.

Correction fluid

⑪ I used purple, mustard, and dark green in shades 4 and 5 to create the flowers.

⑫ I used correction fluid to add highlight to areas I intended to brighten and black coloured pencil in shade 5 to reinforce shadows on the vanity plinth and underneath the bathtub. I also applied black coloured pencil in shades 1 through 3 to reinforce other shadows.

Gardening Space: Living Room and Patio with an Umbrella

My goal with this design was to create peaceful moments in the garden for the resident, such as enjoying a beer while relaxing on the patio, etc. Surrounding the patio are meticulously tended flowers abloom, offering treats for both the eyes and the nose.

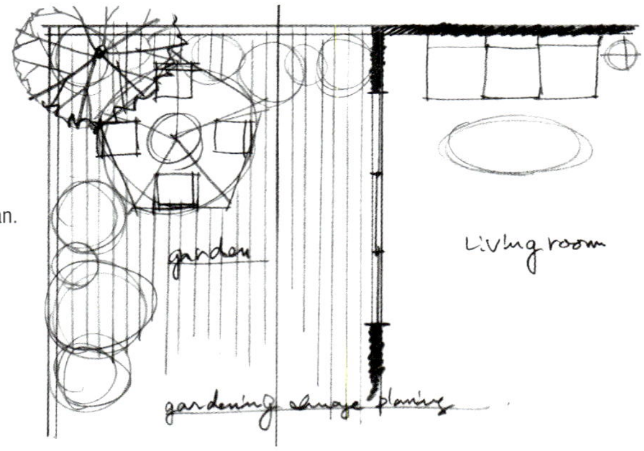

❶ I started by drawing a floor plan.

❷ Next, I produced a one-point perspective under drawing. I added the shrubbery at this point.

❸ I applied brown in shades 1 through 4 to the floor, paying careful attention to modulating the pencil strokes.

Add shadows when colouring the floor.

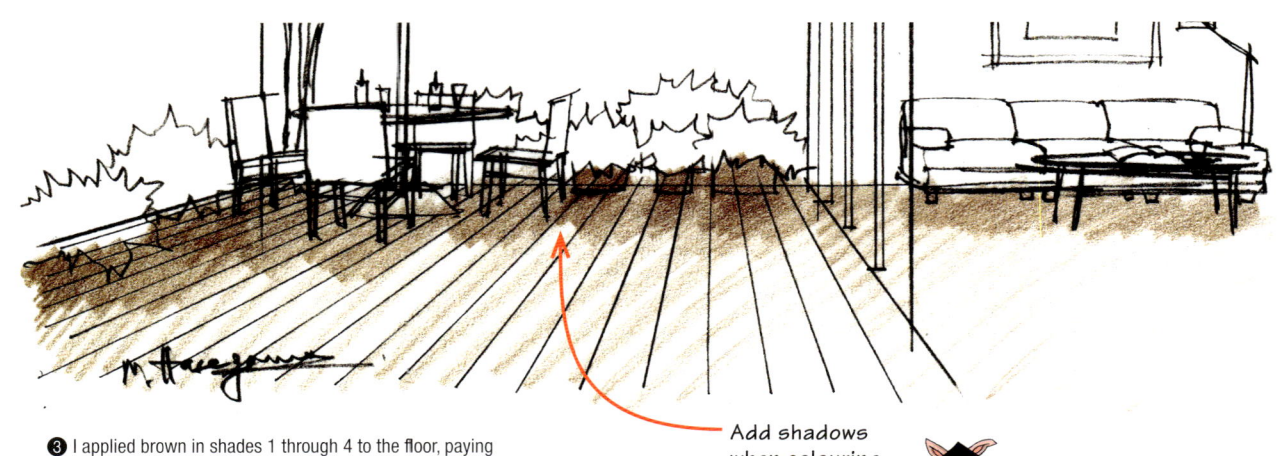

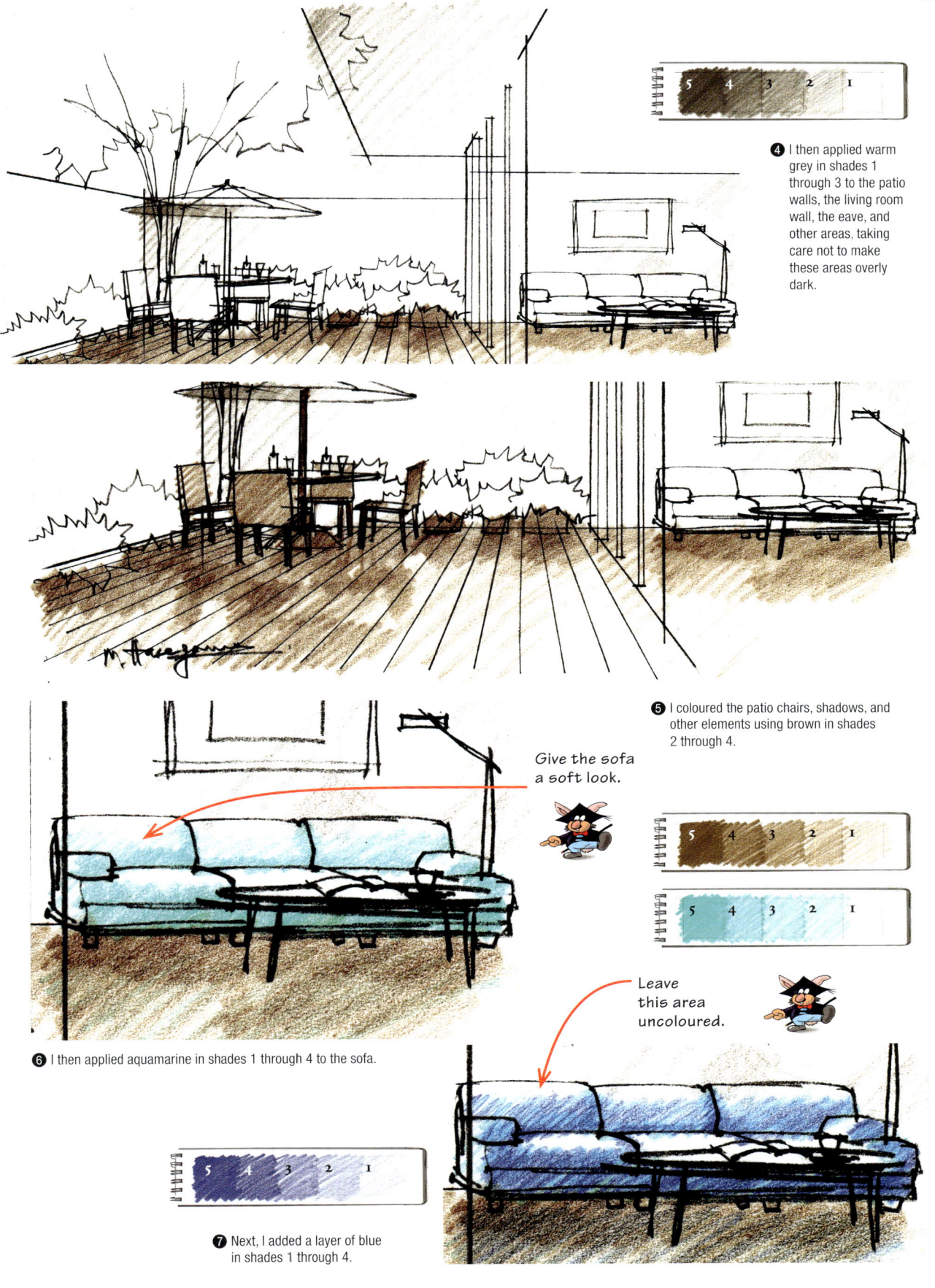

❽ I then created the shrubbery using dark green in shades 1 through 5.

❾ Next, I added a layer of blue-green in shades 1 through 5.

Colour flowers as clustered areas rather than individual dots.

Correction fluid

❿ I used mustard in shades 1 through 5 to create the flowers and beer atop the table.

Currently, home designs tend to place importance on creating a comfortable environment, and gardens have come to play a key role in enriching our lifestyles. The number of people expressing interest in living amongst flowers and plants that they, themselves, have raised is growing. Interior designers and coordinators will find it effective to construct designs that allow their clients to lead comfortable and enriched lives and incorporate their hopes and dreams.

The main difference between sketching gardens and sketching interiors is that gardens requires the portrayal of trees, flowers, plants, water, and other natural elements. I recommend making an effort to observe carefully and sketch grasses, trees, flowers, and other plants on a regular basis.

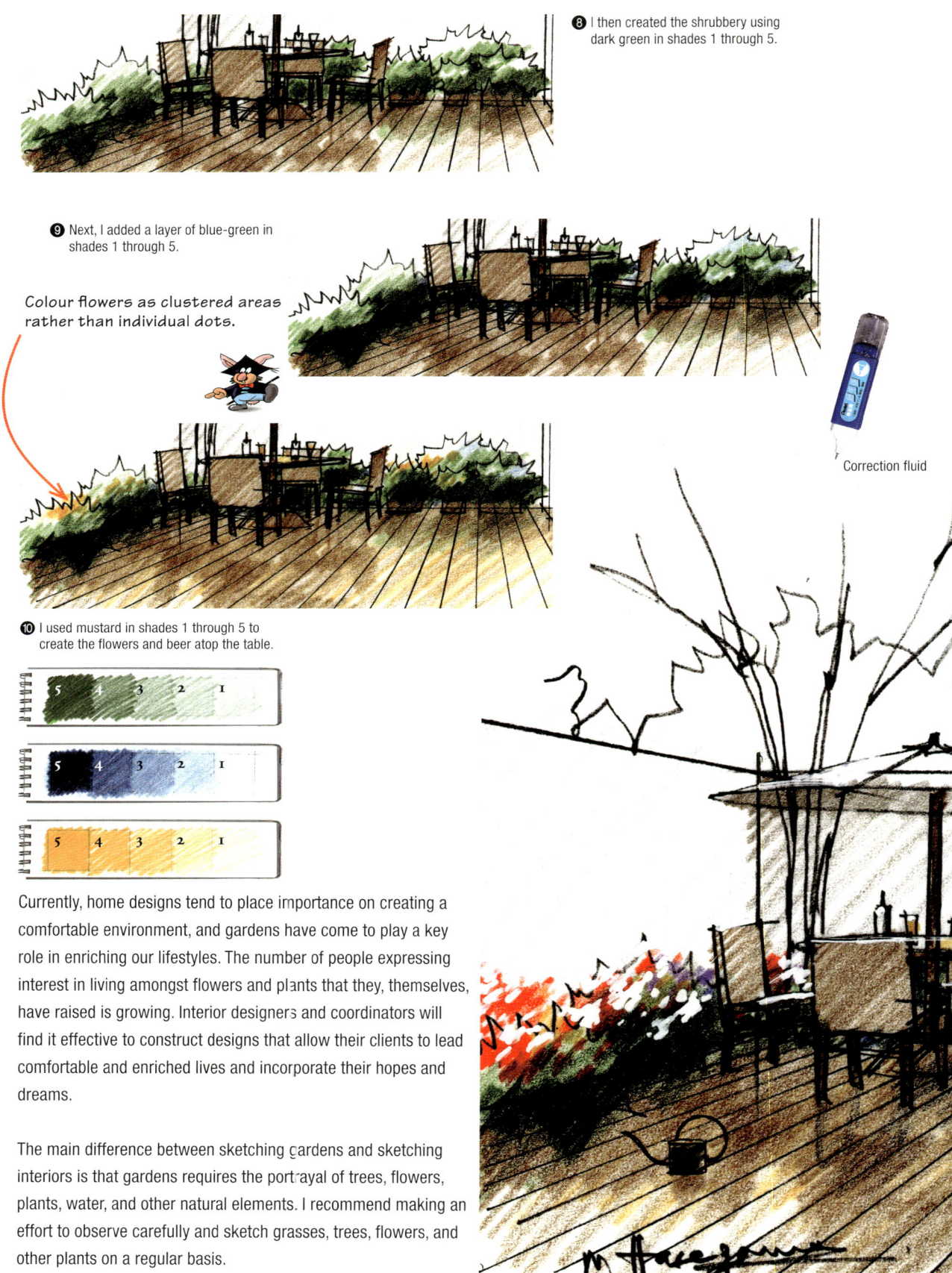

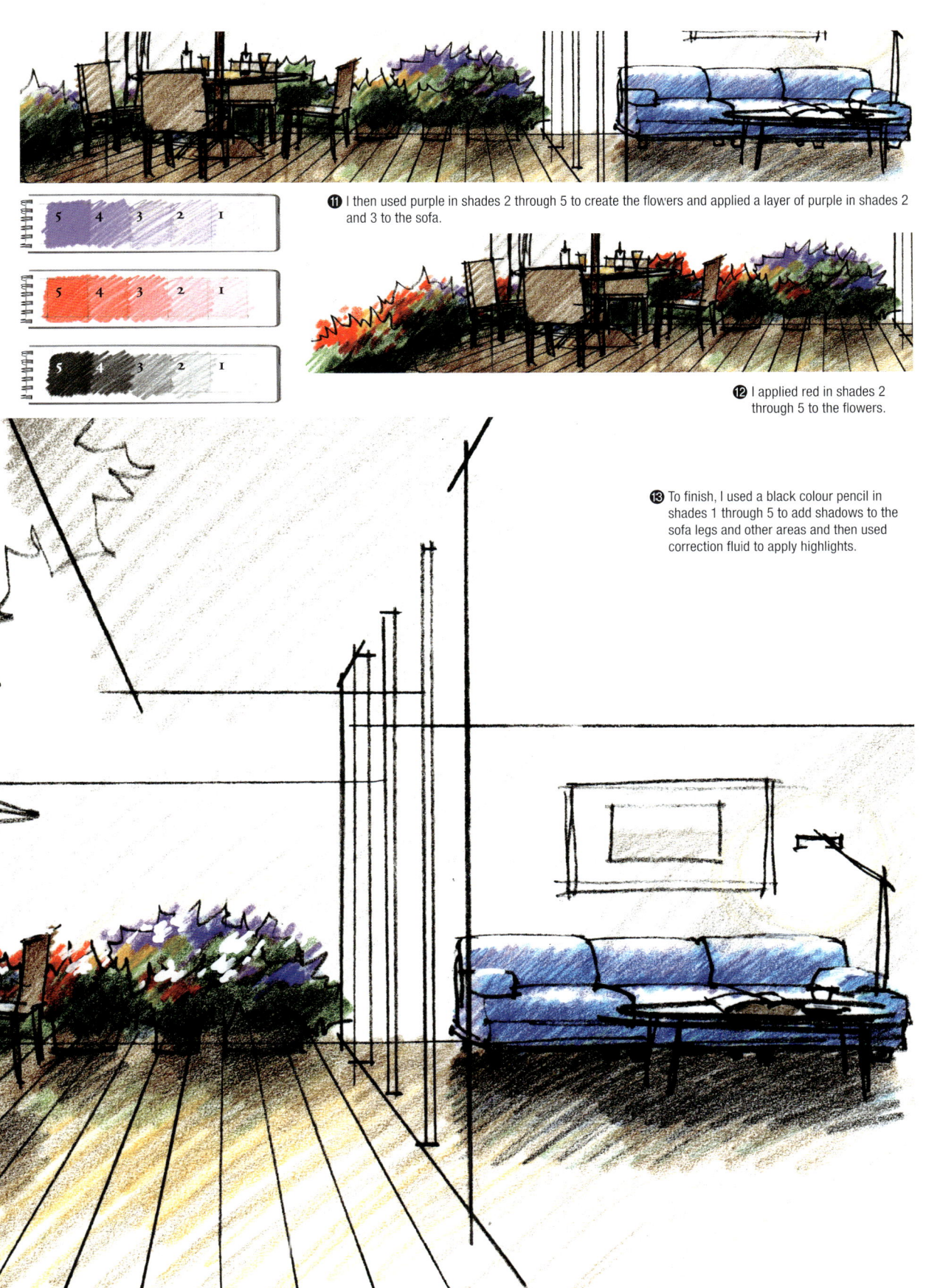

⓫ I then used purple in shades 2 through 5 to create the flowers and applied a layer of purple in shades 2 and 3 to the sofa.

⓬ I applied red in shades 2 through 5 to the flowers.

⓭ To finish, I used a black colour pencil in shades 1 through 5 to add shadows to the sofa legs and other areas and then used correction fluid to apply highlights.

Garden Spaces: Dramatizing Details

While drawing plants is essential in portraying gardens, being able to add details also plays a crucial role. I will not be able to present a wide range of samples in this book. However, I do provide several that should prove to serve as valuable examples. I hope that they will further serve as reference when actually producing sketches for clients.

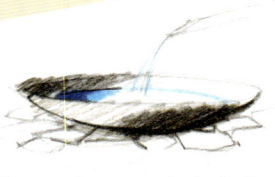

I used brown and warm grey in shades 1 through 5 and black in shades 3 through 5 for the water saucer. I applied light blue in shades 3 through 5 and blue in shade 5 to the water.

I used brown and warm grey, both in shades 1 through 5, to colour this water saucer. I applied dark green in shades 3 through 5 and black in shades 2 through 5 for the foliage. For the water, I used light blue in shades 1 and 2.

I used brown and warm grey in shades 1 through 5 and black in shades 4 and 5 for the water saucer and stones. I applied light blue in shades 3 through 5 and blue in shade 5 to the water.

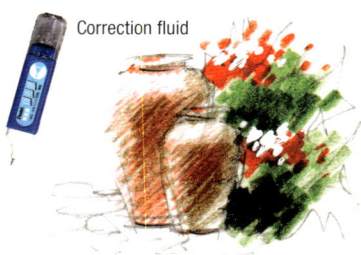

Correction fluid

For these large urns, I used chocolate brown and brown in shades 1 through 5 and black in shades 3 through 5. I applied dark green in 3 through 5 and black in shades 2 through 5 to the foliage, and red in shade 5 to the flowers. I then used correction fluids to add highlights.

Here, I used brown and warm grey, both in shades 1 through 5, and black in shades 3 through 5 to colour the water saucer. For the water, I used light blue in shades 3 and 5 and blue in shade 5.

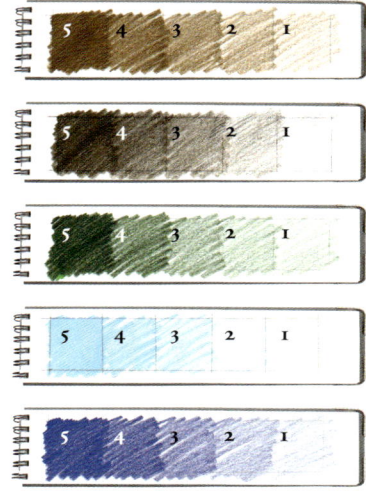

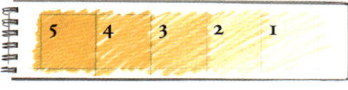
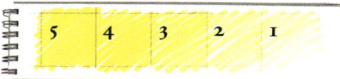
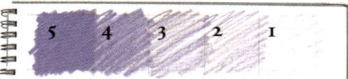
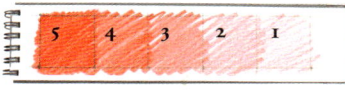

For this *tsukubai*, or ablution water basin, I used brown and warm grey, again in shades 1 through 5 for both, and black in shades 3 through 5. For the water, I used light blue in shades 3 through 5 and blue in shade 5. I applied dark green in shades 3 through 5 and black in shades 2 through 5 to the foliage.

I used brown and warm grey, both in shades 1 through 5, and black in shades 3 through 5 to create the modern stone lantern. I applied dark green in shades 3 through 5 and black in shades 2 through 5 to the foliage.

I used brown and warm grey, both in shades 1 through 5, and black in shades 3 through 5 to create these modern stone lanterns. I applied dark green in shades 3 through 5 and black in shades 2 through 5 to the foliage. For the candlelight, I used yellow and mustard in shades 3 through 5.

I used brown and warm grey, both in shades 1 through 5, and black in shades 3 through 5 to create the modern stone lantern. For the candlelight, I used yellow and mustard in shades 3 through 5.

For the table and benches, I used brown and warm grey, both in shades 1 through 5, and black in shades 3 through 5.

I applied warm grey in shades 1 through 5 to this bench.

For this double bench, I used brown and warm grey, both in shades 1 through 5, and black in shades 3 through 5.

For the bench, I used brown and warm grey, both in shades 1 through 5, and black in shades 3 through 5.

I used brown and warm grey, both in shades 1 through 5, and black in shades 3 through 5 to create this bench.

I applied warm grey in shades 1 through 5 to create shadows for the table and chairs, and mustard in shade 5 to the beer.

Here, I used warm grey in shades 1 through 5 to create shadows for the table, and warm grey in shades 1 through 5 and aquamarine in shades 2 through 5 to the chairs. For the flowers, I applied purple in shade 5 and dark green and black, each in shades 4 and 5.

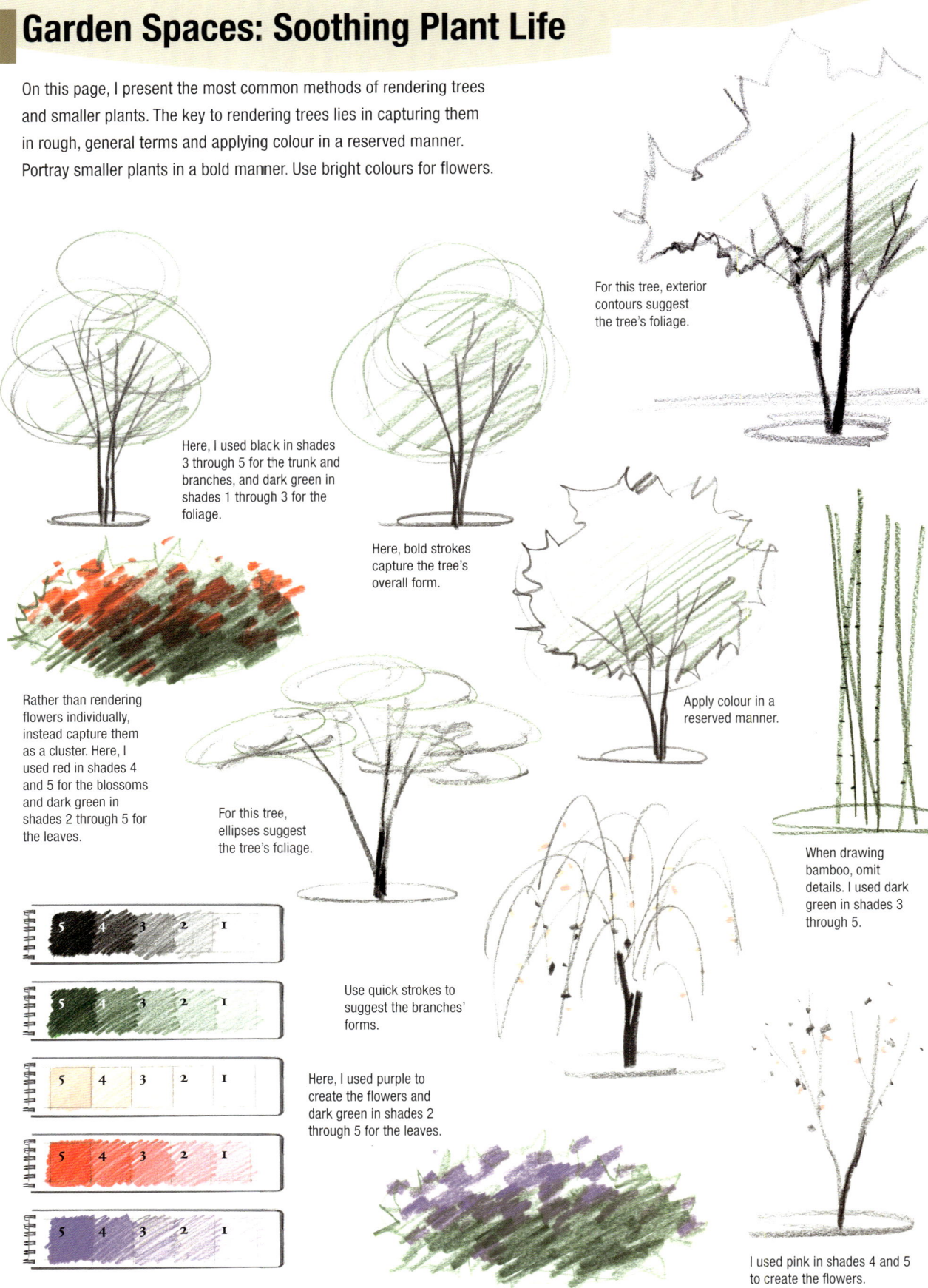

Chapter IV

Floor Plans in Coloured Pencil

This chapter covers techniques in using coloured pencils to create orthogonal floor plans. Adding furniture, flowers, plants, and cars to orthogonal floor plans and then using coloured pencils to portray the space and objects within as three-dimensional turns the floor plans into compositions that are more exciting and easier to understand.

General speaking, from now on the key point to interior design presentation lies in creating the orthogonal floor plans, which are traditionally viewed as indigestible to clients, to engage the client readily and convey a space or house. Floor plans should not be drawn to show how a house will be constructed but rather to present the house or space to the client as a future home or space to live. Previously, many floor plans might include fixtures but not furniture. In this book, furniture is absolutely included.

House with a Garden Patio

Shown here is a floor plan from a two-story house. However, to discuss the steps in colouring a floor plan, we will look at a floor plan showing only one story. This floor plan shows the living room, dining room, kitchen, the plumbing fixtures, and the garden patio. When duplicating the floor plan, take care not to make the floor overly dark and not to over colour the composition. In the case of a flat, orthogonal floor plan, North is always up. Consequently, floor plans should be coloured assuming the light source is located to the bottom right corner (Southeast). Regardless of how the windows, walls, and other components are positioned, fixtures, furniture, and the like should always be coloured so that they appear dark in the upper left corner (use a black coloured pencil) and light in the lower right corner (correction fluid).

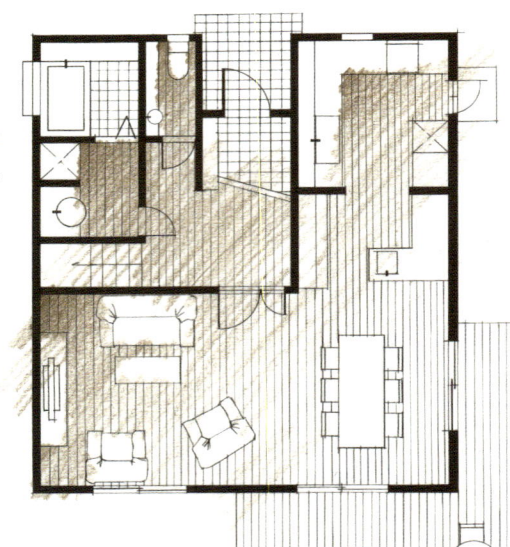

Leave this area uncoloured.

❶ I started by drawing the floor plan (including the fixtures, furniture, lines for the flooring, etc.).

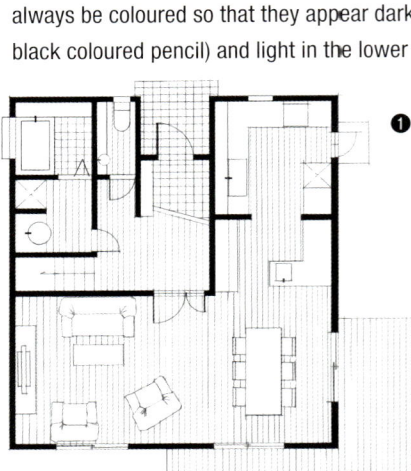

❷ I then coloured the floor using brown in shades 1 through 4.

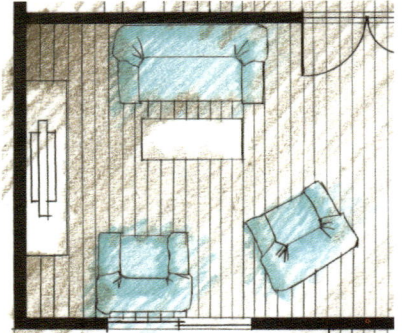

❸ Next, I used grey in shades 2 through 4 to colour the bathroom and foyer floors.

❹ then used aquamarine in shades 1 through 5 to colour the sofa.

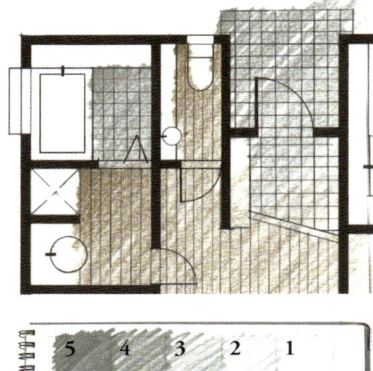

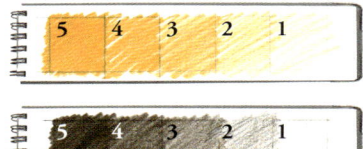

❺ I applied mustard (in shades 1 through 4) and warm grey (in shades 1 through 3) to colour the cabinets, table, and other furniture.

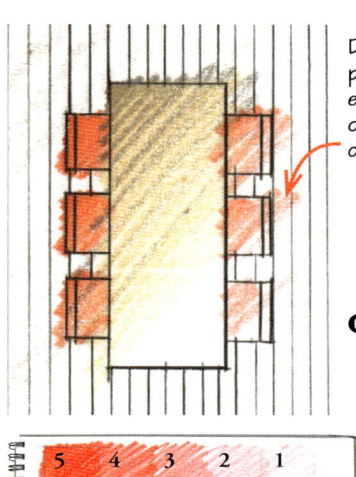

Do not worry if pencil strokes extend outside of objects' exterior contour lines.

❻ I then applied red in shades 1 through 5 to the chairs so that the red became lighter toward the lower right.

❼ I then used aquamarine (in shades 1 through 4) and dark blue (in shades 2 through 5) to colour the bathtub, the kitchen sink, and other first floor sinks.

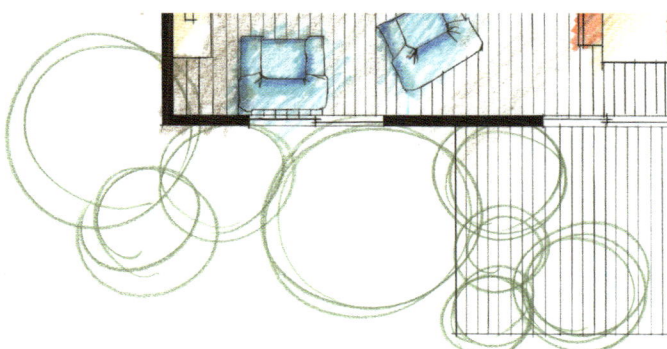

❽ I used dark green in shade 4 to draw the ellipses defining the garden trees' exterior contours.

❾ I applied a gradation of dark green in shades 1 through 5 to make the trees appear three-dimensional.

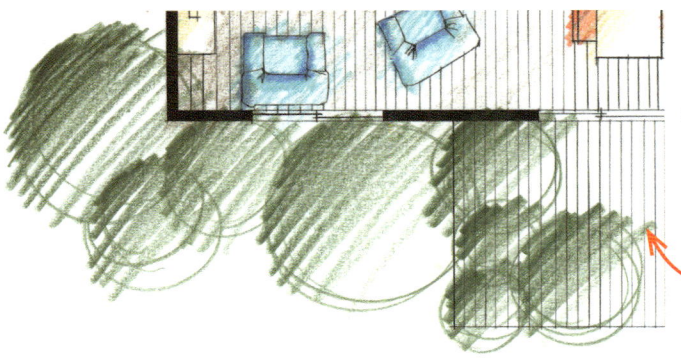

Use quick, bold strokes and do not worry if the strokes extend outside boundaries and exterior contours.

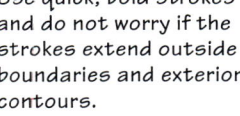

❿ Next, I used dark green in shades 2 through 5 to colour the trees' shadows and the ground.

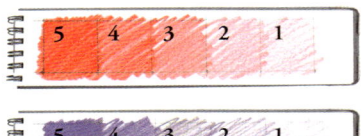

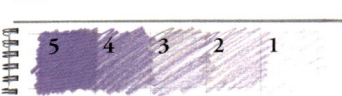

⑫ Avoid drawing wall shadows.

⑪ I then used red and purple in shades 4 and 5 to create the flowers. I applied the colours in clumps of varying sizes rather than dots.

This is a key point!

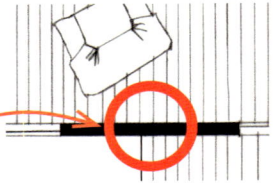

⑬ Pretend there is no wall and omit drawing the shadow.

⑭ I then used black coloured pencil in shades 4 and 5 to draw shadows cast to the tops and the left sides (North is located up on the floor plan) of fixtures and furniture.

Apply shadows to the lower right (interior) of objects that have indented forms.

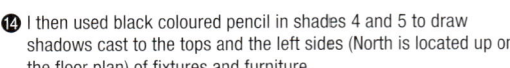

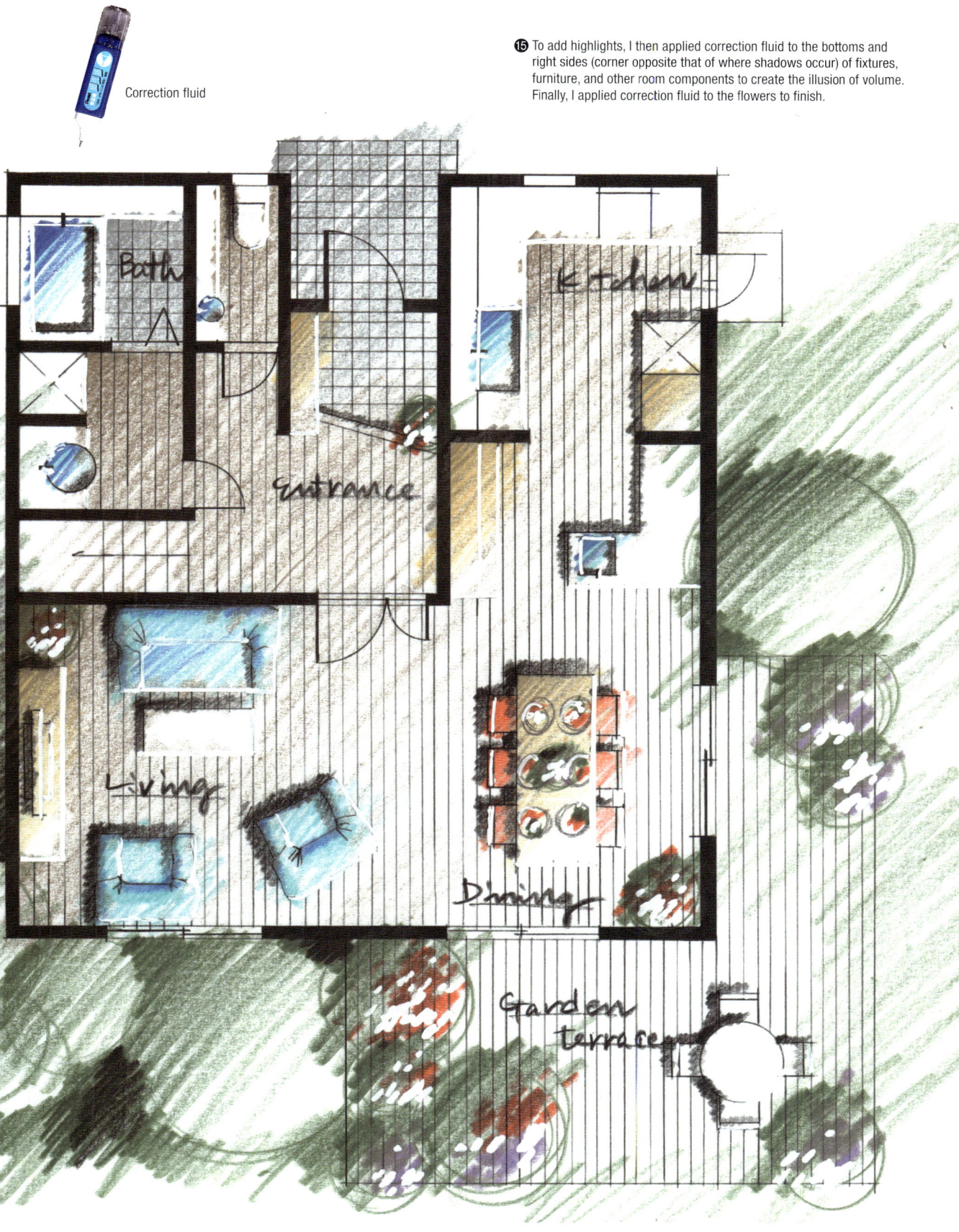

Correction fluid

⓯ To add highlights, I then applied correction fluid to the bottoms and right sides (corner opposite that of where shadows occur) of fixtures, furniture, and other room components to create the illusion of volume. Finally, I applied correction fluid to the flowers to finish.

Condominium Surrounded by Flowers

These pages illustrate the steps I followed to colour a condominium with three bedrooms and two balconies. Plants on the balcony constitute the focal point of this sketch, so I opted for a bright, energetic finish.

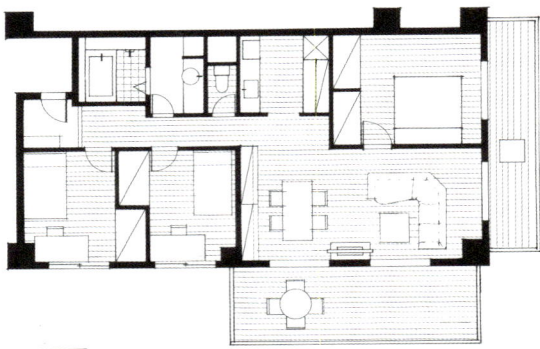

❶ I started by drawing the floor plan (including the fixtures, furniture, lines for the flooring, etc.).

❷ I applied brown in shades 1 through 5 to the living room, dining room, kitchen, and toilet floors and to the balconies.

Do not worry about unevenness in pencil stroke pressure.

❸ I then used grey in shades 1 through 3 to colour the foyer, bathroom, and washroom floors.

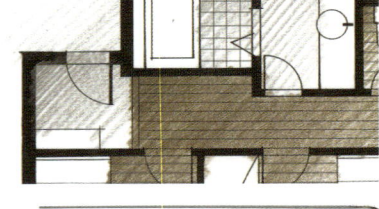

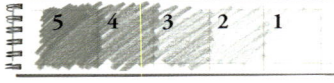

❹ I then applied layers of mustard (in shades 1 through 4) and brown (in shades 1 through 3) to cabinets and other furniture.

❺ I used aquamarine (in shades 2 through 5), red (in shades 2 through 4), and blue (in shades 1 through 5) to colour the bed and sofa.

Modulate the pressure of the pencil strokes.

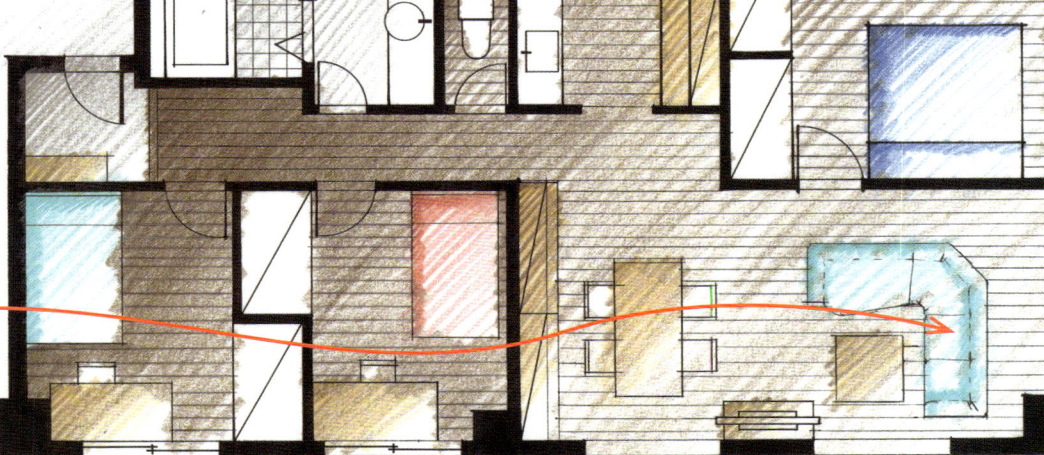

❻ I used blue (in shades 2 through 5) and red (in shades 4 and 5) to colour the chairs.

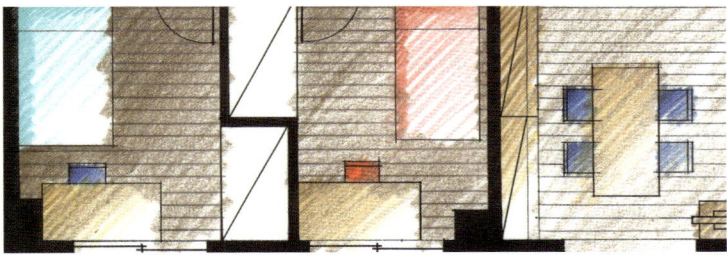

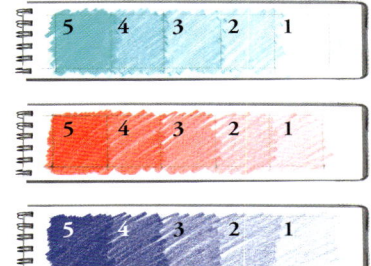

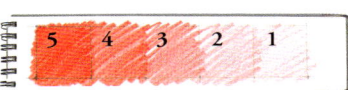
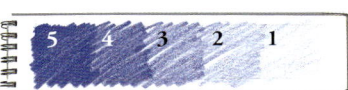

❼ I used warm grey in shade 4 to colour the television.

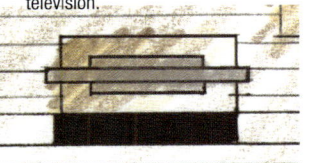

❽ Next, I used blue in shades 2 through 5 to colour the bathtub plus the bathroom and kitchen sinks.

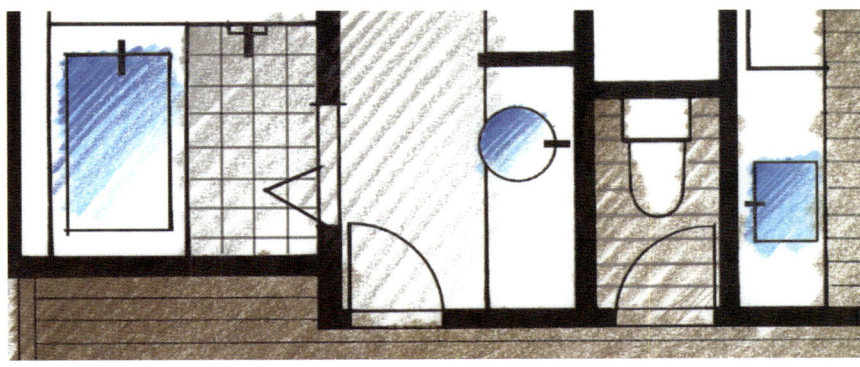

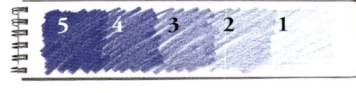

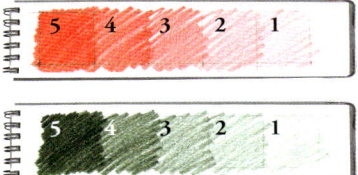

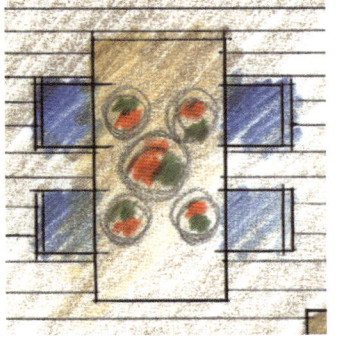

❾ I used red (in shade 5) and dark green (in shade 5) to create food atop the dining room table.

⑩ I used dark green in shades 3 and 4 to draw the plants' exterior contours (circles).

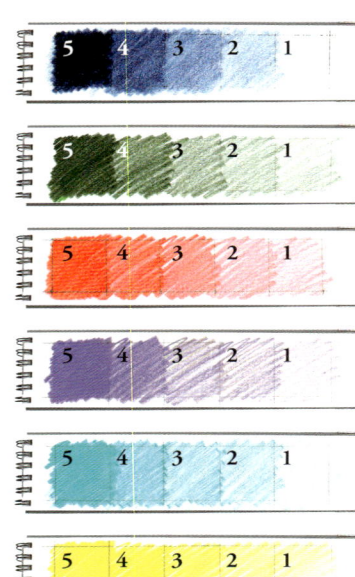

⑪ then applied a gradation of dark green in shades 1 through 5 to the plants to create the illusion of volume.

Do not worry if your pencil strokes extend outside of exterior contour lines.

⑫ I added blue-green in shades 2 through 5 to the plants to make the plants appear thick with foliage and enhance the sense of three-dimensionality.

⑬ I then used red, purple, aquamarine, and yellow in shades 4 and 5 to create the flowers.

14 Next, I used a black coloured pencil in shades 4 and 5 to add shadows to the tops and the left sides of the fixtures and furniture (North is located up on the floor plan).

15 I used correction fluid to suggest bright spots on the flowers.

Correction fluid

16 I then used correction fluid to add highlights to the bottoms and right sides (the sides opposite where shadows form) of furniture to create the illusion of volume. Finally, I labeled each space and room to finish the floor plan.

Rectangular House with a Pond

This is a simple, open, rectangular floor plan of a ranch-style home with virtually all extraneous elements eliminated. This house's distinguishing feature is the intersecting rectangular pond.

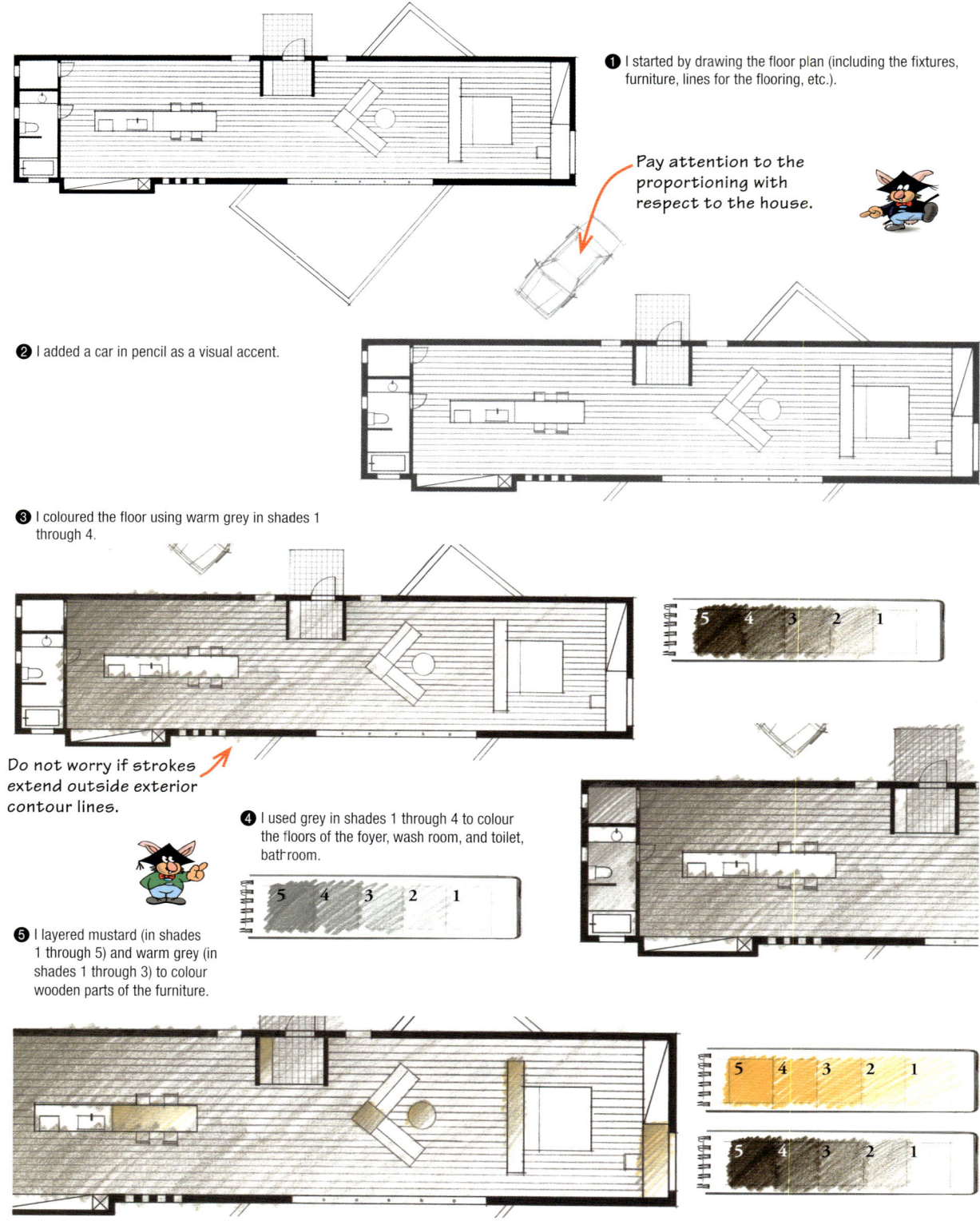

❶ I started by drawing the floor plan (including the fixtures, furniture, lines for the flooring, etc.).

Pay attention to the proportioning with respect to the house.

❷ I added a car in pencil as a visual accent.

❸ I coloured the floor using warm grey in shades 1 through 4.

Do not worry if strokes extend outside exterior contour lines.

❹ I used grey in shades 1 through 4 to colour the floors of the foyer, wash room, and toilet, bathroom.

❺ I layered mustard (in shades 1 through 5) and warm grey (in shades 1 through 3) to colour wooden parts of the furniture.

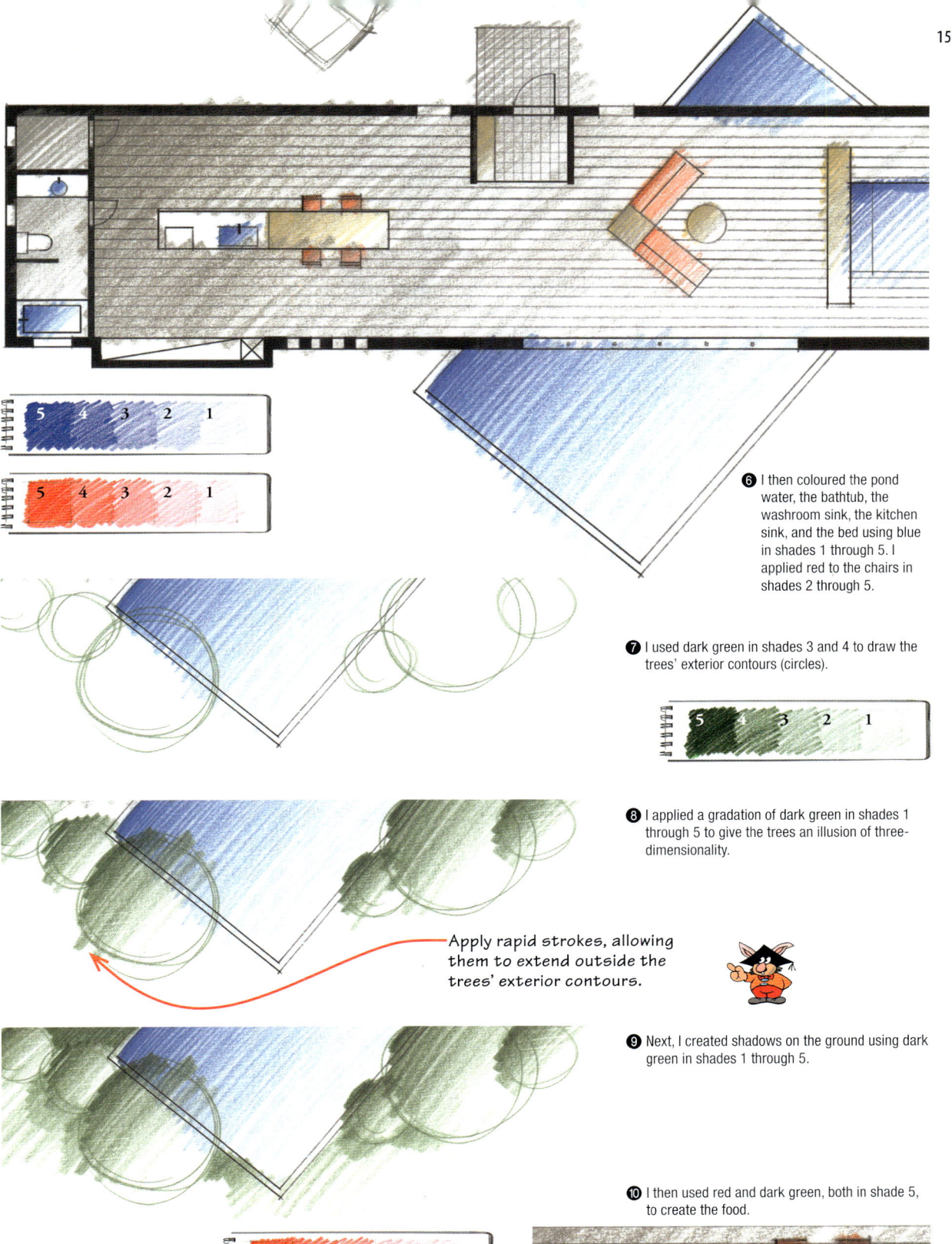

❻ I then coloured the pond water, the bathtub, the washroom sink, the kitchen sink, and the bed using blue in shades 1 through 5. I applied red to the chairs in shades 2 through 5.

❼ I used dark green in shades 3 and 4 to draw the trees' exterior contours (circles).

❽ I applied a gradation of dark green in shades 1 through 5 to give the trees an illusion of three-dimensionality.

Apply rapid strokes, allowing them to extend outside the trees' exterior contours.

❾ Next, I created shadows on the ground using dark green in shades 1 through 5.

❿ I then used red and dark green, both in shade 5, to create the food.

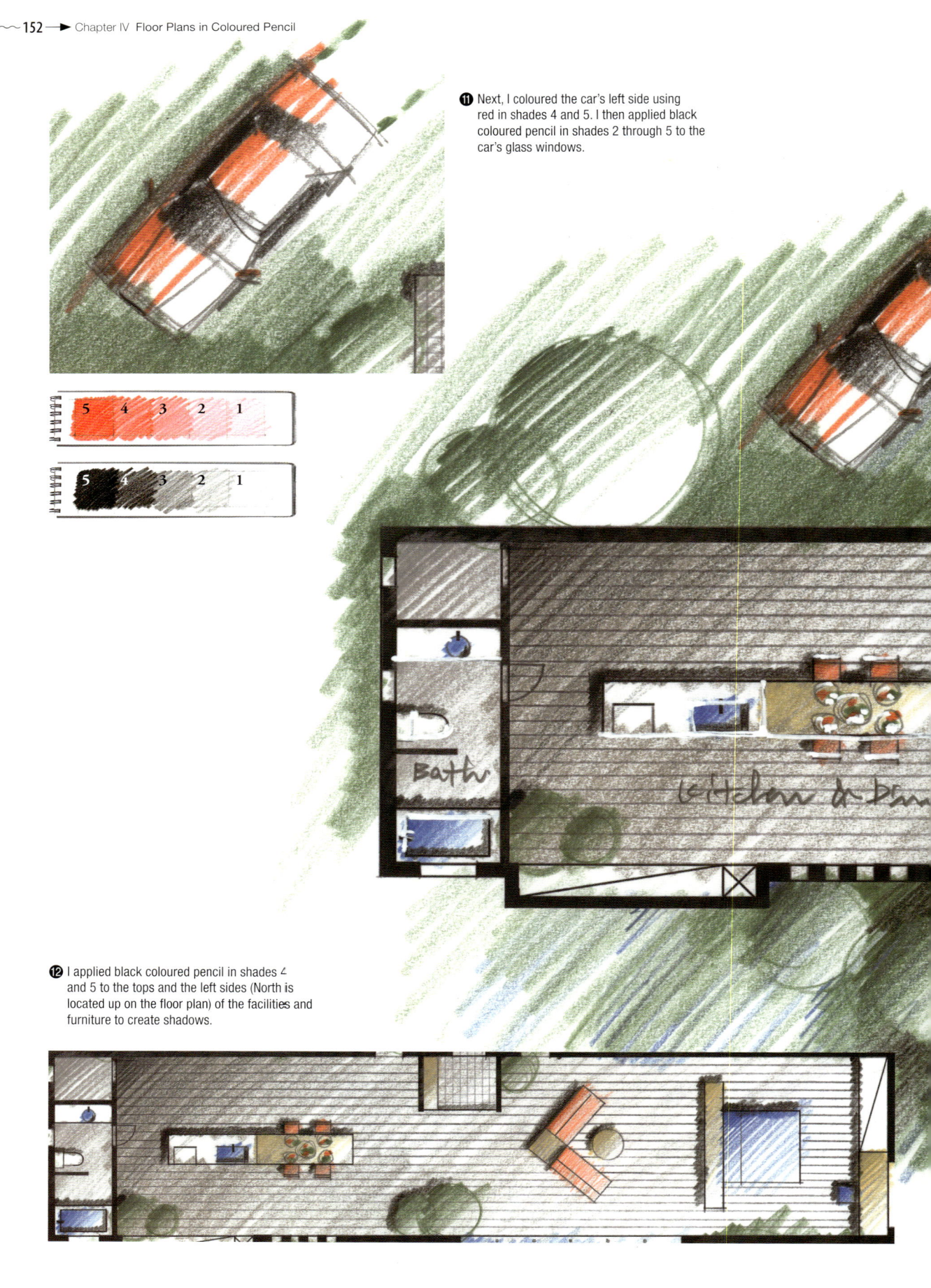

⓫ Next, I coloured the car's left side using red in shades 4 and 5. I then applied black coloured pencil in shades 2 through 5 to the car's glass windows.

⓬ I applied black coloured pencil in shades 4 and 5 to the tops and the left sides (North is located up on the floor plan) of the facilities and furniture to create shadows.

Correction fluid

⓭ I then applied correction fluid to the bottoms and right sides (sides opposite where shadows form) of the facilities and furniture to add highlights, thereby creating a sense of volume. Lastly, I labeled each space and each room to finish.

House Surrounded by Trees

Chapter IV Floor Plans in Colored Pencil

This orthogonal floor plan shows a house encircled by so many trees that it creates the impression of living in a forest. The key point of this composition lies in portrayal of the trees, fixtures, and furniture as three-dimensional objects. I avoided becoming overly fastidious when applying coloured pencil and used bold strokes.

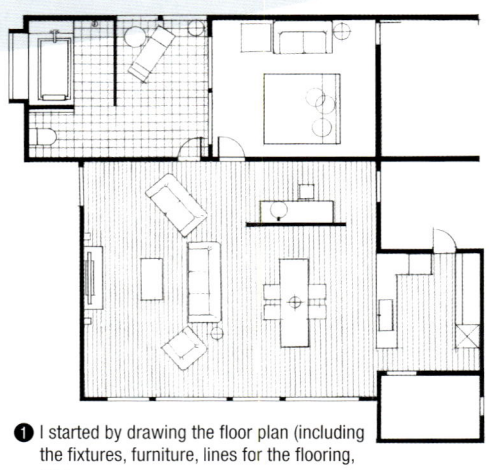

❶ I started by drawing the floor plan (including the fixtures, furniture, lines for the flooring, etc.).

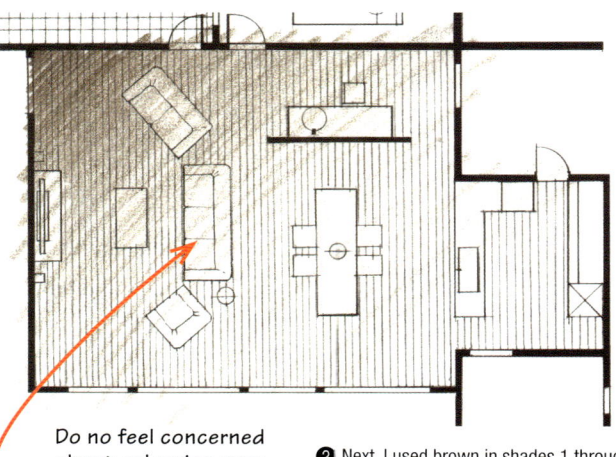

Do no feel concerned about colouring over the sofa, loveseat, and upholstered chairs when colouring to the floor.

❷ Next, I used brown in shades 1 through 4 to colour the floor.

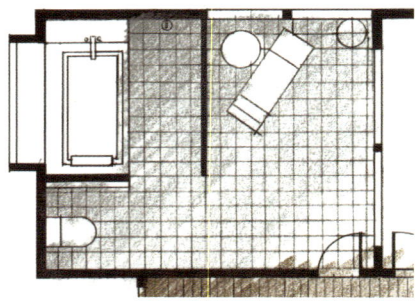

❸ Use grey in shades 1 through 4 to colour the floors of the bathroom, toilet, and lounge area.

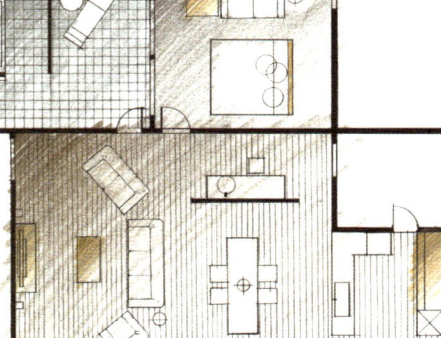

❹ I layered mustard (in shades 1 through 5) and brown (in shades 1 through 3) to colour wooden parts of the furniture.

❺ I then layered mustard (in shades 1 through 5) and brown (in shades 1 through 3) to colour the table. For the sofa, loveseat and upholstered chairs, I used red (in shades 2 through 5). I applied black (in shades 1 through 5) to the chairs. I used blue (in shades 1 through 5) to colour the bed's pillows, and layered light blue (in shades 1 through 4) and blue (in shades 1 through 4) to colour the bathtub and sink.

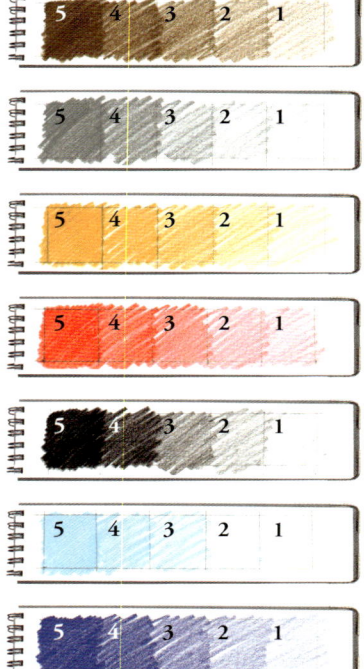

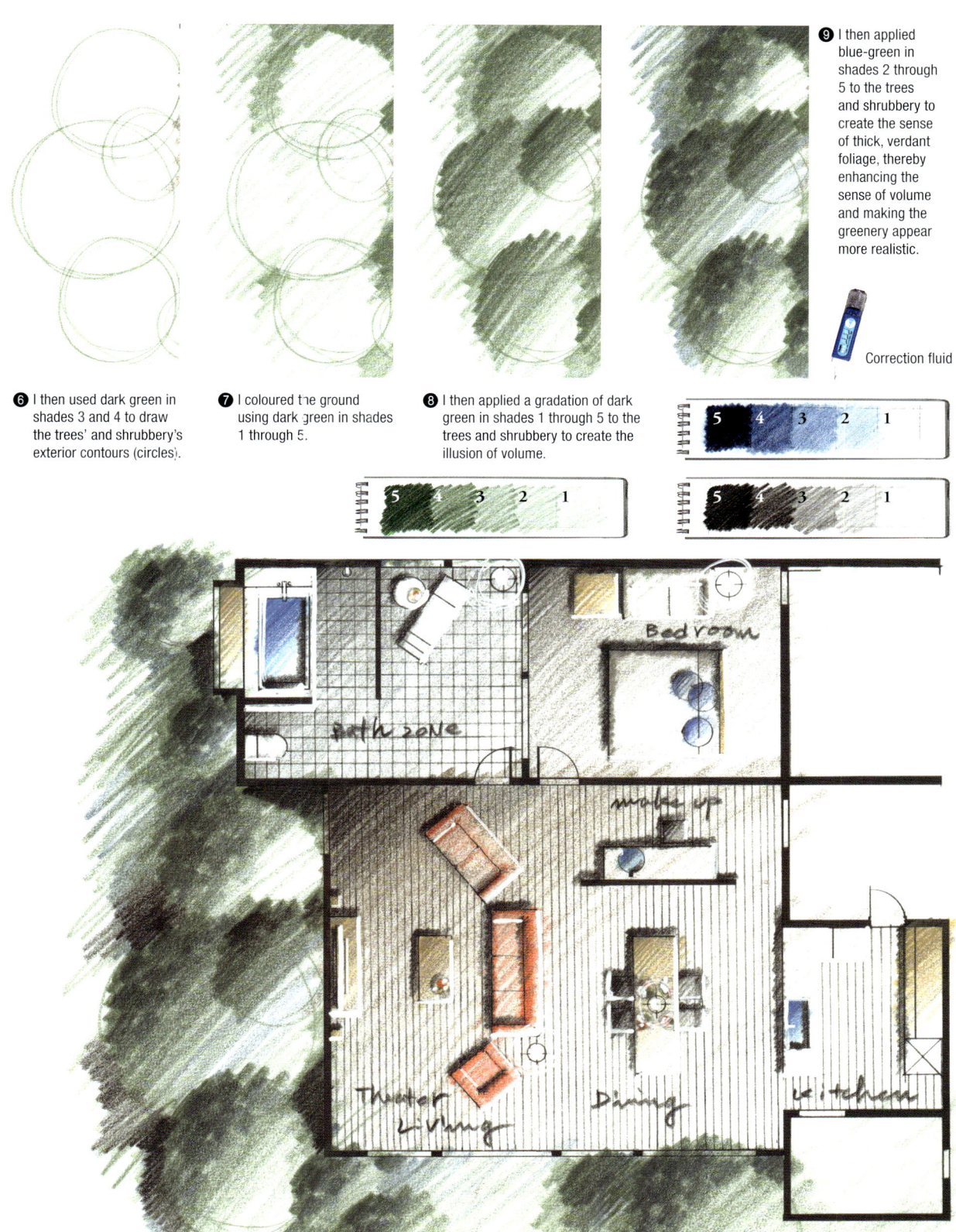

❾ I then applied blue-green in shades 2 through 5 to the trees and shrubbery to create the sense of thick, verdant foliage, thereby enhancing the sense of volume and making the greenery appear more realistic.

Correction fluid

❻ I then used dark green in shades 3 and 4 to draw the trees' and shrubbery's exterior contours (circles).

❼ I coloured the ground using dark green in shades 1 through 5.

❽ I then applied a gradation of dark green in shades 1 through 5 to the trees and shrubbery to create the illusion of volume.

❿ I applied black in shades 4 and 5 to the tops and the left sides (North is located up on the floor plan) of fixtures and furniture to create shadows. I then applied correction fluid to the bottom and right sides (sides opposite where shadows form) of fixtures and furniture to add highlights and create a sense of three-dimensionality. Lastly, I labeled the spaces and rooms to finish.

House with a Piano

I devised this plan to enable the client to enjoy listening to a grand piano from within a spacious living room. This open, large space houses a spiral staircase, a dining area, a kitchen, and a home theater. The key point lied in how to colour the expansive floor using coloured pencil. I used bold, rapid strokes, without showing concern for uneven strokes or for strokes not staying within boundaries and exterior contours.

❶ I started by drawing the floor plan (including the fixtures, furniture, lines for the flooring, etc.).

❷ I added a car in pencil as a visual accent, paying careful attention to its proportioning with respect to the house.

❸ I then used brown in shades 1 through 4 to colour the floors of the living area, the hall to the foyer, etc. I used grey in shades 1 through 4 to colour the floors of the foyer and bathroom.

❹ I layered mustard (in shades 1 through 5) and warm grey (in shades 1 through 3) to colour the cabinets and the dining area table.

Do not become concerned about unevenness in coloured pencil strokes.

❺ I layered aquamarine (in shades 1 through 5) and blue-green (in shades 1 through 4) to colour the sofa, loveseat, and chairs.

❻ Next, I coloured the chairs using blue green in shades 1 through 5.

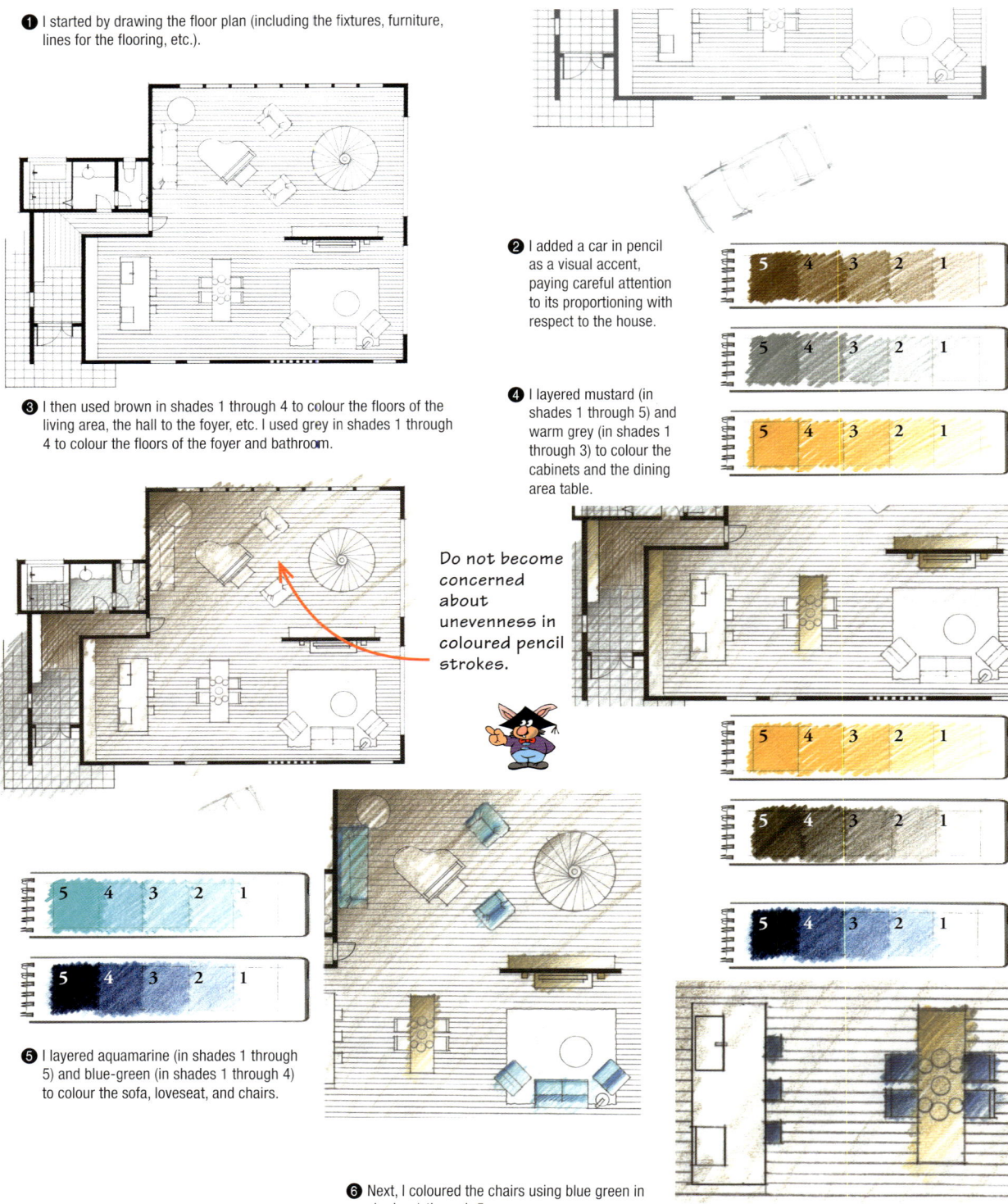

7 I then applied light blue (in shades 2 through 5) and blue-green (in shades 2 through 4) to the bathtub and washroom sink.

8 I used a black coloured pencil in shades 2 through 5 to colour the grand piano, not worrying about the grand piano's proper form and allowed the coloured pencil's strokes to stray outside the piano's exterior contours.

9 I used bold, rapid strokes of dark green in shades 2 through 5 to colour the ground, taking care to avoid the car.

10 I used dark green in shades 3 and 4 to draw the trees' and shrubbery's exterior contours (circles).

Use rapid strokes.

11 I then applied a gradation of dark green in shades 1 through 5 to colour the trees and shrubbery, thereby creating a sense of volume.

12 I then applied blue-green in shades 2 through 5 to the trees and shrubbery to create a sense of volume and make the greenery appear more realistic.

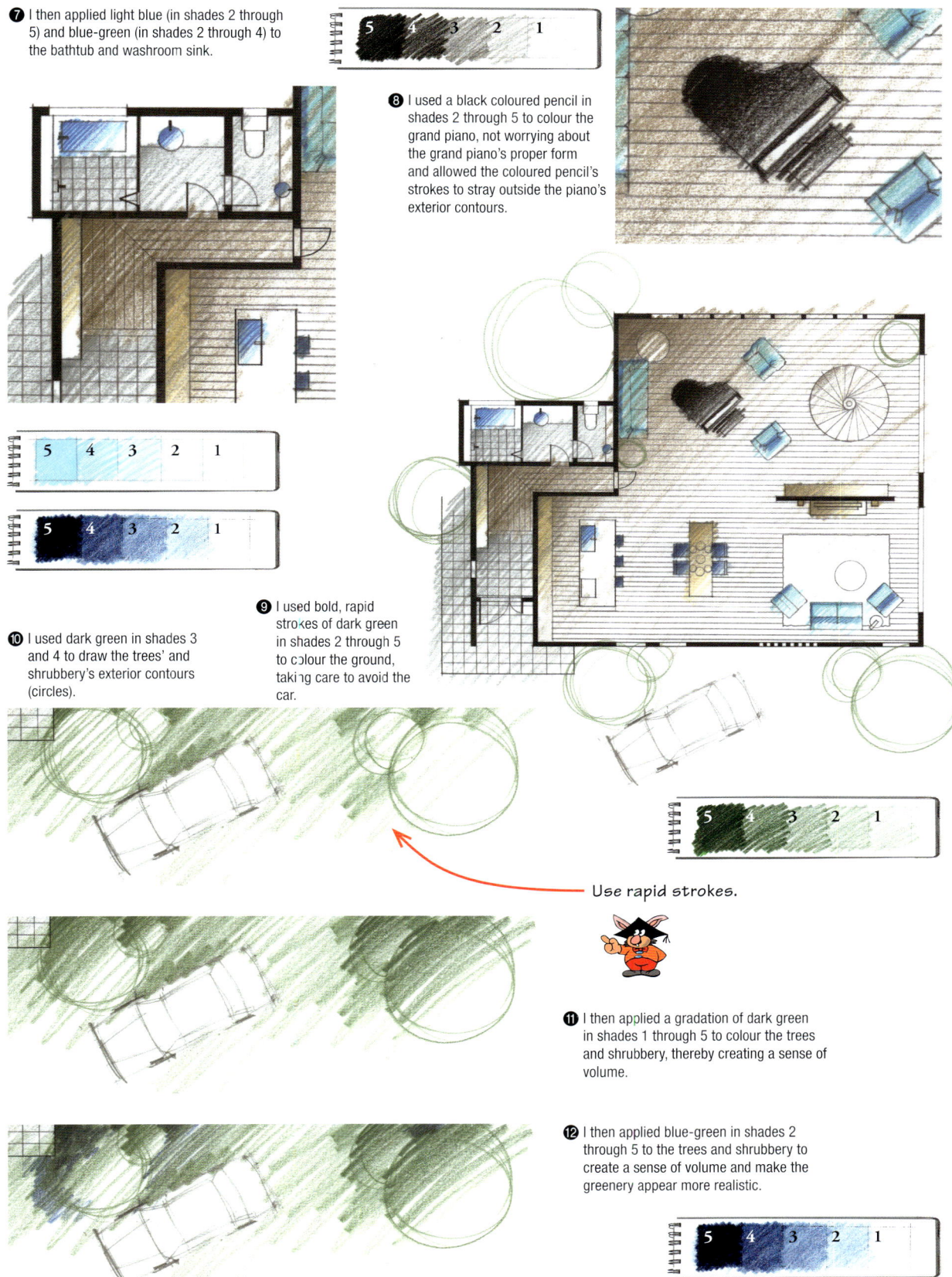

Correction fluid

Use rapid strokes.

⑬ Next, I coloured the car's left side using red in shades 4 and 5. I then applied black coloured pencil in shades 2 through 5 to the car's glass windows.

⑭ I applied black coloured pencil in shades 4 and 5 to the tops and the left sides (North is located up on the floor plan) of the facilities and furniture to create shadows.

Note the shadows that appear at indents.

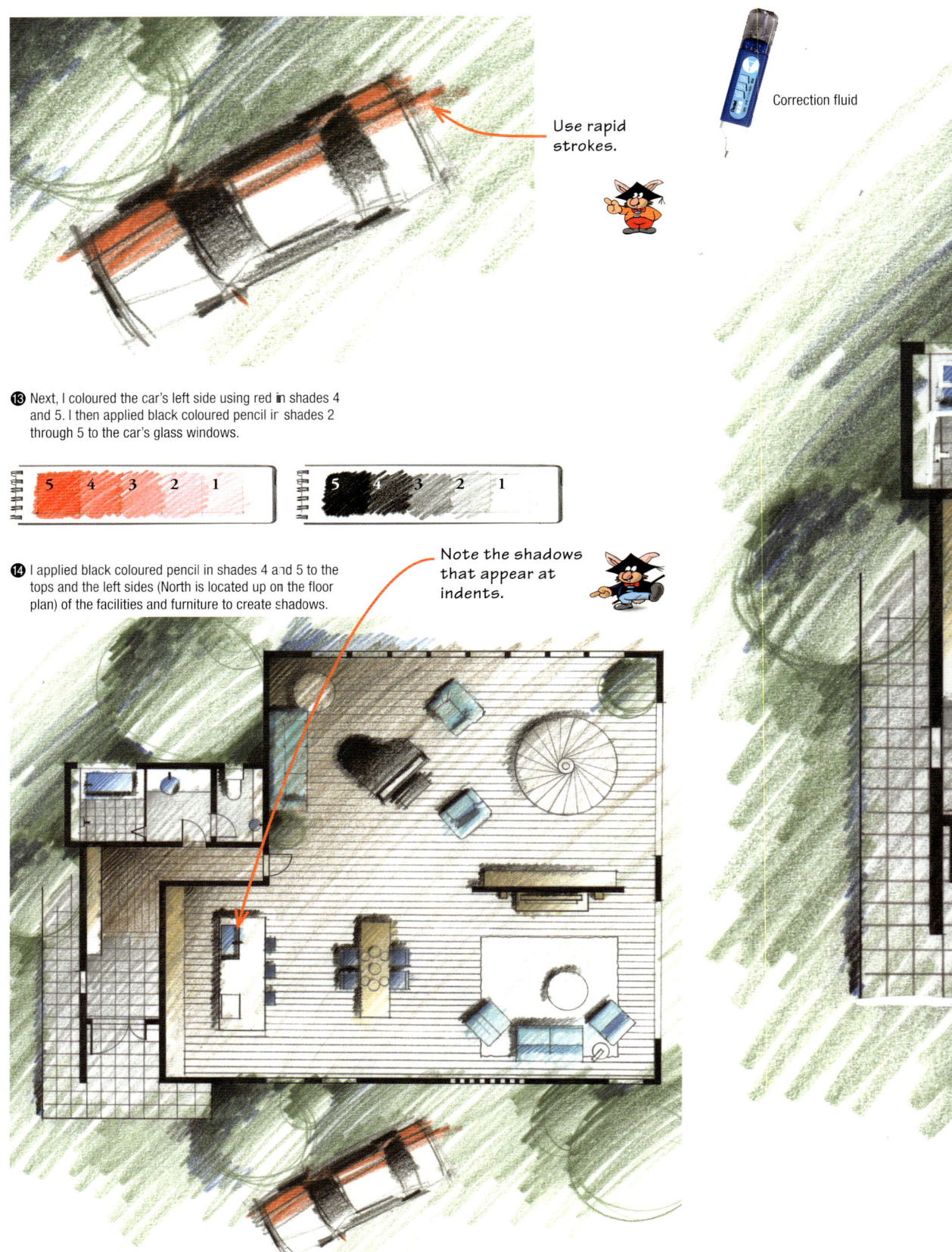

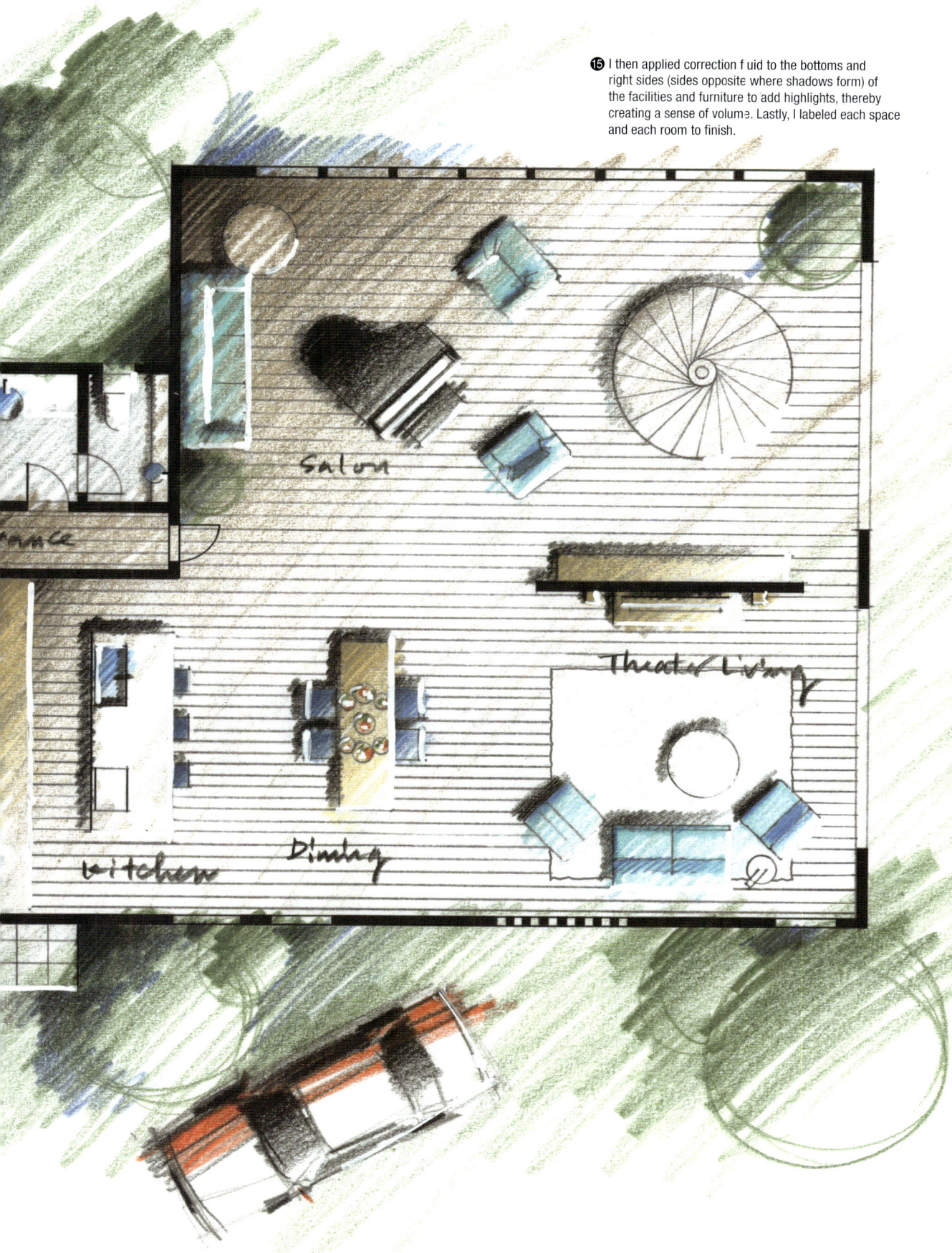

15 I then applied correction fluid to the bottoms and right sides (sides opposite where shadows form) of the facilities and furniture to add highlights, thereby creating a sense of volume. Lastly, I labeled each space and each room to finish.

Afterword

I first encountered coloured pencils as a child. I had one of those two-coloured pencils where one half was red and the reverse side was blue. I remember flipping the pencil over from one side to the other and seeing my pencil leave strokes in red and blue. I also remember the refreshing exhilaration of feeling liberated from a monochrome world of black to a brilliant, colourful world (despite that it was really just red and blue). Later, I encountered coloured pencils in a host of hues, including yellow, green, purple, and so on. Afterwards, I began my relationships with crayons, Cray-Pas, watercolours, poster paints, and other colour media. For some reason, however, my relationship with coloured pencils was not very profound and went no deeper than occasional use.

Coloured pencils are convenient, it is easy to become accustomed to using them, and they provide a light, fresh finish. In terms of performance, coloured pencil adheres well to paper and does not readily diminish in tone when rubbed, which means that it is rather permanent. While coloured pencils do have these advantages, at the same time they seem somehow lacking as a primary medium.

Despite the advantages I wrote above, I tended to use coloured pencils in purely a supplementary manner when sketching perspective drawings for clients during presentations. In my case, I would combine multiple media—pastels, markers (Copic), watercolours, and other media—when creating a single sketch, and would habitually use coloured pencils to draw wood grain, plants and flowers, or tabletop setting details, so I owe a lot to coloured pencils.

The purpose of this book is more about sketching in front of a client during a presentation or even learning techniques for sketching as quickly as possible than about teaching techniques for drawing perspective sketches. It was not long ago that I would not have been able to recommend coloured pencils as a medium for sketching in front of a client.

I frequently sketch as my clients look on. My favorite medium was always pastels.

However, one day purely capriciously, I decided to use coloured pencils. I realized that they really lent themselves well to sketching while someone else was watching.

If a client is sitting right there in front of (next to) you, then you cannot take your time sketching. Pastels particularly do a wonderful job colouring a large area in a short period of time. However, you cannot use coloured pencils to colour in the same way you would pastels. Coloured pencils take forever to colour. Consequently, I would conscientiously use coloured pencils solely to colour small details or specific points.

As a result, my client received the sketch rather well. My client told me the sketch was "easy to understand" and liked it. Because I had distilled its contents down to the key points I wanted to convey in that sketch, it became easy to understand.

The trick is to take care to avoid over-colouring when using coloured pencils. If you are successful, then they are a fantastic medium to use in front of a client.

Since I decided to write this book specifically about coloured pencils, I made an effort to use coloured pencils more in my work. As a result (and this might sound strange coming from me), I discovered that coloured pencils have even more advantages than I realized.

I rediscovered the texture of a coloured pencil stroke — the flavor of coloured pencils, if you will.

It really is important to be able to incorporate your feelings into a sketch and have that recognized by another.

Relaxing the tension in your fingers and using a soft touch produces a soft line. Increasing the tension in your fingers and bearing down on the pencil produces a heavy, dark line.

When I started writing this book, my coloured pencils were brand, spanking new and 16 centimeters long. But, the next time I paid attention to their lengths, they had shortened to 5 centimeters.

This publication is the eighth installment of the Talk series, which started with Interior Colour Talk. I imbued different thoughts and feelings into each book and felt uncompromising toward each in a different way. The most arduous and painful aspect was how to put these thoughts and feelings down in a concrete form so that they might actually be published.

Again, Ota, this book's editor, helped me tremendously in giving me ideas from the planning stage. Thanks to him, I was able to meet the publication deadline. I would like to take this opportunity to thank him from the bottom of my heart.

Noriyoshi Hasegawa

1945: Born in Yokohama, Japan.
1964: Graduated from Kanagawa Technical High School with a major in Design.
1964: Joined Nippon Gakki Co., Ltd. (currently Yamaha Corporation), where he was entrusted with the design of musical instruments, sports equipment, furniture, logos, and a wide variety of other products and graphic designs.
1987: Developed equipment and furnishings for the home.
1988: Entrusted with the design of living spaces.
1992: Appointed as the General Manager of Yamaha Livingtec Corporation's Office of Living Spaces.
2005: Retired from Yamaha Livingtec Corporation.

Current Projects
Hasegawa currently remains active in space planning and perspective drawing projects, and is engaged as an instructor of Presentation Techniques.

Publications
Sketching Interiors: A Step-By-Step Guide
Sketching Interiors, Colour: A Step-By-Step Guide